WORLD BANK LATIN AMERICAN
AND CARIBBEAN STUDIES

Viewpoints

BEYOND THE WASHINGTON CONSENSUS: INSTITUTIONS MATTER

*by Shahid Javed Burki
and Guillermo E. Perry*

**THE WORLD BANK
WASHINGTON, D.C.**

Copyright © 1998
The International Bank for Reconstruction
and Development/THE WORLD BANK
1818 H Street, N.W.
Washington, D.C. 20433, U.S.A.

All rights reserved
Manufactured in the United States of America
First printing September 1998
Third printing September 1999

The findings, interpretations, and conclusions expressed in this paper are entirely those of the author(s) and should not be attributed in any manner to the World Bank, to its affiliated organizations, or to members of its Board of Executive Directors or the countries they represent. The World Bank does not guarantee the accuracy of the data included in this publication and accepts no responsibility whatsoever for any consequence of their use. The boundaries, colors, denominations, and other information shown on any map in this volume do not imply on the part of the World Bank Group any judgment on the legal status of any territory or the endorsement or acceptance of such boundaries.

The material in this publication is copyrighted. Requests for permission to reproduce portions of it should be sent to the Office of the Publisher at the address shown in the copyright notice above. The World Bank encourages dissemination of its work and will normally give permission promptly and, when the reproduction is for noncommercial purposes, without asking a fee. Permission to copy portions for classroom use is granted through the Copyright Clearance Center, Inc., Suite 910, 222 Rosewood Drive, Danvers, Massachusetts 01923, U.S.A.

Shahid Javed Burki is vice president and Guillermo E. Perry is chief economist of the World Bank's Latin America and the Caribbean Regional Office.

Cover illustration by David McLimans

Burki, Shahid Javed.
      Beyond the Washington consensus : institutions matter / by Shahid
Javed Burki, Guillermo E. Perry.
            p. cm. — (World Bank Latin American and Caribbean studies.
Viewpoints)
      Includes bibliographical references.
      ISBN 0-8213-4282-7 (alk. paper)
      1. Latin America—Economic policy. 2. Caribbean Area—Economic
policy. 3. Economic stabilization—Latin America. 4. Economic
stabilization—Caribbean Area. I. Perry, Guillermo. II. Title.
III. Series.
HC125.B7665 1998   98-39051
339.5'098—dc21   CIP

Contents

Tables

Figures

Acknowledgments

THIS REPORT IS THE PRODUCT OF TEAMWORK. THE IDEAS PRESENTED HEREIN WERE INI-
tially discussed with staff members from the Latin American and Caribbean (LAC) regional
office and from the Public Sector Management unit of the World Bank, as well as with spe-
cialists affiliated with other organizations, who participated in a retreat on November 23–24,
1997. We are grateful to all of those who participated in that fruitful event, especially to
Douglass C. North, Andrés Velasco, Allen Schick, Phil Keefer, Florencio López-de-Silanes
and Alberto Chong.

The research and writing of this report were conducted by a group coordinated by the Office of the Chief
Economist for LAC, led by Guillermo Perry. This group was composed of Daniel Lederman (Chapters 1 and
2), Robert Ayres (Chapter 2), Augusto P. de la Torre and Yira Mascaró (Chapter 3), Donald Winkler and
Benjamin Alvarez (Chapter 5), Linn Hammergren and Richard Messick (Chapter 6), and Geoffrey Shepherd
(Chapter 7).

Philip Brock wrote a paper that was commissioned to serve as the foundation for Chapter 3. The chapter extensively incorporates text from that paper. Chapter 4 was commissioned to Rafael La Porta and
Florencio López-de-Silanes.

We thank Conrado García-Corado and Pushan Dutt for their assistance in preparing the data used in
Chapter 1. Marta Cervantes and Gladys Guerricagoitia provided secretarial support in the preparation of
Chapter 2. Charles Griffin, Juliet Literer, and William Mayville assisted in the preparation of Chapter 5.
Finally, Chapter 7 draws extensively from a paper written by Geoffrey Shepherd and Sofia Valencia (1996).
We are also grateful to Eliana Cardoso, Sebastian Edwards, Carol Graham, Phil Keefer, Danny Leipziger,
Ernesto May, Gobind Nankani, Anthony Ody, Lant Pritchett, and many others who took the time to read
portions of the report, to provide comments on earlier versions, or to present their work on institutional
reforms and political economy issues in our monthly seminar series.

Marcus D. Rosenbaum edited the final version of this report.

Shahid Javed Burki and Guillermo Perry

Introduction

I N 1990, A GROUP OF LATIN AMERICAN AND CARIBBEAN (LAC) POLICY-MAKERS, REPRESENTATIVES of international agencies, and members of academic and "think-tank" communities participated in a conference sponsored by the Institute for International Economics in Washington. Their purpose was to evaluate the progress achieved by LAC countries in promoting economic policy reforms after the debt crisis of the 1980s. At the conclusion of the group's deliberations, John Williamson (1990) wrote that "Washington" (at least as represented by those attending) had reached a substantial degree of consensus regarding 10 policy instruments.[1] With but one exception (namely, the protection of property rights) the policy prescriptions of the "Washington Consensus" ignored the potential role that changes in institutions could play in accelerating the economic and social development of the region; it focused instead on the issues of fiscal discipline, liberalization of trade and investment regimes, deregulation of domestic markets, and privatization of public enterprises.[2]

Emerging from the debt crisis, the region's main priorities were to achieve macroeconomic stability and to dismantle the basic elements of the protectionist model of development—priorities that the consensual view saw as necessary to reap the potential benefits from rising global trade and financial flows. Subsequent experience has convincingly demonstrated that the policies prescribed by the Washington Consensus are

paying off. *The Long March*, a document we prepared for last year's World Bank-sponsored conference on development in LAC, which was held in Montevideo, reviewed the existing evidence and concluded that the region's resumption of economic growth in the 1990s had been closely associated with the implementation of many of the policies recommended by "Washington."

The expectation, however, was not only that globalization and the "first-generation" reforms would raise economic growth rates, but that they also would significantly reduce poverty and inequality. Indeed, capital inflows and export growth were expected to promote the development of labor-intensive sectors. This has not occurred. To be sure, the reforms have produced a decline in poverty rates, but this development seems to be more a consequence of the decline in inflation rates and modest growth, rather

than of the distributive consequences of trade and financial liberalization. In particular, the resumption of growth has not been accompanied by strong labor demand in the formal sector (in many countries either formal unemployment or informal employment have increased); export growth has been concentrated in natural-resource intensive industries; and the wage differentials between skilled and non-skilled labor appear to have widened. Consequently, income-distribution problems have not improved in many countries, and have deteriorated in others, which has resulted in poverty rates that remain unacceptably high. In addition, economic insecurity for the poor and middle classes, linked to job insecurity and income volatility, has tended to increase.

The Long March concluded, then, that further reforms were needed to achieve higher sustained rates of growth and to make a more significant dent in poverty reduction. It identified, in particular, the need to focus on improving the quality of investments in human development, promoting the development of sound and efficient financial markets, enhancing the legal and regulatory environment (in particular, deregulating labor markets and improving regulations for private investment in infrastructure and social services), improving the quality of the public sector (including the judiciary), and consolidating the gains in macroeconomic stability through fiscal strengthening. The report showed that such reforms would entail considerable "institutional" reforms.

This report examines the precise nature of the required institutional reforms and provides a framework for their design and implementation. We hope that it will help launch a dialogue among policy-makers, civil society, and the academic community in LAC on how best to design and reform institutions—that is, on how to "supply" institutional reforms to meet new societal demands.

What Is Meant by Institutional Change?

The terms "institutions" and "organizations" are often used as synonyms. This volume, however, does not treat them as such, adopting instead the definitions used by what is being called the "new institutional economics": **Institutions** are *rules* that shape the behavior of organizations and individuals in a society. They can be formal (constitutions, laws, regulations, contracts, internal procedures of specific organizations) or informal (values and norms). In contrast, **organizations** are *sets of actors* who collectively pursue common objectives. Using these definitions, this document focuses on reforming institutions—that is, rules—that determine the non-price incentives for the behavior of individuals and organizations. Specifically, in four key sectors—finance, education, justice, and public administration—the analysis emphasizes rules that may solve information and enforcement problems.

Research conducted for this report revealed that there is much that is still not known about the determinants of institutional change. The document makes it abundantly clear, nevertheless, that analytical tools are available that can facilitate analysis of this important topic. There is no pretense of covering all aspects of institutional reforms here, nor is it intended to produce a detailed manual for action. The more modest objective is to examine how the concepts of the new institutional economics are useful for analyzing and designing institutions (Chapter 1), and to evaluate how political-economy concepts can be used to develop strategies for implementing institutional reforms (Chapter 2). Employing some of the concepts elaborated in Chapters 1 and 2, the report demonstrates that sound institutional reform can be technically and politically viable in the key sectors we discuss (Chapters 3–7).

The Growing Demand for Institutional Reforms in Latin America and the Caribbean

The globalization of national economies, the implementation of the first-generation reforms, and the process of democratization in LAC are contributing to a rise in the demand for institutional reforms. The combination of exogenous factors promoting globalization (such as technological changes and economic and demographic trends in the developed economies) with the implementation of trade and financial liberalization has increased the demand for institutional reforms in LAC along three dimensions.

First, they have increased the demand for institutional reforms on the part of the private sector, which now competes in a global marketplace and has realized that its profitability or competitiveness is affected by the quality and efficiency of the delivery of financial and public services, the quality of education, and the effectiveness of the judicial system. In other words, there is a growing awareness that institutional reforms in these areas are needed to enhance the competitiveness of the private sector, which will in turn contribute to long-term economic growth.

Second, the rapid growth of volatile capital flows has increased the demand for institutional reforms that may help mitigate the risks associated with this trend. That is, globalization, despite its positive features, has increased the vulnerability of countries to developments occurring elsewhere, and there is a growing awareness that new or more effective financial institutions (at both the international and the national levels) are required to reduce this vulnerability.

Third, globalization has increased the demand for institutions that can help reduce income inequality and provide social safety nets for people who are rendered more vulnerable in the new competitive environment. This report, however, does not focus on this last set of topics, but only on those associated with the competitiveness and vulnerability issues—although educational institutions examined in Chapter 5 certainly can affect equity and social protection.

This is a defining moment in the institutional reform process in LAC. In the context of more open economies, institutional reforms and related organizational changes are greatly needed to enhance the competitiveness of the private sector, to reap the potential benefits of the economic reforms undertaken in the last decade, and to reduce the LAC region's financial vulnerability. The greater perception of such needs on the part of many different social actors is creating a rapidly increasing societal demand for institutional reforms.

This heightened demand coexists with a situation in which most LAC countries are lagging in institutional development compared with other countries with which they have to compete in international markets (see Chapter 1). In the following paragraphs we elaborate on some of these issues.

Demands Emanating from Globalization and First-Generation Reforms

The globalization of national economies has been proceeding at a rapid pace in recent years. Merchandise trade flows have grown three times faster than global production during the 1990s, and foreign direct investment (FDI) to developing countries has grown twice as fast as domestic production in these countries (World Bank 1997c). Also, a growing number of corporations now place their assembly plants, establish their offices, and sell their products and services across the world. The countries of the LAC region, liberalizing their trade and investment regimes to reap the potential benefits of such a process, have been active participants in this worldwide transformation.

Globalization has received a substantial impetus in the last decade from the enormous increase in international finance facilitated by the technological revolution in communication and informatics. This information revolution has produced such a reduction in transaction costs for the financial sector that it has created a truly global financial market, stimulated the rapid development of new financial products, and increased the speed at which international capital flows change directions. This process is likely to intensify in the years ahead as savings and demographic trends in the developed world are likely to provide increasing capital surpluses intermediated by large institutional investors with both the capacity and need to invest them across the globe in order to maintain acceptable rates of return and to diversify risks (World Bank 1997d).

Such developments open opportunities for all. They also create new risks. Most developing countries, and LAC countries in particular, have decided to open their economies to trade, investment, and financial flows in order to participate from the potential benefits provided by globalization. But often they have done so without an adequate institutional framework. As the World Bank warned early last year, in such cases the risks can be high (World Bank 1997d). Also, without adequate institutions, the potential benefits of globalization in terms of higher growth and investment rates will either not materialize or be too concentrated, thus exacerbating, rather than easing, inequalities and social tensions.

Stability in Global Economies: Learning from Experience

Recent international experiences have contributed greatly to the demand for reform by the private sector and political leaders. Prime examples are the Mexican peso crisis of 1994-95 and the more recent financial crisis in Asia. Regarding the latter, economies that until a year ago had performed extremely well for decades, and that followed generally sound macroeconomic policies, fell into a profound financial and currency crisis and are today experiencing sharp recessions, rising unemployment, and social unrest. Unsound financial and corporate-governance institutions created perverse incentives that led the private sector in those countries to misuse their access to huge short-term capital inflows, engaging in massive financial and currency risks that rendered them and their economies highly vulnerable to changes in investors' sentiments.

In short, we have learned that in a world of global financial integration, sound financial and corporate-governance **institutions** (in addition to sound macroeconomic policies) are essential for promoting a healthy intermediation and use of international capital flows. Without them, integrated economies are vulnerable to changes in investors' sentiments and thus to financial and currency crises, and private agents may become so exposed to financial and currency risks that a devaluation or an interest-rate hike could have devastating effects on the real economy. That is, good macro policy is not enough; *good institutions are critical for macroeconomic stability in today's world of global financial integration*.[3]

Thus, industrial and financial groups in all emerging markets are now realizing that their interests are exposed to high risks by the lack of sound institutions in these areas. Such a change of perception has already facilitated substantial progress in the reform of financial institutions in LAC since the Mexican peso crisis. (The financial crisis of the 1980s also led a few countries, like Chile and Colombia, to adopt significant reforms in their financial institutions.) Authorities throughout the region are busily engaged in further reform in this area, with strong support from public opinion and the private sector. Chapter 3 discusses the nature of the institutional reforms needed in the financial system (the so-called financial safety net) to respond to this growing societal demand.

It is not yet apparent to what extent the lessons from the Asian crisis will facilitate the reform of corporate governance institutions—i.e., those related to the disclosure of consolidated balance sheets by financial groups, shareholder rights, and the rights of creditors (including bankruptcy laws) that have proved to be so elusive throughout the region. The importance of such reforms for robust capital-market development is demonstrated in Chapter 4.

The inadequacy of present-day international institutions to deal with the new global financial market was also patently revealed in these crisis. However, such a topic is not the object of discussion in this report.

Demands Stemming from Democratization

The increased demand for institutional reforms stems from an array of non-economic and non-financial factors as well. With the important exception of Cuba, there is an ongoing process of consolidation and deepening of democracy throughout the LAC region. Citizens are demanding transparent and efficient governments, improved access to quality education, and reliable and efficient judiciaries. The deepening of democracy has also been accompanied by an increased emphasis on governmental decentralization and the devolution of governmental responsibilities to local governments and communities, which also necessarily entails profound changes in institutions. The importance and complexity of the topic of institutional reform in governmental decentralization (the rules that shape intergovernmental relations and local institutions) warrants a special treatment. It will be the exclusive subject matter of our report next year; hence, it is not examined in this report.

This process of consolidation and deepening of democracy in the region is receiving significant support from the international community. Indeed, the end of the Cold War has

brought renewed global attention to issues such as the access to justice for poor people, the protection of fundamental human rights, and democratic institutions in general. These developments, too, are adding to the new demands for reform of the institutional fabric of LAC countries.

***

In sum, globalization (and the powerful demonstration effects of recent financial crises), previous reforms, democratization in the region, and the end of the Cold War, have opened a "window of opportunity" for implementing comprehensive institutional reforms aiming to alter fundamentally the behavioral incentives for individuals and organizations in the LAC region. These developments have raised the effective demand for institutional reform.

Potential demand for reform, however, is not enough. The "supply" of institutional reform requires considerable ingenuity, both in technical and political terms, to solve the complex incentive issues involved and to overcome the resistance of losers as well as the obstacles to "collective action" that usually weaken the effective support of potential beneficiaries.

Factors Affecting The Supply of Institutional Change: Technical and Political Challenges

What are the main considerations bearing on the supply of institutional change? In the first place, some authors have argued that institutional reform is more difficult to implement than "first-generation" reforms (Graham and Naím 1998). But pessimists disregard the fact that the first stage of reforms in LAC was accompanied by significant institutional reform in several areas such as central bank independence, a shift from import licensing to dispute-resolution (related to anti-dumping and other "unfair" trading) rules in trade, and a complex new set of regulations for competition in the provision of infrastructure and public services. The indexes of institutional reform presented in Chapter 1 also indicate that substantial institutional reform has taken place since the early 1990s, especially in the protection of property rights, by reducing the risks of expropriation of private property and improving contract enforcement.

In addition to technical difficulties, it is undeniable, however, that a number of key political-economy factors may render further institutional—and policy—reform extremely difficult to implement. For example, organized and vocal groups that benefit from the existing institutional setup normally invest resources to mobilize opposition against institutional change (through lobbying, campaign financing, and the press), and, for reasons discussed below, it may prove difficult to mobilize the support of potential beneficiaries.

On the other hand, external or domestic technological, economic, or political shocks—plus the advancement of knowledge—change the way different actors perceive benefits and costs of existing and potential policies and institutions. This may change the resources available to interest groups to invest in favor of or against reform, and they may disrupt the existing political economy—enabling leaders to exploit the "window of opportunity" for institutional reform.

Dealing with Winners and Losers from Institutional Reform

The growing societal demand for institutional reform requires skillful political entrepreneurship to overcome the resistance of losers and to mobilize the support of winners. It is usually more difficult to mobilize winners than losers due to several factors.

First, potential benefits of reform are usually more uncertain and potential beneficiaries more difficult to identify, while potential costs are normally more certain and losers easily identify themselves.

Second, potential beneficiaries of reform are usually numerous, dispersed, poor, uninformed, and unorganized (what we have called "latent" interest groups), while potential losers tend to be more concentrated, rich, informed, organized, and vocal.

Third, appropriate sequencing of reforms from a technical point of view may be "time-inconsistent" from a political-economy point of view. For example, initial reforms may fortify interest groups that later can more effectively oppose the additional promised reforms. Chapter 2 examines some examples of these types of problems in the sequencing of financial reforms.

Overcoming Obstacles to Reform

There are, however, ways of overcoming these obstacles to reform. The mobilization of potential beneficiaries can be enhanced by carefully crafted public information campaigns, in which information about the potential benefits and likely beneficiaries of reform—and even the identification of losers—become public knowledge. In this way, the "asymmetric information" problem that commonly inhibits collective action by potential winners from institutional reforms can be mitigated.

Similarly, resistance of some losers can be overcome or at least reduced through different types of compensation schemes. Reformers may alter the technically optimal design of the reform in order to improve its political viability. This approach brings the danger of making reform possible at the expense of limiting its potential efficiency. However, as discussed in Chapter 2, there are institutional reforms (especially those that provide "choice" and "voice" to beneficiaries) that are sound from both technical and political points of view. Compensation schemes may also be included in careful "bundling" of a package of reforms, in such a way that losers of a particular component of the package benefit from another, thereby lessening their resistance to the proposed reform that may hurt them.

Finally, in those cases in which the optimal sequencing from a technical point of view may create political problems, governments may attempt to "lock in" their future commitments through international agreements or constitutional changes that increase "exit" costs and thus enhance the credibility of commitments. For example, participating in international negotiations under the auspices of the World Trade Organization or Regional Trade Agreements may enhance the credibility of economic and institutional reforms (Burki and Perry 1998).

Chapter 2 provides some guidelines for LAC reformers that may help the design of politically viable reform strategies, taking into account some features related to the political and governmental systems in the region, including political parties and the nature of executive-legislative relations.

Examples of Technical and Political Challenges to Institutional Reform in Four Key Sectors

Institutional change is not something that can be easily achieved, even in purely technical terms. Chapter 3, for example, illustrates the difficult tradeoffs involved in designing a safety-net system for the financial sector, which includes the central bank's role as lender of last resort, deposit insurance, prudential regulation, monitoring, and intervention and closure rules. In principle, a financial safety net should provide reasonable protection against systemic crises, which may develop because of asymmetric and incomplete information available to depositors regarding the quality of their banks' operations and portfolios. At the same time, however, the design of such a safety net should mitigate the moral hazard problem—that is, the incentives, accentuated by the very existence of the safety net, that induce excessive risk-taking by financial firms (which shifts some risks from depositors, and in some cases even from equity owners and debtors, to the government or taxpayers).

By the same token, Chapter 4 demonstrates that countries with civil-law systems, especially from the French tradition, such as most of LAC, have generally found it more difficult to provide adequate legal protection to creditors and minority shareholders and thus exhibit small, shallow, and concentrated capital markets that limit investment and growth opportunities.

In reference to the low quality and low efficiency of LAC public-education systems—as evidenced by the poor performance of LAC students in math and science tests and by the region's high repetition and dropout rates, respectively—observers historically have argued that such neglect was a result of the fact that elites in the region tended to educate their children in private schools, and thus had no interest in public-education reform. As mentioned above, the rise of global competition has now obviously increased the interest of the business community in the quality of public education. Communities are also putting enhanced pressure for improving the quality of public education.

Nevertheless, Chapter 5 makes it clear that reforming the institutions of basic education to achieve more efficiency and higher quality (in particular, changing the governance structure of schools to introduce autonomy and parental control; the incentive structure for teachers and their trainers, including the linking of payment structures to performance; and mechanisms for increasing school competition) remains a daunting task. This is so partly for technical reasons, but also because there are powerful actors (teacher associations and bureaucracies in the ministries of education) that are likely to oppose and effectively block such reforms, unless adequate inducements (for example, in terms of status, empowerment, and remuneration for teachers) are included in the reform package. Equally as important, the latent interests in favor of educational reform (parents and communities) must be effectively mobilized through public-information campaigns and by empowering them with "voice" (shifting decisions and resources to school councils with parental and community

participation) and "choice" (using credit and voucher mechanisms to enable families to choose from a greater number of schools).

A similar development is occurring with regard to the justice sector. The private sector is increasingly demanding more reliable and efficient judiciaries. At the same time, the poor and the excluded are demanding access to justice. The international community is also strongly urging reforms that provide independent and transparent judiciaries that effectively protect human rights. Substantial efforts have already been undertaken in a number of countries to give more independence to the judiciary, to modernize the courts, and to increase the salaries of judges. Results, however, are still inadequate. Chapter 6 argues that there is a need to confront the complex political issues related to the difficult balance between independence and accountability of judicial systems, and to modify the incentive structure in which judges and administrators operate. The chapter explores the potential benefits of requiring the full disclosure of judicial decisions, as well as of alternative reforms in the system of remuneration of judges and judicial sector administrators. It illustrates, among other things, the technical difficulties involved in designing performance-based remuneration policies for judges.

Finally, demand for public administration reform is also accelerating, due to the competitive demands of globalization and the deepening of democracy in the region, as discussed above. Chapter 7 discusses incentive problems that are extremely complex for public administrations, since they are intimately related to a chain of "principals" and "agents," running from voters to elected legislative organizations (congresses, councils) and executive officials (presidents, mayors), and from there to bureaucrats. Thus, public administration institutions are inextricably linked to political institutions.

The chapter examines why LAC countries have had such difficulty in constructing efficient and effective public bureaucracies—in particular why there is such widespread "informality" within the LAC public sector. It finds numerous difficulties related to the inadequacy of political institutions to which administrative behavior is intimately linked. It shows that as the consolidation of democratic institutions advances, especially as political parties modernize, opportunities for efficient reform of core public administrations will increase.

Chapter 7 also analyzes the feasibility of establishing

alternative models of public administration. In particular, the chapter examines the classic hierarchical model (based on checks and balances and highly centralized and strict personnel, budgetary, and monitoring systems, which are characteristic of continental Europe) and the so-called New Public Management model (based on managerial discretion and accountability, performance contracts, and competition for service delivery, which was pioneered by New Zealand and is being increasingly used, wholly or partially, by more advanced countries). It concludes that some features of the classic "hierarchical" model of public administration will probably need to be maintained and consolidated before the region can move to the implementation of New Public Management. It is not a surprise, therefore, that countries with relatively well-functioning hierarchical civil services, such as Chile and Costa Rica, are precisely those in the process of implementing reforms that move them toward the New Public Management model.

From Washington to Santiago

This report thus recognizes that although institutional reforms have become a priority in LAC and are being increasingly demanded by societal actors, their implementation poses significant technical and political challenges. Successful implementation of such reforms undoubtedly hinges on the ability of the region's political and technical leadership. Recent history provides grounds for optimism: The region's leaders have largely succeeded in the design and implementation of the first generation of reforms, and the recent challenges posed by globalization have been met decisively, without backtracking on economic reforms.

More recently, the region's leadership has explicitly accepted the challenge of responding to the increased demand for institutional reforms by adopting many elements of this institutional reform agenda in the Santiago Summit of April 1998. The presidents' declaration begins with ambitious goals for education, followed by explicit support for financial, judicial, and public-sector reforms.[4] This "Santiago Consensus," as coined by the president of the World Bank during the Summit, may play the same catalytic role for the reform agenda of the next decade as the one played by the Washington Consensus earlier in this decade.

President Sanguinetti of Uruguay recently underscored this point when he emphasized that such a consensus has emerged due to the widespread achievement of democratization, economic stabilization, and resumption of growth in the region. He thus highlighted the fact that democratization and the success of first generation reforms, both broadly endorsed throughout the region, are enabling regional leaders to focus on the institutional and social agenda.[5] As the countries of Latin America and the Caribbean confront the new millennium, it will be seen increasingly that "institutions matter."

Notes

1. According to Williamson (1990), the 10 policy instruments proposed by the "Washington Consensus" were fiscal discipline; public expenditure priorities in education and health; tax reform; positive but moderate market-determined interest rates; competitive exchange rates; liberal trade policies; openness to foreign direct investment; privatization; deregulation; and protection of property rights.

2. Williamson, however, concluded that, though he would have thought this was part of a tacit consensus, the region in practice had little concern with improving the protection of property rights, and little had been achieved in this area.

3. On the Mexican crisis see the articles in Edwards and Naím (1997), among others. On the Asian crisis see International Monetary Fund (1998), World Bank (1998a), and Perry and Lederman (1998).

4. "Declaration of Santiago," Second Summit of the Americas, Santiago, Chile, April 18, 1998.

5. Speech delivered at the Inter-American Development Bank, May 1998.

PART 1
Institutional Reform:
Why and How

CHAPTER 1

Institutions Matter for Development

THE SANTIAGO CONSENSUS ACKNOWLEDGES THAT THE POLITICAL AND ECONOMIC ENVIronment is ripe for launching a new set of institutional reforms in education, finance, justice, and civil service. One of the most difficult challenges, however, is to develop a coherent framework for analyzing and designing these new institutions. In this chapter (combined with the Technical Appendix), we attempt to clarify key concepts—discussing why institutions matter for development and examining empirical evidence that links institutional development to economic performance.

What Do We Mean by Institutions and Organizations?

A variety of meanings are commonly attached to the word "institution." Although it is often used as a synonym of "organization," we find useful the distinction made by the "new institutional economics" literature. It defines **institutions** as *formal and informal rules and their enforcement mechanisms that shape the behavior of individuals and organizations in society.*[1] By contrast, **organizations** are entities composed of people who act collectively in pursuit of shared objectives. Thus, *organizations* and individuals pursue their interests within an *institutional* structure defined by formal rules (constitutions, laws, regulations, contracts) and in-

formal rules (ethics, trust, religious precepts, and other implicit codes of conduct)—see Boxes 1.1 and 1.2. Organizations, in turn, have internal rules (i.e., *institutions*) to deal with personnel, budgets, procurement, and reporting procedures, which constrain the behavior of their members. Thus, institutions constitute the incentive structure for the behavior of organizations and individuals.

For economic analysis it is useful to distinguish between two sets of institutions: markets and hierarchies. **Markets** are a set of institutions (rules and their enforcement mechanisms) that set the stage for conducting discrete and impersonal transactions, without requiring a continuous contractual relationship. These rules can range from definitions of location and timing for conducting certain transactions, to more complex rules set out by contract law, financial-credit laws, and courts and arbitration procedures

that attempt to enforce such rules. Some of these rules regulate actors who provide market-enhancing services, such as accountants, auditors, lawyers, and others.

Hierarchies are sets of rules for making transactions based on vertical lines of decision-making authority. For example, organizations often operate under internal rules that establish levels of responsibility and accountability, where some members are entrusted to monitor the performance of others. The specialized literature on institutional economics has pointed out that hierarchies are set up to establish contractual obligations—such as those between managers and their employees in private and public organizations—to produce goods and services with lower transaction and monitoring costs than would be required in pure market transactions (see definitions in the Technical Appendix) (T. Moe 1984, O. Williamson 1981).

BOX 1.1
Examples of Formal Institutions

Laws and regulations are formal rules that determine the incentive structure and thus affect the behavior of individuals and private organizations, such as firms, in the operation of markets.

Contracts of civil servants, as is the case with contracts among private individuals or organizations, and personnel, budgetary, procurement, reporting, and audit procedures are the formal rules that affect the incentives within public organizations.

Constitutional laws, which also affect the incentives of politicians at the various levels of government, are the formal rules that determine the political and fiscal responsibilities of and the relations among the various levels of government (i.e., federal, provincial, city, and other governments).

Examples of Informal Institutions

Trust or the tendency to cooperate among individuals who encounter each other infrequently is an informal rule based on the fact that individuals usually have a good sense of what type of behavior will ensure mutual cooperation. Trust plays an important role in the functioning of large public and private organizations.

Ethics or **values** also tend to constrain individual behavior by establishing informal codes of conduct.

Political norms that are often implicit usually constrain the behavior of politicians and civil servants.

BOX 1.2
Examples of Organizations

Political organizations include legislative chambers and committees, political parties, government agencies, and the judiciary.

Economic organizations include private firms, trade unions, and business associations.

Social organizations include non-governmental organizations (NGOs), schools, and parent-teacher associations (PTAs).

Why Do Institutions Matter for Development?

Neoclassical economics assumes, among other things, that markets are "perfect"; all actors are assumed to have complete and freely acquired information about the quality and prices of the goods and services in all transactions, as well as about other actors' reliability. So individuals and firms can choose efficiently what to buy or sell and from whom. It also assumes that there are no enforcement problems; that is, once a decision is made it is carried out smoothly and cost-free. In this ideal situation, the supplier would indeed deliver the product and service in the agreed quantity and quality, and the buyer would pay the corresponding amounts in a timely fashion.

There are a few markets for which this description is reasonably accurate—what institutional economists call spot-market trading (Williamson 1994). For example, shopping for groceries at supermarkets on a periodic basis is usually done in circumstances that closely mimic the neoclassical assumptions. Shoppers consume the products over a few days and over time become familiar with the quality and prices of different goods—sometimes we are even allowed to taste them in the store. Shoppers can even try a few different supermarkets and get information from neighbors and friends. Though we may make some mistakes in the process, basically we can choose what we want. And we get what we pay for, as we take the goods with us when we leave the market. If we don't like them we won't buy them again; in some cases we may even return them. The supermarket, in turn, gets compensated on time, as shoppers are not allowed to leave the premises without paying, though there may be a few cases of shoplifting, bad checks, and credit cards (which are actually issues associated with the more complex world of finance).

In practice, however, there are many sets of rules for making transactions within organizations and elsewhere that fall somewhere between markets and pure hierarchies. By way of illustration, consider the New Zealand model of civil service reform, where public servants now face a set of incentives that reward or punish performance relative to explicit objectives or outcomes, which is complemented by a system for reporting and monitoring performance (see Bale and Dale 1998, Schick 1998). In this way, public servants must operate in a hierarchy, but with institutional features that mimic the incentives of competitive markets, namely by establishing a link between performance and rewards. (See Chapters 6 and 7.)

Many markets—in fact, some of the most important ones—are a long way from this bucolic description of spot-market transactions. This is especially true with capital and durable goods and services that are consumed over a long time. In such cases, transactions are not repeated often enough among a fixed number of partners to permit perfect and cost-free information-gathering through feedback, and enforcement is often a more complex and costly matter. In extreme cases, the problems of **information and enforcement** may be so severe as to preclude the existence of markets and leave no option besides the direct provision of certain goods or services by the government, or people must live without such goods or services. In the following paragraphs we consider a few examples of long-term contracting in two of the most important services for growth and development in today's global economy—the financial and the education sectors.

Information and Enforcement Problems in a Market: The Financial Sector

Before approving loans, bankers want to be sure that their clients will be able and willing to pay them back. Borrowers' ability to pay depends on the quality of the investments that the borrowers make with the funds, and also on their overall earnings and wealth, so to assess these factors banks require potential borrowers to provide financial statements and describe how they will use the loans. Bankers then charge fees and interest rates according to their credit-risk analysis; consumer credit is normally riskier and commands a higher premium, and poor or small firms either do not get credit approved, or get it at higher costs than wealthier individuals or firms. When clients have an established reputation with the bank, this fact alone may be sufficient to get loans approved. When clients and the bank do not have an ongoing relationship, the bank will try to get information on their past behavior from other sources, such as credit bureaus, rating agencies, or commercial references. Also, the bank probably will require such borrowers to put down collateral, which is why there needs to be an enforcement mechanism to ensure the bank that it will be able to collect the collateral in the event the clients default on the loan.

Both formal and informal institutions are crucial for the operation of credit transactions like the one described above. If there is a culture of "non-payment" in a society, if there are no credit bureaus, if creditor rights are weak, and

if the courts take forever to foreclose on collateral, a lot of potential borrowers with the ability and willingness to pay will be cut off from credit altogether—either because banks will not be able to distinguish between "good" and "bad" potential clients, or because they will be less willing to take chances. From the point of view of the banker, the perceived risks may simply be too high because of inadequate information and enforcement procedures.

In this type of situation, bankers will lend only at very high rates. But at very high interest rates few creditworthy businesses can afford to borrow. Thus, only businesses with very high potential returns, or very risky ventures, or those that do not intend to pay will demand credit. (This is the **adverse selection** problem discussed in the Technical Appendix.) Knowing that only risky borrowers will come knocking at the door, bankers may not lend at all—or they may lend only to clients they know personally or ones that are economically related to the bank. The economy as a whole, therefore, will face massive credit rationing (or **incomplete markets**; see the Technical Appendix), which will severely limit its growth potential.

The availability of information regarding the past behavior and credit-worthiness of potential borrowers may go a long way toward reducing the extent of credit rationing in an economy, because it helps banks distinguish among different types of clients. Nevertheless, having all the relevant information, through private or public services that provide credit and earning histories, will not solve the problem of enforcement; every now and then a "good" client defaults on a loan. Moreover, when the stakes are high enough in any given transaction, the borrower may have an incentive to cheat. Bankers know this, and thus credit rationing is not eliminated as long as there is a problem with enforcement.

Bank depositors face even more acute problems of information and enforcement. They usually do not have enough information to evaluate the quality of the bank's overall loan portfolio, and thus have to "trust" the bank, either because they know it well or because they have faith in those who supervise it. Imperfect information can lead to a loss of trust, and can cause depositors to withdraw their deposits even from solvent banks. Such panics can cause those sound banks to fail and may lead to a systemic financial crisis. This realization has led to the creation of various types of explicit safety nets, including deposit insurance institutions, as well as implicit safety nets that often are implemented during times of banking distress. As will be discussed in Chapter 3, such safety nets should be accompanied by effective systems of information collection, client monitoring, and risk management in order to ameliorate the effects that such schemes have on the incentive of depositors not to monitor the banks by themselves (Kane 1989)—which leads to the **moral hazard** problem discussed in the Technical Appendix.

Even more difficult information and enforcement issues are present in the equities markets. Unless there are good disclosure rules, rating agencies, and specialized investment assistance services, potential buyers of equities can know little about the financial status and prospects of a firm issuing stock. They will be likely to presume that company managers are offering new stock above its "real" price and either will not buy it at all, or will offer to buy it at a price too low for the managers to accept. Thus, equities markets do not develop without solving the information problem. And even then, if shareholders' rights are not protected and guaranteed through an effective enforcement mechanism, equities markets tend to remain shallow.

In general, financial sectors are highly regulated and tightly supervised everywhere, and banking safety nets, financial laws, and practices are crucial for the depth, efficiency, stability, and the very existence of financial markets. These and other issues will be discussed in more detail in Chapters 3 and 4.

Information and Enforcement Problems in Hierarchies: The Education Sector

Information and enforcement problems are even more severe in the case of education. "Consumer" choice is limited, among other things, by the fact that quality and relevance can be fully evaluated only after the individual has finished the educational process. There are no repeated transactions to learn from, and it is extremely costly to change schools. Parents usually have to rely on certifications, evaluations, and statistics provided by governments or non-governmental agencies—or just on casual information—to decide where to send their children to school. Once they make a decision (if indeed they *can* choose) they have to rely on the school director and on the government, or on their own participation in the management of the school, for "enforcement." Households implicitly rely on school managers and government policies to ensure that their children are receiving minimally adequate education.

Hence, the education system can be viewed as a series of **principal-agent** relationships (see the Technical Appendix): The households and parents are the principals who entrust civil servants, teachers, or school managers (the agents) to defend the interests of their children. In so doing, monitoring and enforcement institutions are crucial for ensuring that the agents will indeed act according to the children's interests.

Due to the severity of informational and enforcement problems and to the character of education as a "public good," many societies rely on hierarchical governmental organizations to deliver educational services, at least for basic education.[2] The existence of such governmental organizations, however, does not automatically resolve the information and enforcement problems. There must be adequate ways for the civil servants in a ministry of education to know how well a particular school or teacher is performing and to take appropriate corrective actions or create appropriate incentives for school managers and teachers. In addition, bureaucratic appointments and rules are often designed with political purposes in mind, which do not always result in efficient institutions that allow this to happen (see the section on political-economy issues below). Indeed, as will be discussed later in Chapter 5, Latin American and Caribbean educational systems suffer from numerous problems that are symptomatic of a lack of information and enforcement, including teacher absenteeism and even illiteracy, high desertion and repetition rates among students, and blatantly poor instruction.

The problems of information and enforcement of commitments are also present in large private corporations. Indeed, economics and legal literature on **transaction costs** (see the Technical Appendix for definitions), dating back at least to the 1930s, has been preoccupied with the effects of such costs on organizational choices for private business rather than governments (Coase 1937). In particular, the transaction-costs literature has focused on the key question of when firms should procure services and inputs in a market and when they should produce them themselves. For example, should a firm that makes automobiles also make auto parts, or should it buy the parts from external suppliers? To make this type of decision, managers must consider the frequency with which the firm requires auto parts, the degree of uncertainty affecting the delivery and quality of the parts, and the specific investments that are required to produce such parts. On the one hand, the production of auto parts may require certain machines and workers with specific skills that are expensive to acquire, but on the other hand, the outside suppliers may work with unknown quality controls and may have commercial interests that do not necessarily coincide with those of the auto-producing firm. It is not surprising, therefore, that automobile producers across the globe have chosen different strategies for acquiring auto parts; some produce them in house, others have a pre-determined pool of suppliers, while others try their luck in the auto-parts market without having made specific commitments with any particular supplier. The right decision can only be based on accurate information and on the ability to enforce contracts or commitments with suppliers.

***

At this point it should be clear that information and enforcement problems underscore the need for appropriate institutions both for markets (for their efficiency and in many cases for their very existence) and for hierarchies, or organizations. *Institutions matter for development because they determine the efficiency and existence of both markets and organizations, public or private.*

In addition, institutions determine the level of investment in both physical and human capital and the dynamics of innovation, since they determine the perceived risks by individuals and other economic agents of conducting investments and undertaking risks. Thus, both the rate of capital accumulation (physical and human) and their quality and efficiency depend on formal and informal institutions. And thus, we expect institutions to influence the rate of economic growth.

Finally, institutions are absolutely necessary with respect to the production and quality of public goods, like clean air or security in the streets. Unlike private goods, there are no efficient ways to exclude these public goods from people who do not help finance them; this generates the well-known problem of free riders and "market failures" that require specific institutions (rules) and organizations to collect taxes or contributions, as well as to ensure the quantity and quality of the public goods and to deliver them. *Good institutions, in summary, should provide rules that are clear, widely known, coherent, applicable to all, predictable, credible, and properly and evenly enforced.*

Institutions Matter: The Evidence

We have already discussed how institutions matter for economic performance. Here we will provide some empirical

evidence about the relationship between institutional development and economic growth, stability, and poverty reduction; we will review some contributions to the emerging empirical literature, and we will evaluate LAC in relation to other regions of the world.

Issues of Measurement and Some Illustrations

A first issue that arises is how to measure institutional development. The recent empirical literature on the subject has tended to rely on subjective and objective indicators of the quality of institutions around the world. The **subjective indicators** come from surveys of international and domestic investors (Brunetti et al. 1997a) or from international economic and political consultants who deal with the business climate of numerous countries on a daily basis (many studies listed in Table 1.1 use this type of indicator). Some studies have used **objective indicators**, too; they assess whether certain legal provisions are present to get a broad measure of the overall quality of institutions in the financial sector and in corporate governance structures (La Porta et al. 1998a).

In this chapter (Figures 1.1–1.17) we rely on the subjective measures provided by the *International Country Risk Guide (ICRG)*. Given our understanding of the importance of contract enforcement, property rights, and the incentives affecting the behavior of bureaucrats, we have chosen five individual indicators to measure institutional development: (1) the perceived risk of expropriation of property, (2) the perceived degree of contract enforceability, (3) the extent to which there are mechanisms for peaceful dispute-resolution or the perceived degree of the rule of law and order, (4) the perceived quality of public bureaucracies, and (5) the perceived incidence of corruption in government. In addition, we constructed a composite index of institutional development, which is the sum of the scores given to each country for each of the five indicators listed above. The Technical Appendix at the back of this publication details the variables used in our analysis.

Despite the fact that these subjective indicators have been used in a plethora of empirical studies (to be discussed below), they suffer from a number of noteworthy weaknesses. Two of them are particularly important for our current purpose of examining the link between these indicators and economic activity: First, these indicators reflect the perceptions of ICRG analysts, which undoubtedly are affected by objective economic or political conditions. Consequently, the indicators may be contaminated with the influence of factors or events that are not necessarily reflections of institutional quality. Second, among the factors that may influence the perception of the analysts is economic performance, which may bias estimates of the relationship between these indicators and economic growth. It is also important to note that the five indicators tend to be correlated with each other, and with other indicators of institutional quality and political stability (see Knack and Keefer 1995). These considerations should be kept in mind while interpreting the evidence presented below.

Figures 1.1a and 1.1b illustrate the relationship between our composite index of institutional development and economic growth (the rate of growth of GDP per capita). The upward sloping line shows that, on average, higher scores in institutional development are associated with higher rates of growth. Figure 1.1a shows the fitted line from a simple linear regression. While this method is straightforward, it suffers from several weaknesses, includ-

ing the fact that growth is determined by a variety of factors not limited to institutional development—factors which may be caused by economic growth.

To deal with these issues, Figure 1.1b shows what could be considered the "true" relationship between growth and institutional development. We have followed Greene (1993, p. 180) to estimate the partial correlation coefficient between growth and our composite index of institutional development. In a nutshell, we followed a three-step econometric procedure that attempts to isolate the impact of institutional quality on growth. The intuition of the procedure is that we must first determine how much of the variation in growth rates across countries is due to other economic factors (such as inflation, trade, the size of the financial sector, the terms of trade, and its volatility). Then, we must determine how much of the variation in our composite index is also associated with these other economic factors. Once we have isolated the portion of growth and institutional development that is

FIGURE 1.1a

Institutional Development and Economic Growth

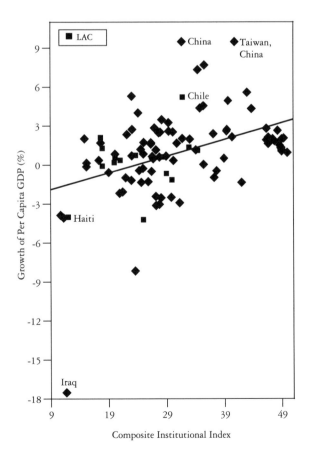

FIGURE 1.1b

The "True" Partial Coefficient Between Growth and Institutional Development

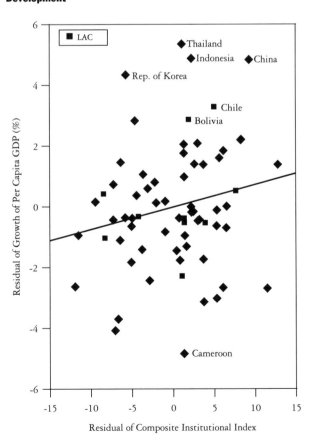

not associated with these other factors we can attempt to measure the extent of the "true" relationship between economic activity and institutional development.[3] As you can see in Figure 1.1b, this more elaborate procedure confirms the positive relationship between growth and institutional development.[4]

A Brief Review of Recent Empirical Studies

Table 1.1 lists recent empirical studies that examine the relationship between various indicators of institutional development and economic performance. The evidence is clear regarding the relationship between institutions and economic growth: Improvements in institutions promote economic growth, thus confirming our own estimates.

The first section of Table 1.1 lists studies that have evaluated the relationship between various institutional indicators and economic growth. Most of these studies have found evidence that the subjective indicators of the quality of formal institutions are positively associated with indicators of economic performance. Moreover, there are two (La Porta et al. 1997b and Knack and Keefer 1997b) that examine the effects of informal rules, namely trust, on economic performance, and find that trust (more than formal social organizations) tends to promote economic growth.

The second part of Table 1.1 lists studies that have examined the relationship between institutional measures (mostly objective qualitative measures compiled by La Porta et al. 1998a) and financial development and stability. Levine (1997c) took the extra step of estimating the indirect effect of these measures on economic growth by assessing the effects of institutions on financial deepening, which in turn promotes economic growth. In the area of financial development, we have included one study that examines the role of institutional development on the probability of experiencing a financial crisis (Demirgüç-Kunt and Detragiache 1998), and another on the impact of explicit deposit-insurance schemes on financial development (Cull 1998). The former confirms our contention that institutions are important for maintaining financial and macroeconomic stability, because the authors show that institutional development (measured with our same subjective indexes for the rule of law, corruption, and contract enforcement) reduces the probability of financial crises after financial liberalization (defined as the elimination of interest-rate ceilings). Cull found that explicit deposit insurance schemes tend to promote financial development

in subsequent periods of time *ONLY* when the general subjective indicators of institutional quality, such as the rule of law, are sufficiently high.

The third and final part of Table 1.1 lists two recent studies by Chong and Calderón who have analyzed the relationship between institutions and inequality and poverty reduction. In this respect note that the subjective indexes of institutional development tend to reduce poverty, despite an apparent ambiguous relationship between institutions and inequality.[5]

LAC's Progress in Institutional Development

After this brief review of the empirical evidence, it is worthwhile to assess where the LAC region stands in terms of institutional development relative to other regions and relative to its recent past.[6] Figures 1.2–1.7 show the evolution of the six institutional indicators (the composite index plus its five components) for the various regions of the world, based on the simple averages of the indicators by region. (Note that for negative criteria, such as repudiation of contracts and corruption, a high score in these indexes means a *lack* of them; for positive criteria, such as law and order or quality of bureaucracy, a high score means *more* of them. For a more detailed explanation, see the Data Appendix. Also see the Data Appendix for the list of countries in each regional group.) From Figure 1.2 we can see clearly that LAC is lagging behind most regions of the world, except for Sub-Saharan Africa, in terms of the composite index of institutional development, despite the significant recent progress achieved since 1990. Also, it is apparent that other regions, namely the Middle East/North Africa and Asia, have experienced rapid improvements, also since the late 1980s, thus showing that institutional development can actually occur quickly.

Figures 1.3 and 1.4 show the evolution of the indicators related to the risk of repudiation of contracts and expropriation, respectively. They show clearly that LAC has made very rapid improvement, probably because of structural reforms, including privatization, that have been implemented across the region since the late 1980s.[7] However, it is also clear from these two figures that while LAC has experienced progress on both fronts, it is still lagging behind other regions, especially regarding contract enforceability, as shown in Figure 1.3.

In contrast, Figures 1.5–1.7 show that LAC's progress in terms of corruption, law and order, and the quality of

TABLE 1.1

Empirical Evidence of the Role of Institutions for Economic Growth, Financial Development, Inequality, and Poverty

AUTHORS	METHODOLOGY	MAIN FINDINGS
I. INSTITUTIONS PROMOTE ECONOMIC GROWTH		
Knack and Keefer (1995)	Cross-country regressions using two subjective indexes of institutional development. One composite index combines variables such as quality of the bureaucracy, corruption in government, rule of law, expropriation risk, and repudiation of contracts by government. The other combines variables such as bureaucratic delays, nationalization potential, contract enforceability, and infrastructure quality.	Institutions that protect property rights are crucial for economic growth. Institutional development increases the rates of convergence between developed and developing countries.
Mauro (1995)	Cross-country regressions using subjective indexes of corruption, the amount of red tape, the efficiency of the judicial system, and various categories of political stability.	Corruption is negatively linked with economic growth.
Brunnetti, Kisunko, and Weder (1997a)	A survey of business establishments around the world to construct an index of the "credibility of rules," composed of "the predictability of rule-making, subjective perceptions of political instability, security of persons and property, predictability of judicial enforcement, and corruption." Cross-firm and cross-country regressions test the relationship between the credibility index and economic growth.	Credibility promotes investment and economic growth.
Chong and Calderón (1997a)	Geweke decomposition to test the causality and feedback between institutional measures (such as contract enforceability, nationalization potential, infrastructure quality, bureaucratic delays, and a composite index of the above four) and economic growth.	Improving institutional development promotes economic growth in developing countries.
Knack and Keefer (1997a)	Cross-country regressions using institutional variables such as the rule of law, the pervasiveness of corruption, the risk of expropriation, and contract repudiation.	Institutions are important determinants of "convergence"—weak institutional systems prevent poor countries from "catching up."
Knack and Keefer (1997b)	Cross-country regressions using indicators of trust and civic norms from the World Values Surveys by Inglehart (1994). The indicators can be interpreted as proxies for the quality of informal institutions.	Trust and civic cooperation have significant impacts on economic performance.
La Porta et al. (1997b)	Cross-country regressions using measures of trust from the World Values Surveys.	Trust has important effects on economic performance.

the bureaucracy has been much less pronounced than that achieved in terms of contract enforceability and expropriation risk. Indeed, the region has barely made any improvements on the corruption and bureaucratic-quality fronts. These indexes highlight the critical importance of reforming the public administration in LAC (see Chapter 7).

However, the regional averages mask the diversity that exists within the LAC region. Figures 1.8–1.13 show the evolution of these indicators for four sub-regional groupings within LAC. Figure 1.8 shows that all sub-regions have experienced moderate progress in terms of the composite index, with no apparent laggard among the sub-regions, though the Southern Cone countries stand clearly above the rest.

Figures 1.9 and 1.10 confirm our previous statement that the LAC region has made substantial progress in terms

of reducing the risk of contract repudiation and expropriation, and this progress has been evenly distributed across LAC sub-regions, though the Southern Cone fares better, and the countries of the Andean Community (i.e., the Northern Cone countries) are second. Figures 1.11–1.13 also confirm our contention that LAC's progress in terms of the other three institutional indicators has been modest across the board, with some clear exceptions. For example, Figure 1.11 shows that Central American countries fare better than the rest of the region in terms of lower levels of perceived corruption, and that they and the Caribbean countries have experienced the most significant improvements in terms of reducing the extent of perceived corruption. Figures 1.12 and 1.13 shows that the Southern Cone countries fare better in terms of rule of law and quality of the bureaucracy, but that Central America and Panama as

TABLE 1.1

(Continued)

AUTHORS	METHODOLOGY	MAIN FINDINGS
II. INSTITUTIONS PROMOTE FINANCIAL DEVELOPMENT (AND ECONOMIC GROWTH)		
La Porta et al. (1997a)	Cross-country regressions using measures of legal rules protecting investors and the quality of their enforcement (measures include rule of law, shareholder rights, one-share equals one-vote, and creditor rights). The data on these qualitative, but objective variables (except for rule of law) are presented in La Porta et al. (1998a).	Countries with better investor protections have bigger and broader equity and debt markets.
Levine (1997c)	Panel regressions using institutional variables (such as creditor rights, enforcement of contracts, and accounting standards) as instrumental variables.	Countries with more developed institutions (legal and regulatory systems) have better-developed financial intermediaries, and consequently grow faster.
Cull (1998)	Cross-country regressions in levels and differences.	Explicit deposit insurance is positively correlated with subsequent increases in financial depth if adopted when government credibility and institutional development are high.
Demirgüç-Kunt and Detragiache (1998)	Panel logit regressions using rule of law, corruption, and contract enforcement as measures for institutional development as determinants of the probability of financial crisis after interest-rate liberalizations.	Banking crises are more likely to occur after financial liberalization. However, the effect of financial liberalization on the fragility of the banking sector is weaker when the institutions are more developed.
III. INSTITUTIONS, INEQUALITY, AND POVERTY		
Chong and Calderón (1997b)	Cross-country regressions using measures of risk of expropriation, risk of contract repudiation, law and order, corruption in government, and quality of bureaucracy for institutional development, and measures proposed by Foster, Greer, and Thorbecke (1984) for poverty.	Improvements in institutional efficiency reduce the degree, severity, and incidence of poverty.
Chong and Calderón (1998)	Cross-country regressions using a composite index of institutional efficiency based on measures of corruption of government, quality of bureaucracy, law-and-order tradition, risk of expropriation, and risk of contract repudiation.	For poor countries, institutional efficiency is positively linked with income inequality, and for rich countries it is negatively linked with income inequality.

a group experienced the fastest improvement in terms of the quality of its bureaucracy.

Figures 1.14–1.17 show the evolution of the composite institutional indexes by country, and some outliers are worth mentioning. Chile, first, and Costa Rica, second, stand out in their groups, and in the overall sample, as having better institutions than the rest. In contrast, Haiti, Honduras, and Paraguay stand at the bottom of their groups. Rule of law and corruption have improved substantially in some countries, while they have strongly deteriorated in others.

So far we have focused on our subjective indicators of institutional performance. The *World Development Report 1997* (World Bank 1997a) presented other subjective indicators based on worldwide private-sector surveys conducted in 1996 (see Brunetti et al. 1997b). Figures

1.18–1.20 respectively show the percentage of respondents to the surveys in each region of the world who thought that the authorities tend to be incapable of protecting persons or property from criminal actions, that unexpected changes in laws and policies affect business, and that the unpredictability of the judiciary materially affects business practices. Clearly, LAC also seems to be behind other developing areas, especially with regard to the insecurity of property and the reliability of the judiciary. This evidence, combined with the aforementioned gap in terms of our law-and-order indicator, reinforces the need to consider innovative approaches to reforming LAC judicial systems (see Chapter 6).

As a whole, the evidence presented here shows that the LAC region still suffers from an "institution gap," relative to other developing countries, despite recent accomplishments

FIGURE 1.2

Composite Institutional Index by Regions, 1984–97

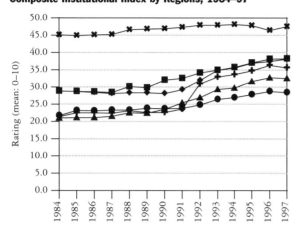

FIGURE 1.5

Corruption in Government Index by Regions, 1984–98

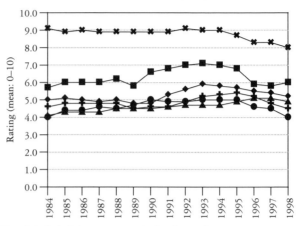

Note: A rise in the index represents a reduction of corruption.

FIGURE 1.3

Risk of Repudiation of Contracts Index by Regions, 1984–97

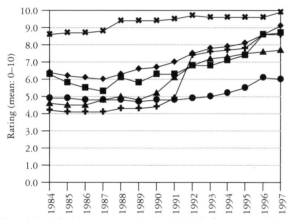

Note: A rise in the index represents a reduction in the risk of contract repudiation.

FIGURE 1.6

Law-and-Order Index by Regions, 1984–98

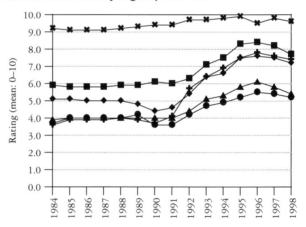

FIGURE 1.4

Risk of Expropriation Index by Regions, 1984–97

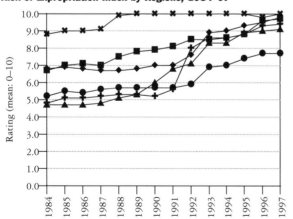

Note: A rise in the index represents a reduction in the risk of expropriation.

FIGURE 1.7

Quality of the Bureaucracy Index by Regions, 1984–98

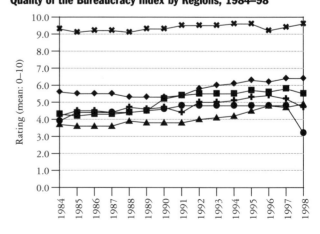

◆ Asia   ■ Europe and Central Asia   ▲ LAC   ✛ Middle East and North Africa   ✖ OECD   ● Sub-Saharan Africa

FIGURE 1.8

Composite Institutional Index by LAC Sub-regions, 1984–97

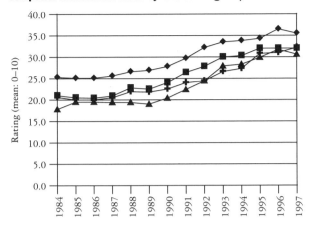

FIGURE 1.9

Risk of Repudiation of Contracts Index by LAC Sub-regions, 1984–97

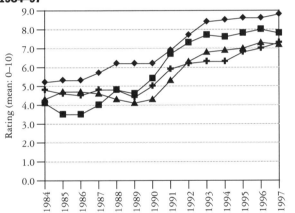

Note: A rise in the index represents a reduction in the risk of repudiation of contracts.

FIGURE 1.10

Risk of Expropriation Index by LAC Sub-regions, 1984–97

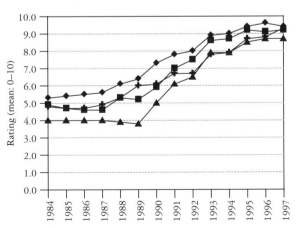

Note: A rise in the index represents a reduction in the risk of expropriation.

FIGURE 1.11

Corruption Index by LAC Sub-regions, 1984–98

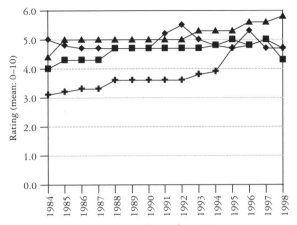

Note: A rise in the index represents a reduction of corruption.

FIGURE 1.12

Law-and-Order Index by LAC Sub-regions, 1984–98

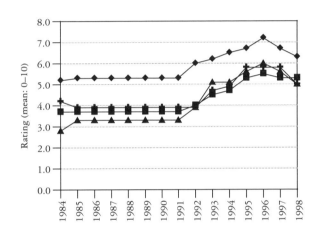

FIGURE 1.13

Quality of the Bureaucracy Index by LAC Sub-regions, 1984–98

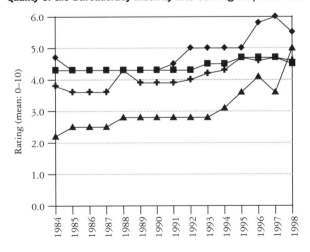

◆ Southern Cone ■ Northern Cone ▲ Central America and Panama ✛ Mexico and the Caribbean

21

FIGURE 1.14

LAC: Southern Cone Composite Institutional Index, 1984–97

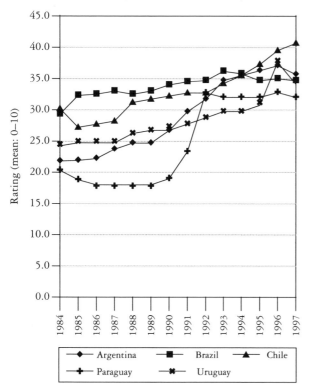

FIGURE 1.16

LAC: Central America and Panama Composite Institutional Index, 1984–97

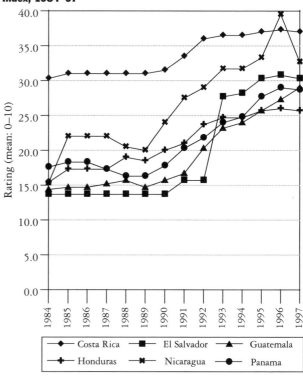

FIGURE 1.15

LAC: Northern Cone Composite Institutional Index, 1984–97

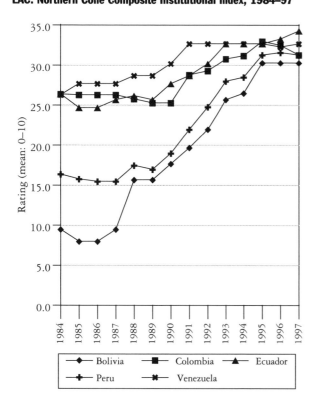

FIGURE 1.17

LAC: Mexico and the Caribbean Composite Institutional Index, 1984–97

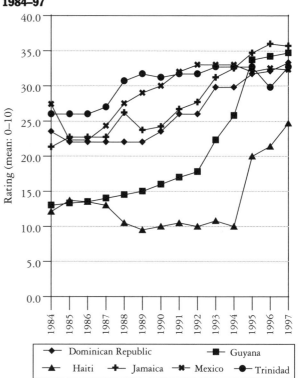

FIGURE 1.18

Insecurity of Property Index by Regions

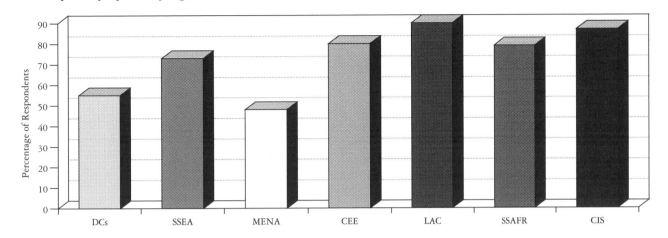

FIGURE 1.19

Unpredictable Changes in Laws and Policies Index by Regions

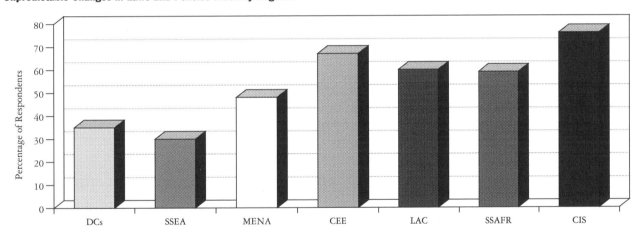

FIGURE 1.20

Unreliable Judiciaries Index by Regions

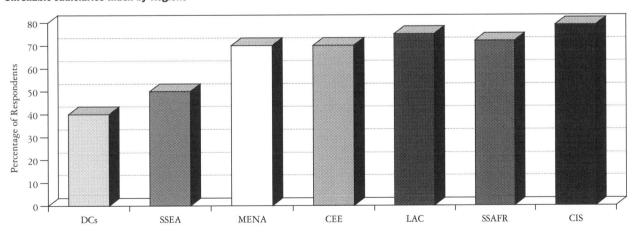

Note: Indexes reflect the percentage of survey respondents who thought that this consideration was an important obstacle to conducting business.

Key: DCs = Developed Countries   SSEA = South and Southeast Asia   MENA = Middle East and North Africa   CEE = Central and Eastern Europe
     LAC = Latin America and the Caribbean   SSAFR = Sub-Saharan Africa   CIS = Commonwealth of Independent States

in the areas of expropriation risk and contract enforcement. So, much remains to be done to improve the quality of institutions—and thus to help accelerate the pace of long-term growth and reduce short-term instability. The remaining question is how policy-makers can promote institutional change, which can be a challenging task indeed.

Notes

1. North (1990) and O. Williamson (1985) are well-known contributions to this extensive literature. North (1990, p. 73) defines organizations as "purposive entities designed by their creators to maximize wealth, income, or other objectives defined by the opportunities afforded by the institutional structure of the society."

2. Education is a "public good" in at least two aspects: First, when a public school is set up, all households in that jurisdiction can benefit from it. Second, and more generally, education tends to promote social peace and economic prosperity in the long run, which benefits all households, regardless of whether they have contributed to the financing or administration of the schools, or even whether they have children in school.

3. The econometric procedure was the following: First, we estimated the relationship between growth and a set of standard explanatory variables—the initial level of educational attainment in the population, the initial level of GDP per capita in constant dollars, the initial ratio of investment-to-GDP, the average ratio of trade over GDP, the average inflation rate, the initial level of M2 to GDP, the average variation of the terms of trade, and the standard deviation of the terms of trade. (See the Data Appendix for a detailed description of these variables.) From this procedure, we calculated the portion of the growth rate that was not associated with these control variables (the residuals). Second, we ran a similar regression that estimated the effects of these control variables on the composite index of institutional development, and similarly estimated the por-

tion of institutional development that was not explained by the control variables (again, the residuals). Finally, we estimated the linear relationship between the two sets of residuals, which gives us a measure of the "true" relationship between growth and institutional development. It is worth pointing out that to some extent we have dealt with the issue of causality by using the initial level of the composite institutional index (corresponding to the year 1984) in these regressions.

4. The coefficient of the composite institutional index in the simple regression shown in Figure 1.1a is significant at the 1 percent confidence interval. The "true" partial coefficient shown in Figure 1.1b is significant at the 11 percent confidence interval. The residuals exercise was also done using data for two sub-periods separately (1984–89 and 1990–95), and on the pooled data for both subperiods. The results of these exercises confirmed the positive and significant relationship between growth and institutional development.

5. According to Chong and Calderón (1998), one potential explanation for the apparent positive relationship between formal institutional development and inequality is that in some developing countries informal institutions tend to predominate in the business transactions of the poor. Hence it is possible that the development of formal institutions benefits the formal sector more than the informal sector. But this is just an untested hypothesis, and the results of this study are based purely on cross-country regressions, which do not tell us anything precise about the potential dynamic effects of institutional development on poor countries over time.

6. In last year's *The Long March,* we also used ICRG data to assess LAC's progress in institutional reform (or governance), and in that occasion we complemented the analysis with indicators provided by the *Business Environment Risk Intelligence (BERI).* Unfortunately, this latter service has been discontinued, and thus we were unable to update that data.

7. See Burki and Perry (1997) and Inter-American Development Bank (1996) for a review of progress achieved in structural reforms.

CHAPTER 2

Institutional Reform Is Possible

CHAPTER 1 DISCUSSED HOW IMPORTANT EFFECTIVE INSTITUTIONS ARE FOR ECONOMIC performance, and how urgent institutional reform is for Latin American and Caribbean countries. It demonstrated that efficient institutions should provide clear, widely known, coherent, predictable, credible, and properly and evenly enforced rules. Although predictability and stability of institutions are important for promoting investment, stimulating growth, and reducing poverty and inequality, institutional adaptation and change also are important. Such adaptability ensures that the incentive structure accommodates changes in technology, social preferences, external factors, and institutional innovations elsewhere.

Given the importance of institutional change, this chapter turns to the question of how such change occurs and how to accomplish institutional reform. Political economy becomes a crucial consideration in this regard, as it often has a determining impact on the nature and extent of institutional reform at different times and under different circumstances. The political economy of institutional change in Latin America and the Caribbean remains a relatively underexplored area of inquiry. Nevertheless, disparate studies in recent years have pointed to some key factors that appear to facilitate institutional change in the region as well as those that might impede it. This chapter attempts to point out some of the most salient political-

economy factors likely to affect the potential for institutional change, and to show how these factors, if taken seriously into account, can enhance both the analysis and the undertaking of such change.

Factors Increasing the Demand for Institutional Change

An increase in the effective demand for institutional change comes from many sources, not all of them political—technological innovations; external economic shocks; natural or manmade disasters; and foreign experiences, good or bad, that have powerful demonstration effects.

One prominent example in contemporary Latin America and the Caribbean that has already been discussed is globalization. Countries in the region now trade a higher share of domestic production with the rest of the world and

receive greater volumes of foreign investment as a share of domestic investment than they did two decades ago. As noted in the introduction, this increasing activity in the global economy has led entrepreneurs and firms to realize that their international competitiveness is critically affected by the quality of domestic institutions. Both the spread of the Mexican peso crisis of 1994–95 and the more recent Asian financial crisis demonstrated the increased vulnerability of national economies to external shocks in a world characterized by rapidly increasing financial integration. In addition, globalization has brought with it potentially adverse distributive effects, which need to be offset by new institutional structures (i.e., social safety nets and improved access to quality education for vulnerable groups).

On another front, the end of the Cold War and the global and regional emphasis on democratization and the advancement of human rights have created demands for more accountable and transparent political institutions and a reformed judiciary. In Latin America and the Caribbean, the devolution of power to local governments, the popular election of mayors, the increased importance of national legislatures, and the emergence of grassroots organizations and new political parties are all manifestations of these increased demands.

Developments such as globalization act as facilitators of institutional change; they provide the dynamic context in which such change takes place. They increase the societal perception that it is "time for a change." For example, the economic crises of the 1980s led to the widespread acceptance and subsequent adoption of liberal trade and investment regimes recommended by technical experts inside and outside the region. In turn, the adoption of these new policies required changes in the rules governing international trade, and even led to the dismantling of some organizations, such as import-licensing agencies, and to the creation of new ones, such as antitrust agencies and those that evaluate the impact of "unfair" trade practices. In short, the prevailing institutional structure can become widely perceived as incongruent with the way the world (or a country or region or sector) is evolving. Factors that might previously have narrowed the parameters for change—most notably the accumulated weight of history and culture—become, or appear to become, less constraining. The effective demand for institutional change is thus increased.

In the long run, the main factor propelling the demand for institutional change is learning or the accumulation of knowledge (North 1990). Over time, actors evaluate the functioning of institutional arrangements based on their own experiences. Accumulated knowledge helps actors develop more effective rules to overcome the underlying problems that existing rules were designed to solve and enables them to identify new problems requiring institutional solutions. Without social learning a society can be trapped for decades or more in a perverse equilibrium characterized by low-quality institutions, slow accumulation of knowledge, and meager growth and institutional change. The role of social learning in institutional change points to the crucial importance of education over the long run. Regardless of the underlying forces increasing the effective demand for institutional change, education is critical for promoting an adaptive institutional structure.

The Supply of Institutional Change: The Role of Societal Actors, Interest Groups, and Collective Action

The factors affecting the "supply" of institutional change—including how much change takes place, at what pace, and along what dimensions—are numerous and varied, and we do not attempt to present a comprehensive list. There are many complex technical issues involved, but we focus here on the political-economy factors affecting the likelihood that increased demands for change actually will yield results. This is because the nature of the institutional changes undertaken is likely to turn significantly on how the demands for change previously cited are (or are not) processed by the political system. The ensuing discussion focuses on three broad areas: societal actors and the factors affecting their ability to act collectively; political organizations like political parties that serve an important intermediary role between such societal actors and the formal institutions and organizations of government; and some characteristics of the formal institutions themselves.

Societal Interests in Change

In attempting to understand why and how institutional change takes place, it is necessary to identify and accurately characterize the major societal-level interests at stake in such change. Obviously, these will vary from country to country (and even from region to region within countries) as well as from sector to sector.

In this connection, it is necessary to understand what societal actors—with what interests—are attempting to effect institutional change. It is necessary to assess what resources—financial, organizational, and political—they are capable of bringing to the table of reform. And it is necessary to assess who benefits and who loses from current institutional arrangements, and who would benefit and lose from the changes. In short, it is essential to have a clear understanding of the major social cleavages surrounding institutional change, and to know the nature and intensity of the demands of the main societal actors.

Bardhan (1997) explains how a society's institutional arrangements "are often the outcome of strategic distributive conflicts among different social groups," and how, therefore, inequality in the distribution of power and resources can sometimes block necessary reform of these institutions. The flip side of this, of course, is that changes in the relative capacity of organizations to influence institution-building may *lead* to institutional changes. Emerging powerful organizations may deem the existing institutional structure to be inconvenient for their own interests; or existing organizations or interest groups see either their net benefits derived from the existing institutional structure sharply reduced or their own capacity to oppose institutional change weakened (both of these effects appear in times of economic or financial crisis). In addition, economic crises and other exogenous developments such as technological changes can change the perceptions of interest groups or organizations about the costs and benefits of particular institutions. Hence, not only can changes in the relative capacity of organizations bring about institutional change, but also changes in the perceptions of influential organizations can lead them to support or reduce their opposition to institutional reforms.

The recognition that organizations may lead the way in changing institutions is an important ingredient of institutional change. Of particular importance is the political concept we can call the "private interest" theory. This theory emphasizes that private interest groups can seek policy and institutional changes (or prevent such changes) to serve their own interests. This approach thus echoes that of Bardhan in emphasizing the role of distributive conflicts among interest groups as an important determinant of institutional change.

Collective Action

One prominent way of addressing these concerns in the economic literature on institutions is through a focus on the costs for individuals and, especially, organizations to act collectively in pursuit of their interests (see Olson 1965). "Collective action" is costly for each member of a group, yet the benefits from collective action accrue to all members. Thus, there is an incentive for individuals or organizations to be free riders and let others pay the organizational and coordination costs for group activities, including political lobbying (Becker 1983).

Olson (1965) identified several characteristics of interest groups that affect the likelihood of a group's being formed and how effective such a group would be. For example, the smaller the number of members, the greater the likelihood that collective action will take place, because the smaller the group, the lower the costs of coordinating and enforcing membership requirements. Likewise, if the members are geographically concentrated, the costs of collective action

are smaller. Hence, the costs of collective action are associated not only with the resources needed to pursue a particular objective (e.g., political campaign contributions, lobbying, etc.) but also include the costs of monitoring the behavior of members to prevent free riders. Any factors that may reduce such costs usually enhance the ability of members to act collectively as a group.

In addition, the pattern of distribution of the costs and benefits of particular institutional reforms also influence the likelihood that affected interest groups will act collectively to support or oppose such reforms. It is often argued that reforms that yield benefits to a large number of people but that have negative consequences for specific groups will be especially difficult to implement. When the benefits are dispersed, according to the argument, they will seem small relative to the costs of acting collectively (Becker 1983), so support for the reforms will tend to be weak and poorly articulated. To clear and concentrated losers, however, there will be strong incentives to cover the costs of collective action to oppose the reforms.

Latent Interest Groups

An important implication here is that in any society we may find groups of individuals or organizations that have a common interest but are unable to organize themselves as an effective interest group; Olson (1965) referred to these groups as "latent" interest groups. That is, for many potential beneficiaries of a particular institutional reform the costs of collective action may be too high, and their collective voice will not be heard in policy debates. The costs of collective action and the resources necessary to promote it, however, are not the only impediments to collective action. Lack of information regarding the details and consequences of policy prescriptions is often an obstacle, too. In other words, voters may clearly understand what their interests are, but they may not know the specific details and technical issues of policy debates.

Such latent interest groups seem especially numerous in Latin America and the Caribbean and may be linked to many factors, including the inequality in the distribution of income and wealth for which the region is unfortunately well known. Indeed, such inequality may be the key barrier to collective action for many actors in Latin American and Caribbean society. Many potential interest groups have lacked both the incentives and the resources to engage in effective collective action.

Within Latin America and the Caribbean, many such latent interest groups have historically been "bought off" or co-opted by the clientelistic distribution of ad hoc and piecemeal "pork" and favors on the part of politicians, particularly at the local level. Such patron-client ties, arguably the prevalent form of political representation in much of the region over an extended period of time, are antithetical to the development of more structured, broader-based, and more effective political organizations. The proliferation of grassroots organizations throughout the region in recent years, however, has the potential to significantly alter the pattern just described. It could greatly intensify the effective demand for institutional change stemming from the societal level and could greatly increase the possibilities for constructing pro-change coalitions.

Coalition Building

An emphasis on the constellation of societal forces at play, and on how such forces do or do not engage in collective action in pursuit of their interests, leads to a concern with coalition building and the construction of pro-change or pro-reform coalitions. The key concern is how to build such pro-change or pro-reform coalitions in specific countries and sectors. What is the role of compensation mechanisms, and what are the roles played by timing, sequencing, and uncertainty?

A number of analysts have examined the factors that seem to account for the building of "pro-poor" coalitions in the context of the political economy of poverty reduction. A central conclusion of these analyses is that it is necessary to include payoffs for non-poor groups as well (Ascher 1984; World Bank 1990). Some institutional changes appear to pit the poor against the non-poor directly, but frequently the fortunes of both groups are linked, and coalitions can be formed that cut across the poor/non-poor divide. Coalitions may form, for example, along sectoral lines (e.g., agriculture vs. industry) or geographic lines (e.g., the interests of Brazil's Northeast versus those of the more developed southern region). Where institutional reforms to benefit the poor have been effected in Latin America and the Caribbean, their success has generally turned on the stance of white-collar workers, professionals, and small- and medium-size business interests.

Compensation Schemes

More generally, there are various types of compensation schemes that can be used to compensate losers and winners from reforms to reduce their opposition and raise their support (Edwards and Lederman 1998). Table 2.1 describes five types of compensation mechanisms that have been used in various situations.

- The first type is *direct compensation*, which is usually in the form of fiscal transfers or subsidies to losers from specific reforms. For example, adjustment assistance schemes are commonly implemented jointly with trade liberalization programs. In the case of Chile, for example, the government offered a minimum employment program in the 1970s to alleviate (although meagerly) the unemployment caused by trade liberalization and cutbacks in public employment.

- *Indirect compensation* may emerge out of economic forces (such as the devaluation of currencies that usually follows the implementation of stabilization and trade liberalization policies), or may be deliberate policy measures that compensate groups affected by a particular reform through the adjustment of a different policy instrument that indirectly raises their revenues or reduces their costs of production or organization. In several cases of education reforms, for instance, the centralized structure of collective bargaining of teachers' salaries and salary levels have been maintained in order to reduce the opposition of teachers' unions to other education reforms.

- *Cross compensation* entails changes in other policies that raise revenues or reduce costs of potential supporters not affected by the change in the policy under consideration. For example, Bolivia's capitalization program raised public support for privatizations, while the privatizations themselves would not necessarily have negatively affected the population at large (in fact, they should provide overall benefits).

- *Exclusionary compensation* relies on exemptions from reforms to certain groups that would otherwise block the reform effort. A case in point is the Chilean military's non-participation in the privatized social security system.

- Finally, *political compensation* can be achieved, for example, by incorporating leaders of opposition groups into reform-oriented governments.

The fact that winners and losers can be compensated for either not opposing or actually supporting institutional reforms also implies that reform proposals can include several policy changes in a single package. Hence, proposed reform packages can have "built-in" compensation mechanisms, whereby one element hurts the interests of one group, but another offers compensation.

Time-Inconsistency and Other Complications

The consideration of compensation schemes, however, brings further political complications. For example, are "promised" compensation schemes to be implemented in the future sufficient to placate opposition to institutional reforms? This type of question is the so-called "time-inconsistency" problems that are common in discussions of macroeconomic policy choices (Kydland and Prescott 1977). Promised compensation schemes can be derailed if the initial reforms strengthen certain interest groups that subsequently oppose the implementation of the compensation mechanisms. Time-inconsistency (i.e., when elements of the reform package or compensation schemes are not credible over time) can also produce a status quo bias as potential supporters may withdraw from the coalition when promises of benefits are not credible. Box 2.1 discusses how a technically optimal sequence of financial-sector reforms can suffer time-inconsistency problems due to political factors.

Graham and Naím (1998) have also argued that the timing of the costs and benefits of institutional reforms presents special political challenges. For example, they argue that a key difference between stabilization programs and institutional reforms is the timing of the costs and benefits of the reforms in question. Macroeconomic stabilization has immediate positive consequences embodied in the reduction of inflation and perhaps in the acceleration of growth. In the case of institutional reforms, it can be argued that some of the benefits become apparent only after an extended gestation period, while the costs of the reforms (felt mainly by well-organized interest groups) are absorbed up front. In this context, it may be politically difficult to implement institutional reforms—more difficult, at least, than macroeconomic stabilization programs.

However, it should also be noted that stabilization in Latin America and the Caribbean (or "first generation" reforms) has been accompanied by a variety of other reforms, including trade liberalization, which also produce up-front costs and delayed benefits. Moreover, some institutional reforms may have immediate positive effects for their main beneficiaries. For example, the introduction of education vouchers immediately helps the families that can

TABLE 2.1

The Political Economy of Reform and Compensation Mechanisms

MECHANISMS	MAIN FEATURES AND SOME EXAMPLES
A. Direct Compensation	*Groups directly affected by the reform policy are compensated through the transfer of cash or financial securities.* In this way the authorities expect to see a reduction in the extent of opposition from that group to that particular reform. Examples of this type of compensation mechanisms include the distribution of shares of privatized firms to workers in that particular firm, and adjustment assistance programs to workers who lost their jobs as a consequence of trade liberalization. The increase in take-home pay following a social security reform is another good example of this type of direct-compensation scheme.
B. Indirect Compensation	*This mechanism implies compensating groups affected by a particular reform through the adjustment of a different policy that indirectly raises their revenues or reduces their costs of production.* In some cases this type of indirect compensation is "automatic," and is the result of normal economic forces at work. In others it is the result of specific policy measures. One of the most important indirect compensation mechanisms is the real exchange rate. By devaluing the real exchange rate, import-substituting sectors are partially compensated, while exporters experience an additional boon. Providing tax exemptions to sectors affected by deregulation constitutes another common form of indirect compensation.
C. Cross Compensation	*This mechanism entails transferring resources—either directly or indirectly—to groups not directly affected by the reform,* in order to obtain their political support. Transferring shares of privatized firms to the population at large—as in Bolivia's capitalization program—is a good illustration of this mechanism at work.
D. Exclusionary Compensation (i.e., Exemptions)	*This mechanism entails excluding certain powerful groups from the effects of a reform, or implementing policies that in effect exempt some sectors from the reform in order to diffuse their political opposition.* By allowing these groups to maintain certain privileges, they are not likely to become active antagonists. The special treatment given to the Chilean armed forces regarding that country's social security reform is a classic example of this type of compensation mechanism.
E. Political Compensation	*This mechanism encompasses political "carrots and sticks"*—for example, the appointment of influential representatives of certain groups to high-level government jobs, which often sends a (symbolic) signal to interest groups that their concerns will be addressed.

Source: Edwards and Lederman (1998).

BOX 2.1

Time-Inconsistency Problems in the Political Economy of Financial-Sector Reform

Consider the relationship between five banking sector reforms: the privatization of state-owned banks, interest-rate liberalization, allowing foreign ownership and foreign direct investment in the sector, liberalization of cross-border financial services, and strengthening of prudential regulation and supervision. Suppose that a reform-oriented government decides to implement all five policies but must make a decision about their sequencing. Ideally, privatization, interest rate liberalization, allowing foreign competition and ownership in the domestic banking sector, and the strengthening of regulation and supervision should be done prior to the liberalization of cross-border financial services to avoid provoking a financial crisis. Reformers may realize that all five reforms benefit national welfare in the long run, yet they may face political and fiscal constraints in the implementation of the five policies with the optimal sequence.

In order to raise fiscal revenues at the time of privatization, governments often grant protection against foreign competition in the domestic market. Yet another problem is that interest-rate liberalization usually hurts some important interest groups that benefited from the artificially low rates of the previous system. Consequently, reformers may decide first to conduct the privatization, the interest-rate liberalization, and the liberalization of cross-border financial services (which offers the opportunity for domestic entities to tap cheaper foreign financial markets), and to postpone the implementation of the foreign-ownership reform and the regulatory reform until a later date. The time-inconsistency problem arises in this context because it is likely that the newly privatized banks will flourish in the protected environment and will grow also in political influence, thus making them capable of blocking the promised opening of the domestic

banking sector to foreign ownership or the regulatory reform. In other words, the promises of opening the sector to foreign competition and improving regulation and supervision are not credible in this context.

It is not surprising, then, that many Latin American reformers have chosen to permit borrowing from foreign banks directly by opening other aspects of the capital account early in the reform process, since this policy provides access to cheaper foreign financing, without necessarily promoting foreign competition in the domestic sector. In this sense, the capital account liberalization is a form of indirect compensation mechanism: It compensates the formerly privileged domestic borrowers for the increase in interest rates (and the trade liberalization that many LAC countries have implemented at the same time). Unfortunately, this early opening of the capital account can be detrimental to the medium-term stability of reforming economies (see Edwards 1984 and McKinnon 1991). Another common decision taken by reformers in the region has been to sell public banks to financial groups that also owned real-sector firms, many of which had benefited from the subsidized credit schemes—again reflecting the use of an indirect compensation mechanism that raises the support for the reforms on the part of these affected interest groups (on Chile's experience, see Edwards and Lederman 1998).

In other venues we have suggested that a way of avoiding the time-inconsistency problem in financial reforms is to commit to the opening of the domestic sector in the context of international negotiations. For example, reformers could promise to open their domestic financial sectors in the context of international trade negotiations, which would raise the costs for future governments of not implementing the needed reforms (see Perry 1997).

use the coupons to purchase better education. The introduction of consumer choice and competition in health services will have similar positive effects. In fact, institutional reforms that enhance the ability of individuals or organizations to use "exit" or "voice" strategies to provide proper incentives to their "agents" can be politically popular. Indeed, choice (exit) and empowerment (voice) are good

and popular policies. In any case, while the timing of the costs and benefits of institutional reforms may pose some political challenges, these can be overcome through a variety of reform strategies, including the use of the compensation mechanisms discussed above.

Another important consideration that has been raised by Fernández and Rodrik (1991) is that uncertainty about the benefits from reforms may lead voters (or individuals, or even interest groups) to reject proposals for reform. Such uncertainty may arise when various reforms are introduced together (thus making it more difficult for individuals to assess the net benefits from reforms) or when there is imperfect information regarding the details and consequences of the policies. It has already been pointed out that latent interest groups may be the result of lack of information, especially regarding the technical details and distributive consequences of policy or institutional reforms. These considerations raise the need to couple reform proposals with public information campaigns. Nonetheless, reform "bundling" may be necessary to offer "something for everybody." This may be needed to raise political support or reduce opposition to specific institutional reforms (Tommasi and Velasco 1996).

The Intermediation of Societal Interests

So far the discussion has emphasized the nature and interests of societal actors, whether and how they are likely to organize collectively around their interests, whether they are potential winners or losers from the process of institutional reform, and how their support can be garnered through various compensation mechanisms and related actions. But whether pro-change or pro-reform coalitions can be built is not only a matter of the societal interests at stake.

Another important factor has to do with the intermediating role of political leaders and political organizations, such as political parties. Such intermediaries "aggregate" the interests collectively articulated by the actors in civil society. This is a crucial political function because it facilitates the harmonization of the often contradictory interests of groups in civil society and thus facilitates the adoption and implementation of public policies that command support beyond the narrow political interests of any one group. In the literature on pluralist political systems, political parties are seen as the essential "interest aggregators." Political parties also provide ideological frameworks and lenses through which their supporters can interpret and assess the numerous and complex policy issues without having to possess detailed knowledge on each and every one.

Political parties have attracted considerable attention from analysts of politics in Latin America and the Caribbean. Although broad, region-wide generalizations are obviously difficult to make, it is apparent that many political parties and party systems in the region fail to meet the criteria for effective interest aggregation.

Mainwaring and Scully (1995) suggest four criteria for "institutionalized" party systems. First, there must be some stability in the rules and nature of inter-party competition; parties should not simply appear and then just as quickly evaporate. Second, the major parties should have stable roots in society if they are to structure political preferences over time. Third, the major political parties must accord legitimacy to the electoral process, with the expectation that elections will be the primary route to governing. Fourth, party organizations matter; parties are not simply the vehicles of ambitious politicians but acquire an independent status and value of their own.

Employing these criteria, the authors note sharp differences among the party systems of countries in the region. While Chile, Costa Rica, and Uruguay, for example, appear to have party systems that are relatively well-institutionalized, Bolivia, Brazil, Ecuador, and Peru do not. Other countries in the region fall somewhere in between.

Brazil is often taken as an example of party fragmentation. One recent analysis concludes that, in Brazil, "party leaders have little control over their members, and many, perhaps most, deputies spend the bulk of their time arranging jobs and pork-barrel projects for their constituents. Parties in Brazil rarely organize around national-level questions" (Ames 1998, p. 4). Brazil, however, is certainly not the only country in the region in which political parties do not appear to perform the interest aggregation function particularly well. Why not?

The reasons given in the literature are numerous:
- Some observers place at least part of the blame on electoral systems, particularly on some kinds of proportional representation that appear to encourage a lack of discipline on the part of party politicians.
- Others focus on internal party decision-making structures and processes that they say contribute to party oligarchies. (The advent of internal party primaries in some countries has, however, partially countered this argument.)
- Others see the problem more rooted in long-standing cultural and historical persuasions, such as the alleged tendency toward "personalism" as a basis for political affiliation.
- Some political parties have been "captured" by relatively narrow class or sectoral interests, making them in effect little more than glorified interest groups.

• Some focus on the previously discussed history of clientelism in the politics of the region; patron-client relationships place a premium on personal ties and political kinship, and correspondingly downplay the role of formal party organizations.

Noting the apparent shortcomings in many political parties, some have argued that countries in the region are facing a "crisis of representation" (Domínguez 1997). This may be an exaggeration; it is difficult to argue that there is less representation in Latin America and the Caribbean today than existed in the heyday of authoritarian and military regimes. Nevertheless, it is an important question whether the formal democratization of politics in the region has been accompanied by "effective" advances in representation, particularly of the lower socioeconomic strata. The role of political parties is important in this debate; in their absence or their reduced effectiveness, it would become more difficult for the citizenry's interests and demands to be aggregated, processed, and ultimately dealt with by governmental leaders.

Governmental Institutions in the Change Process

The formal institutions of government also affect the possibilities for institutional change.[1] For example, constitutions and other formal rules can determine the nature of checks and balances between the different parts of government as well as the structure of the political system in terms of the number of political parties and the like, and they may determine which specific political actors control institutional reforms. According to G. Cox and McCubbins (1996), "political actors' incentives are significantly influenced by the rules regulating electoral competition, while their capabilities are determined jointly by their electoral success and the constitutionally stipulated powers of the various governmental posts that are at stake (either directly or indirectly) in elections."

Chapters 6 and 7 of this volume deal with two important governmental organizations—the judiciary and the bureaucracy. Here the focus is on the executive and legislative branches of government in Latin American and Caribbean countries that have presidential (not parliamentary) political systems. Such systems have two defining characteristics: (a) The chief executive is popularly elected, and (b) the terms of office of the president and the legislature are fixed. Neither the executive nor the legislature alone may shorten the other's term, except in extraordinary circumstances.

Noting that the region is characterized by presidential systems of government is not the same, however, as arguing that it is marked by "presidential dominance." In fact, there are wide variations in the powers of the president vis-à-vis the legislative branch. There are, for example, significant differences in the extent to which the presidents have veto power, can promulgate decrees without resorting to the legislature, and retain the exclusive power of introducing legislation, at least in some key policy domains. To complicate matters, such powers can differ according to the subject of proposed changes. For example, even presidents with generally strong veto powers may lack such powers when it comes to budgetary matters, and even presidents with generally broad decree powers may lack such powers with regard to particular issues. In addition, there are variations in the procedures for amending the constitution in the different countries of the region.

These differences are captured in Table 2.2, which provides a summary of presidential powers over legislation in selected countries. A "proactive" president is one who can establish—or attempt to establish—a new status quo. A "reactive" president is one who only can attempt to defend the status quo against legislative attempts to change it.

The relative power of the president, however, is not only determined by the formal allocation of authority as spelled out in the constitution. What also matters greatly is the president's partisan support in the legislature. This also varies substantially across countries, as shown in Table 2.3. The mean level of presidential support in the legislature, whether on the part of the president's own party or on the part of a coalition of parties supporting him, has been low historically in Bolivia, Brazil, Chile, and Ecuador. Presidents have been far from commanding majority support in the legislature in these countries. Moreover, even where support for the president in the legislature hovers near a majority, such support is frequently vitiated by a lack of discipline in the president's own party or the coalition of parties supporting him. While the nature of social cleavages and other historical factors undoubtedly plays an important role in determining the extent of party proliferation within the legislature, research has also demonstrated the importance of such factors as concurrent elections for the presidency and the legislature, various kinds of proportional representation, and characteristics of the institutions

TABLE 2.2

Summary of Constellations of Presidential Powers over Legislation in Latin American Constitutions

PRESIDENT'S CONSTITUTIONAL LEGISLATIVE AUTHORITY	CONFIGURATION OF POWERS	EXAMPLES
Potentially dominant	Decree, strong veto, exclusive introduction	Chile 1980-89[a] Colombia 1968–91
	Decree, strong veto	Argentina[b] Ecuador[b, c]
Proactive	Decree, weak veto, exclusive introduction	Brazil 1988[b] Colombia 1991[b] Peru 1993[a]
	Decree, weak veto	Peru 1979[a]
Reactive	Strong veto, exclusive introduction	Brazil 1946 Chile pre-1973 Uruguay
	Strong veto	Bolivia Dominican Republic El Salvador Panama
Potentially marginal	No veto (on annual appropriation bills)	Costa Rica[b] Honduras[b] Mexico[b] Nicaragua Paraguay Venezuela

Notes: Decree—the president may establish new law without prior congressional authorization (therefore not including decrees of a regulatory nature). *Strong veto*—override requires more than a majority of all members. *Exclusive introduction*—certain important bills in addition to the budget must be initiated by the president, or congress may not increase items of expenditure in budget proposed by the president.
a. Decree restricted primarily to fiscal matters.
b. Different veto provisions apply on different types of bills. The Colombian president has strong veto powers over the budget but weak power over other forms of legislation. No other presidents have veto power over budgets. Veto powers over other forms of legislation are strong in Costa Rica, Honduras, and Mexico, and almost absolute in Ecuador.
c. The Ecuadorian president's veto may not be overridden if he or she vetoes the entire text, although Congress may request a referendum on the bill; if the president objects only to specified parts of a bill, the veto (of the whole bill) may be overridden by a two-thirds veto.

Source: Mainwaring and Shugart (1997, Chapter 1).

(rules) of the legislative branch (Mainwaring and Scully 1995; Mainwaring and Shugart 1997).

A recognition of both the formal constitutional and partisan powers of the president leads to a more complete understanding of the president's ability to effect change, including institutional change. Table 2.4 combines a consideration of each kind of power and produces some instructive results. For example, the only country in which the president has strong constitutional powers accompa-

nied by at least moderately strong support in the legislature is Argentina. In several other cases, presidents with strong constitutional powers have had relatively low support in the legislature, rendering decisive governmental action difficult. Interestingly, many countries' presidents actually have relatively low levels of formal constitutional powers and their strength derives principally from the partisan support they enjoy in the legislature. This is the case, for example, with the president of Mexico, traditionally considered perhaps the strongest chief executive in the region. From a comparative perspective, the Mexican president has relatively limited formal powers but has been immensely fortified by his leadership of the Partido Revolucionario Institucional (PRI), the formerly hegemonic political party in the Mexican system. If future political developments in Mexico lead to more power-sharing with other political parties, then it is likely that Mexican presidential power will diminish due to the formal constitutional provisions. More broadly, Table 2.4 demonstrates that in many countries of the region the vaunted power of the president is closely tied to electoral outcomes and partisan configurations in the legislature.

Attention to executive-legislative relations is arguably even more important in the current institutional context in the region. The democratization of regional political systems has, in theory at least, increased the importance of the legislative function. Thus, issues that have long been prominent in the study of executive-legislative relations in the advanced industrial democracies—such as the internal decision-making structures and processes of the legislature, the adequacy of legislative staffs and of legislative access to independent information sources, and the nature of legislative oversight of executive decision-making—may take on added significance in Latin America and the Caribbean as well.

Chapter 7 suggests that the nature of executive-legislative relations may be an important element of achieving viable bureaucratic reform. Other studies have demonstrated their importance for a considerable array of policy domains. A fruitful line of inquiry has been one that emphasizes the alignment of incentive structures in such a way that politicians' interests in short-term political survival can be harmonized with their desire to promote more encompassing social or political objectives (such as institutional reform). Geddes (1994), for example, has demonstrated that the adoption of more meritocratic presidential

TABLE 2.3

Presidents' Parties' Mean Share of Congressional Seats in Latin America

(percentages)

COUNTRY AND PERIOD YEARS		NO. OF ELECTIONS	PRESIDENT'S PARTY		PRESIDENT'S COALITION	
			LOWER CHAMBER	UPPER CHAMBER	LOWER CHAMBER	UPPER CHAMBER
Argentina	1983–93	6	48.3	52	49.1	52
Bolivia	1980–93	4	33.9	47.2		
Brazil						
Ia	1945–50	3	34.8	44	52.2	48.6
Ib	1954–62	4	26	26	44.8	52
IIa	1985–90	4[a]	26.9	25.6	37	31.8
IIb	1994	1	12.1	13.6	35.4	42
Chile						
I	1932–73	18	23.3	20.8	41.6	41.2
II	1989–93	2	31.7	28.3[b]	58.3	46.3[b]
Colombia	1945–49, 1974–94	11	55.2	56.3	55.2	56.3
Costa Rica	1953–94	11	49.6	—	51.8	—
Dominican				69.1		
Republic	1962, 1966–90	8	55.6	—		—
Ecuador	1978–94	7	22			
El Salvador						
I	1985–91	4	47.5	—		—
II	1994	1	46.4	—		—
Honduras	1981–93	4	54.2	—	54.2	—
Mexico	1982–91	4	65.8	95.8	65.8	95.8
Nicaragua	1984–90	2	65.4	—		
Paraguay	1993	1	47.5	44.4	—	—
Peru						42.2[c]
	1980	1	54.4	43.3	54.4	43.3
	1984–90, 1995	3	47.1	40[c]	47.1	41.7[c]
Uruguay	1942–71, 1984–94	11	45.6	43.8		
Venezuela	1958–93	8	41.1	47.4	43.2	47.7

Notes: a. Includes the indirect presidential election of 1985.

    b. For Chile II, appointed senators were included in calculating the president's share of Senate seats. If one takes only elected seats, the percentage increases to 34.2% for the president's party and 56.6% for the coalition.

    c. Does not apply to 1995; Peru moved to a unicameral legislature with the constitution of 1993.

Source: Mainwaring and Shugart (1997, Chapter 11).

appointment strategies to bureaucratic posts in many countries of the region has been crucially affected by some fundamental features of the political landscape, including the size of the president's party, the discipline of party members, and whether the president is attempting to build a political machine while in office. Such studies emphasize that the harmonization of short-term political survival goals with the broader "public interest" in institutional reform is likely to be at the heart of reforming institutions through the mechanisms of the political process.

Some Guidelines for Reform

The discussion in this chapter indicates that a full-blown theory of the political economy of institutional change still remains elusive, despite the contributions of economists and other social scientists. In focusing upon institutional

change as the factor to be explained (i.e., the "dependent variable" in social science terminology), it is clear that there are various explanatory levels—broadly speaking, societal, intermediary, and formal/governmental—that facilitate understanding of why and how such change occurs. But a systematic appreciation of the precise relationships among these levels, or of their analytically independent contributions to the explanation of varying outcomes, remains a daunting task.

Nevertheless, this survey of some of the key emphases in the study of the political economy of institutional change has highlighted a range of relevant factors that need to be taken into account by those—be they societal actors, governments, or international agencies—who may be interested in promoting reforms aimed at improving the quality of domestic institutions. Taken together, they

TABLE 2.4

Relationship Between Presidents' Constitutional and Partisan Powers in Latin America

CONSTITUTIONAL POWERS OVER LEGISLATION	PRESIDENT'S PARTISAN POWERS			
	VERY LOW	MEDIUM LOW	MEDIUM HIGH	VERY HIGH
Potentially dominant	Chile, 1989 Ecuador	Colombia, 1968	Argentina	
Proactive	Brazil, 1988	Colombia, 1991 Peru		
Reactive	Brazil, 1946 Chile, 1925	Bolivia	El Salvador Uruguay	Dominican Republic
Potentially marginal			Costa Rica Paraguay, 1991 Venezuela	Honduras Mexico Nicaragua

Source: Mainwaring and Shugart (1997, Chapter 11).

constitute a few basic guidelines for institutional reformers. Borrowing from central concepts in institutional economics and political economy, the guidelines are as follows:

- *Pay systematic attention to the nature of prospective winners and losers from institutional reform* (e.g., trade unions in the formal sector with respect to labor market reform, diverse rural interests regarding "market-based" land reform, teachers' unions regarding education reform, various subcategories of the financial sector regarding financial reforms, etc.). Be aware of the main cleavages that appear to separate such winners and losers— sometimes, for example, these may have a regional dimension, sometimes a sectoral base, sometimes a base in social classes linked directly to their position in the productive structure. In any event, monitor closely the nature and intensity of support or opposition as manifested by public opinion polls, proclamations of interest groups, public demonstrations, and the like.

- Based on well-informed assessments, *attempt to craft compensation schemes that are politically viable and thus credible.* In addition, it may be necessary to make promises about future compensation schemes, which may be key ingredients for both the effectiveness of the reforms and for their political sustainability. One way to enhance the credibility of compensation schemes is to raise the costs of "exit" from commitments by future governments through adherence to

international treaties or similar commitments, such as the signing of summit declarations.

- *Empowering the beneficiaries is good policy and smart politics.* Graham and Naím (1998) have suggested that institutional reforms are more likely to be supported if the potential beneficiaries participate in the design of the new institutions. One way to do this is through "voice," in Hirschman's (1970) terminology, which is a feedback device by which principals exert control on the decision-making process of their agents and organizations. As is discussed in greater detail in Chapter 5, one way of improving the performance of schools in the region is to provide greater participation to parents in the schools' management. Empowerment (or voice) then becomes a means to ensuring that the school acts according to the interests of the households, which is particularly important when the "exit" or choice strategy is not available. It is also safe to argue that the beneficiaries will welcome such policies. In the context of financial reforms, protecting minority shareholders' rights is also a voice strategy for reform, which should not face severe political obstacles on the part of public opinion. The decentralization of state functions to local governments is another example where local communities can potentially gain voice over public bureaucracies in the context of democratic (choice) politics.

- *Providing choice to beneficiaries is also good policy and smart politics.* Some of the assertions stated above about empowerment also apply to the provision of "choice" or "exit" strategies for beneficiaries. If principals are not satisfied with the quality of services provided by their agents or organizations, they can desert and look for the services elsewhere. The threat of exit is a complement to the provision of voice or empowerment strategies for institutional reforms, since the threat of exit strengthens the voice strategy. In the case of education, for example, the use of education vouchers may be a good (and politically popular) complement to empowerment strategies, where the schools have to respond to the demands of parents, especially if public-education subsidies for schools are linked to children's enrollment (as in the case of Chile, for example).

- *Public-information campaigns should be part and parcel of reform efforts.* A frequent issue that emerges out of the political-economy perspective is that latent interest groups are politically inactive as a consequence, in part, of the costs of collecting information about the potential costs and benefits of particular reforms. If reforms are viewed as a collective good, however, there is clear justification for reformers to spend resources explaining the details and likely consequences of proposed policy initiatives. This role is particularly important in the context of democratic regimes, where voters have political voice and exit strategies available but may not use them to defend their interests effectively.

- *Pay careful attention to the political support for prospective reforms at the intermediate level, particularly among key political leaders and political party organizations.* Assess the possibilities for "deals" and tradeoffs among them. Be particularly aware of the "political cycle"—i.e., how windows of opportunity for institutional change might open (or close), depending upon impending elections.

- *Have a clear understanding of the constitutional—i.e., formal/governmental—facilitators and obstacles to institutional change and reform* (e.g., the possibilities of introducing reforms via presidential decree, the realistic scope for reform in situations in which a strong legislative branch shares important powers with the president, the potential for creating autonomous or semi-autonomous agencies as relatively non-political

enclaves within the formal structure of government, etc.). Such an understanding, simple as it seems but important as it is, could facilitate ex ante calculations of the feasibility of institutional reform—of labor market reform in Argentina, to take but one example, or of administrative and social security reform in Brazil, to take another. With a clear understanding of the constitutional forces in play, and of their close relationship to partisan forces particularly in the legislature, think creatively about how to exploit the opportunities and overcome the constraints.

- *Focusing on reforming incentive structures is good policy and smart politics.* Perhaps the most difficult reforms to undertake from a political standpoint are those that aim to change or reduce the size of public employment. This is the case for two reasons: First, the losers have human faces that become the symbols of the costs of such reforms, and second, the public jobs are often part of the political game by which supporters of certain leaders get rewarded. Consequently, reforms of the civil service and societal organizations (e.g., schools) should focus on the incentive structures rather than on changing personnel or installing the latest technology. This approach may not only be more politically viable than wholesale changes in personnel, but may also be the most appropriate approach from a technical standpoint, based on the emphasis placed on incentives by the new institutional economics.

* * *

In sum, the analysis in this chapter indicates that reforming institutions in the countries of Latin America and the Caribbean is far from an impossibility. To the contrary: The increased demand for more effective institutions in the region can be matched by commensurate supply. What is required from would-be institutional reformers is sustained political commitment and carefully tailored strategies for putting such commitment into operation in specific sectors. Policy analysts, using some of the tools of the trade discussed in this chapter, have an important role to play in helping reformers craft such strategies. The combination of historical trends that have raised the demand for institutional reforms, and the fashioning of astute reform strategies that are sound from both technical and political points of view, present Latin American and Caribbean countries with a historic opportunity to close the "institution gap" that currently afflicts the region—a gap that both threatens the consolidation of the vital reforms already undertaken and impedes the implementation of the "second generation" reforms that are crucial.

Note

1. The discussion in this section draws extensively from Mainwaring and Shugart (1997), especially Chapters 1 and 11.

PART 2
Institutional Reform in Markets: The Case of the Financial Sector

CHAPTER 3

Institutions, Governance, and Incentives in Banking: Safety Net Arrangements

A CONSENSUS HAS DEVELOPED IN THE LAST FEW DECADES THAT WHEN IT COMES TO THE performance of the financial sector, institutions play an essential role—especially because of the relevance for this sector of information issues, agency problems, transaction costs, and property rights. While there is general agreement on the importance of having an adequate institutional framework for well-functioning financial markets, how to achieve it remains a challenge. The general purpose of this chapter is to illustrate incentives and institutional issues in banking systems by reference to broadly defined safety-net arrangements—including lender-of-last-resort facilities, deposit insurance, capital requirements, supervision, and exit policies—because safety nets tend to be, de facto or de jure, an important component of financial systems.[1] We endeavor to highlight those aspects that are of greater relevance to LAC countries.

A useful framework to tackle the key issues systematically is that provided by **agency theory** and the **theory of incomplete contracts**. *Information and incentives in banking*, the first section in this chapter, deals with the conceptual aspects of asymmetric information and agency issues, illustrating them principally by reference to loan and deposit contracts. *Banking regulation and safety nets* starts reviewing the information and incentives issues that motivate regulation. Safety nets have evolved over time, but not in a linear way;

in any one country the existing safety-net arrangement has been shaped by that country's history, including the nature of financial crises and regulatory pressures. Thus the rest of the section takes a historical perspective, first focusing on instances of prudential regulation without ex ante safety nets, and then considering illustrations of pressures for safety nets even before the introduction of central banks. A discussion of central banks and the provision of safety nets (both ex ante and ex post) follows, with special attention given to the shift of risks to the government that results from safety nets and to the trade-offs involved between this shift of risks and financial deepening.

Throughout this chapter, the structure of incentives that emerge from safety nets in banking systems is considered to depend principally on the strength of a tripod consisting of **capital**, **monitoring**, and **closure**. The underlying argument is that even if there is no ex ante provision for safety nets, these tend to surface ex post in one form or another—and frequently in an improvised manner. Given that safety-net arrangements seem to be here to stay, and because of the complexities they involve, the careful design of ex ante safety nets is crucial. Although extensive research has been done on capital requirements and monitoring (including prudential regulation and official supervision as well as market monitoring), closure mechanisms have had relatively less attention in the academic literature. *The safety-net tripod: capital, monitoring, and closure* reviews these three crucial aspects of safety nets, emphasizing the complexities involved in closure.

Fire protection and fire fighting: designing exit policies discusses elements of effective exit policies, drawing on an analogy with good fire protection and fire-fighting policies.

By this analogy, effective bank exit policies need to be supported by preventive regulation, monitoring, and capital requirements (building codes and inspections), early detection mechanisms and prompt corrective rules (smoke alarms, fire extinguishers). They should include carefully designed bank intervention and bank failure resolution capacities (fire-escape routes, fire drills, and fire departments) so as to avoid disorderly evacuation and unnecessary panic if the worst comes to pass. Insolvent banks and unfit bankers should not be allowed to remain in operation ("condemned" buildings are not suitable to be inhabited).

Bank resolution is a broad term that goes beyond plain vanilla liquidation and closure mechanisms. We describe alternatives and explicitly discuss deposit insurance, focusing not only on its role in curbing panics and contagion risks, but mainly on its role as a potentially important tool for bank-failure resolution.

The adequate design for safety nets needs to deal with the day-to-day issues related to individual banks' idiosyncratic risks as well as with systemic risk. A commonly observed occurrence in banking systems is that the rules of the game regarding ex ante risk-shifting toward taxpayers tend to change or be ignored once the going gets tough. *Safety nets, systemic risk, and catastrophe insurance* explores systemic risk and the difficult decision of rules versus discretion that a government faces in the event of a potential systemic crisis. If difficult theoretically, this issue appears all the more complex in practice. We review a few lessons from experience and discuss alternative ways to address this problem. The chapter ends with a summary and concluding remarks.

Information and Incentives in Banking

Information problems are particularly important in financial markets because financial transactions take place over time. Financial markets deal with a promise to pay in the future, which involves uncertainty and risks. Information problems arise when the agents involved (investors or depositors, financial institutions, and borrowers) have asymmetries in information about the likelihood of compliance with the promises kept—that is, when one of the parties has less, or less accurate, information than the other party.[2]

Banks have a dual function, as delegated monitors on the asset side and liquidity providers on the liability side (Dewatripont and Tirole 1994), which gives rise to two agency relationships: lender-borrower and bank-depositor.[3] Banks act as delegated monitors of firms when they engage in their lending activities: Numerous depositors, instead of monitoring each one of the borrowing firms, delegate such monitoring to a bank, whose ability to stay in business largely depends on its capacity to exploit economies of scale because of the natural monopoly aspect of information-generation. "Know your client"—the basic rule of good banking—presupposes that banks are able to gather and accumulate sufficient information, which, on the one hand, enables them to assess the risk of debtors and, on the other, limits debtors' ability to shift easily from one bank to another.

On the liability side, banks must provide liquidity for depositors. Depositors do not always know when they will need cash, although not all depositors have liquidity needs at the same time. The bank must provide cash when it is needed, while channeling funds from a pool of typically short-term and small deposits to longer-term and larger-scale investments.

Loan Contracts

To lend money, banks write a loan contract, which, based as it is on information possessed only by the bank, is not easy to trade in markets.[4] Writing a loan contract is the formal equivalent of writing a put option on the assets of the debtor firm: The firm pays if it can and defaults (delivers, or puts the assets to the creditor) if it cannot pay. Given asymmetric information, the problem for a bank is to determine the ex ante profitability of the projects to be carried out by borrowers. To the extent that the bank (principal) cannot distinguish between projects, it would charge a "lemons" premium across all projects, taking into account the probability of mistakenly funding a bad project.[5] As a result, borrowers (agents) with good projects have an incentive to look elsewhere for funding, leaving the bank with a worse pool of borrowers from which to choose. If this **adverse selection** or **hidden information** problem is severe enough, lending may not take place. An increase in the lending interest rate tends to increase adverse selection (Stiglitz and Weiss 1981).

In addition to, and independently of, the adverse selection problem, asymmetric information creates **moral hazard**, as borrowers have an incentive to take risks aimed at capturing potential gains under good states of the world, while not losing more than the capital they have invested in the project in bad states of the world. To this end borrowers could engage in **hidden actions** that increase the probability of default after the loan has been made.

Deposit Contracts

If a loan contract is the formal equivalent of a put option on a debtor's assets, a deposit contract is the formal equivalent of a put option on a *bank's* assets. Banks pay a return on deposits that includes an implicit premium to cover the probability of default (the premium on the implicit put option). Asymmetric information between depositors and the bank's owners and managers once again gives rise to selection and moral hazard problems. If depositors cannot distinguish between good and bad bankers, the **adverse selection** problem will create a "lemons" premium that penalizes good banks and favors the entry and expansion of bad banks. Once depositors give their money to a bank, **moral hazard** arises, as the bank has an incentive to undertake hidden actions that help bank owners at the expense of depositors.

Moral hazard implies that bankers have incentives to undertake riskier lending with the expectation of capturing the upside potential, while keeping the downside limited to the amount of bank owners' net worth invested in the bank. In addition, they may even misrepresent earnings and engage in old-fashioned looting. Akerlof and Romer (1993) argue that moral hazard may induce bank managers and owners of undercapitalized and inadequately monitored banks not only to "go for broke" (i.e., to bet for the resurrection of the bank by undertaking riskier activities, which may *not* hurt depositors or taxpayers if the low-probability bet happens to pay off) but also to "go broke" (i.e., to defraud and loot the bank, with depositors and/or taxpayers always losing in the process).

Mitigating Agency Problems

As discussed, there are two common ways in which a debtor firm can hurt the creditor bank: misrepresentation of assets (leading to a problem of adverse selection) and misuse of those assets once the loan is approved (the result of moral hazard). Both banks and firms find it advantageous to create non-price solutions—that is, institutions—to mitigate these problems and, thus, enable the credit system to operate.[6] Screening devices, debtor information centers (credit bureaus) and loan covenants play a central role in this connection. A standard covenant in a loan contract is a restriction on the amount of debt that a firm can have, the collateral required, and an injunction that loans from other lenders be reported to the bank. These restrictions are a form of capital requirement, since they limit the leverage of the firm.[7] Loan contracts normally also require some form of monitoring—for instance, to ensure that the debtor firm is audited by an independent auditor, that the bank has a representative on the firm's board of directors, or that debtors that share liabilities within a group monitor each other's behavior. Finally, many loan contracts are short term but rolled over so that the bank can force the firm to default and seize assets (closure) if it becomes clear that the firm will not be able to pay back the loan. This provision limits the bank's losses from actions the firm could take to run down the value of its assets once it ceases to be a viable enterprise.

Capital requirements, monitoring provisions, and **closure mechanisms** in loan contracts lower the cost of intermediation by allowing the bank to sort out prudent borrowers from risky borrowers, and by influencing the incentives of prudent borrowers once loans have been made. Successful use of these measures results in **financial deepening**: more projects are undertaken, and their adoption does not depend on self-financing. At the same time, bank financing of these projects results in financial **risk shifting** between private agents: Firms with limited liability bear only part of the downside risk for their projects, with banks assuming the remainder of the risk.

Even if introduced spontaneously by private agents without inducement from the government, capital, monitoring, and closure would mitigate selection and moral hazard problems in loan contracts only to the extent that a society and its government are capable of providing a minimally reliable set of public goods and services that facilitate **contract enforcement** at reasonable costs. This would imply that property rights are well-defined, bankruptcy rules are clearly specified in the law and custom, and judicial systems can be counted upon to facilitate collateral repossession and execution of guarantees, as well as to deter and punish breaches of contract.[8] Governments have a significant role to play in strengthening the institutional framework needed for loan-contract enforcement, although the required effort to succeed in this is not independent of a country's legal heritage. La Porta et al. (1997a, 1998a) show that covenants establishing the rights of creditors over debtors are weaker and less enforceable in countries whose legal heritage can be traced to the civil-law tradition, particularly the Napoleonic Code, than in countries with common-law tradition (see Chapter 4).[9]

Although a parallel can be made between the information asymmetries involved in loan contracts and deposit contracts, the fact is that the associated selection and moral hazard problems are much more difficult to mitigate through voluntary actions by private agents in the case of deposit contracts. To be sure, unregulated banks have an incentive to create mechanisms to mitigate the effects of asymmetric information, given that the "lemons" problem may lead to equilibrium where there are no bank deposits.[10] In effect, as a partial voluntary solution, a bank may be willing to submit to an external audit, in order to create publicly available and credible information about assets, reserves, loans to related parties, and other data that signal the quality of the bank. In addition, banks may issue demandable debt, such as bank notes or demand deposits, rather than time deposits. In the absence of lender-of-last-resort facilities (see below) or credible deposit insurance, demandable debt creates a sequential service constraint of first-come, first-served (Mishkin 1991) that makes it worthwhile for some depositors to invest resources in monitoring the bank. Demandable debt reduces the problem of free riders, since depositors that rely on others to monitor are less apt to recover their funds if there is a run on the bank. Depositors would vote with their feet if the bank is not viable, forcing its closure.

These voluntary non-price solutions tend to be insufficient in the case of deposit contracts because the free-rider problem is more severe, as implied by the theory of collective action (Olson 1965). This theory suggests that, due to the free-rider problem, larger groups, such as those made up of numerous depositors, tend to be less effective in achieving a common objective than smaller and more concentrated groups, such as those made up of relatively few banks. Once a depositor invests in the costly activity of gathering information on a bank, such information cannot be hidden from other depositors in a sustainable manner. The very actions that would result from such information (e.g., a run on the bank) immediately discloses the information. Also, individual depositors usually have relatively small claims on banks, so it normally does not pay for them to engage in costly information-gathering activities. Hence, no depositor has an incentive to enforce covenants in deposit contracts that mimic the covenants imposed by

banks in loan contracts, and each depositor has an incentive to free ride on the information-generation efforts of other depositors, enjoying the benefits without incurring the costs. A market failure thus arises that provides a basis for official regulation.

Banking Regulation and Safety Nets

The rationale for banking regulation is the need to address externalities that the market does not adequately deal with, either through the price mechanism or via non-price arrangements set up voluntarily by private agents.[11] In particular, regulation addresses the market failures that arise from information asymmetries. As with all market failures, those stemming from asymmetric information in the banking system create a wedge between private and social interests: The "invisible hand" of the market fails to produce a convergence of the two. Because the key market failure to be dealt with is the one that constrains monitoring of banks by depositors, there is a case for a governmental supervisory agency to monitor banks as the representative of all depositors.

This is the representation hypothesis introduced by Dewatripont and Tirole (1994). The main argument is that to ensure adequate monitoring, control over banks should shift from soft claim holders (equity-holders) to tough ones (debt-holders) in case of mediocre performance. This is because stockholders will tend to "gamble for resurrection" during difficult times and will thus not be tough monitors when it is needed the most. Nevertheless, debt-holders (depositors), especially small ones, typically do not monitor banks, as explained above. Thus, governments can monitor banks as representatives of depositors, with significant gains to society's welfare.

The type of government intervention called for is centered on prudential regulation and supervision[12]—that is, on the set of norms and monitoring policies and procedures that encourage greater "prudence" in risk-assessment, risk-taking, and risk-management by banks and their clients. The goal of prudential regulation is to promote financial deepening while complementing market-originated monitoring and enhancing overall governance in the system. The appropriate design and implementation of prudential regulation and supervision is a complex subject, especially because of the challenges posed by rapid financial innovation and other changing market realities. Sound prudential regulation places emphasis on complementing and supporting market forces (Caprio and Klingenbiel 1996). Optimal government regulation should mimic the mechanisms of a perfect market (Klein and Leffler 1981) with a view to creating **incentive compatibility**, i.e., such alignment of incentives facing the various agents that removes the wedge between private and social benefits. As indicated in the discussion on loan contracts above, appropriate prudential regulation in the banking system would need to cover well the three dimensions of capital, monitoring, and closure (see *the safety-net tripod: capital, monitoring, and closure* for more details).

As we will illustrate subsequently, prudential regulation in banking systems needs not provide for an explicit safety net and may not even entail an implicit one. However, the existence of a safety net (explicit or implicit) not only presupposes prudential regulation but also heightens the need for it. This is because, by definition, safety nets in banking are sets of organizations and institutions that imply risk-shifting toward taxpayers, which gives rise to a form of implicit social contract whereby the official supervisor undertakes to maintain tight prudential oversight over banks to control taxpayers' exposure to losses. This risk-shifting is nonetheless taken as the price to be paid for enhancing systemic stability and curbing socially costly externalities associated with bank runs, payments system failure, generalized credit collapse, etc. Although it is frequently argued that the best safety net is one that results in market participants' behaving as if the safety net did not exist, well-designed bank safety nets *should* alter behavior and deepen financial intermediation by shifting some risk to the government.[13]

A well-functioning safety net must balance its institutional components—lender-of-last-resort facilities, deposit insurance, capital requirements, prudential oversight, and bank-closure (exit) policies—so as to carefully control the risk borne by taxpayers, while achieving the financial deepening that results from the strengthened ability of the system to withstand such disturbances as contagious bank runs. Ultimately, a well-designed safety net would improve social welfare. The proper balance between the safety-net components becomes more feasible to the extent that the safety-net architecture does not blunt, but rather supports the monitoring, discipline, and governance provided by the market. By the same token, when a safety net's institutional components are poorly designed or inadequately implemented, then it becomes dysfunctional and exacer-

bates moral hazard problems, which, if sufficiently severe, increase systemic instability, thereby undermining the safety net's raison d'être (Calomiris 1997).

The design of safety nets is also complicated by the recurrent emergence of ex post safety nets in the midst of crises, the "too big to fail" phenomenon, and the relevance of aggregate systemic risk—rather than idiosyncratic, loan-specific risk—for banks in volatile economies such as those of Latin America. In effect, there is the historical observation that, to the extent that a formal safety-net arrangement fails to anticipate political and economic pressures during a crisis, an ex post safety net will emerge in which risk-shifting is driven by governmental discretion rather than rules. Also, even if risk-shifting to taxpayers is excluded or rigorously minimized by ex ante rules of the game, behavior does tend to be influenced by the rather pervasive perception that an implicit safety net exists to cover 100 percent of the liabilities of at least those banks considered to be "too big to fail." Finally, with much of the risk faced by banks in Latin America being of the aggregate kind (e.g., terms-of-trade shocks), the issue arises as to the conditions under which deposit insurance can be thought of as a form of catastrophic insurance, with the government having a comparative advantage in handling aggregate risk.

The issues and themes mentioned above will be explained further in the next subsections through a selected historical recounting of how safety nets emerged, even when they were not explicitly stated ex ante and even prior to the creation of central banks.

Prudential Regulation without a Safety Net

Prior to the development of a bank safety net, banks have more often been subject to a "light" amount of prudential regulation rather than no regulation at all. The key similarity between no regulation and light regulation is that the closure mechanism is generally triggered by bank runs, and the government remains outside of the compensation process for bank creditors. The key difference is that under light regulation the government creates laws and norms that commit banks to more stringent prudential practices than banks could insure depositors without such regulation.

The main features of "light" regulation can be seen by examining free banking legislation in the United States in the nineteenth century. After enactment of the 1838 New York State Free Bank Law, free bank legislation in most states created a form of "narrow banking." States would give bank notes to free banks in exchange for U.S. government bonds or approved state bonds. Free banks would circulate bank notes and, equally importantly, take deposits to make loans. Free banks were subject to minimum capital requirements and sometimes "double liability" requirements (shareholders were personally responsible for an additional amount up to the par value of bank capital in case of the bank's liquidation). The comptroller of a state could, upon petition by depositors, order the detailed inspection of a free bank and have the results published.

Between 1838 and 1863 many free banks failed in the United States. Only a small portion of note holders lost money, but deposit holders lost much more. Despite each state's role in the regulation of free banks, state governments avoided becoming insurers of bank notes or deposits.[14] Thus, free banking and other forms of narrow banking worked successfully in the nineteenth century United States in the sense that they protected the means of payment (bank notes) and did not result in government bank rescues in crisis times. Despite the fact that depositors did lose deposits during crisis times and banks failed, there appears to have been no effective pressure for a safety net to be provided by the government. Part of the lack of government response was tied to successive U.S. governments' commitment to the gold standard. Part of the lack of response may also have been associated with the decentralized federal form of government. As these characteristics are unusual from the perspective of the small open economies of Latin America, a historical example from Chile in the nineteenth century will help illustrate how the borrowers of financial institutions with no explicit safety net could generate enough pressure on the government to create an ex post safety net.

Pressures for Bank Safety Nets before Central Banks
The earliest documented ex post governmental safety net in Latin America was created in Chile about 140 years ago. During the early 1850s foreign gold rushes had created pressures to increase grain exports from the Central Valley of Chile to California and Australia. But large Chilean landowners who wanted to expand their production had no access to long-term credit, largely because existing mortgage laws were poorly defined in legal terms. In addition, potential lenders were faced with the lack of reliable information on the holdings, quality, and legal status of land-

holdings. Asymmetric information potentially leading to adverse selection, coupled with the lack of a legal mechanism to enforce contracts, resulted in a "lemons" problem where no long-term lending took place.

This is a clear example where, even in the lending side, there is room for government intervention to strengthen the broader institutional framework affecting the definition of property rights and the enforcement of contracts. In effect, the Chilean Congress responded in 1856 by creating a "special" mortgage that gave clear rights to the lender. Property registries were set up to make information on mortgages, sales, and censuses readily available to the public. In addition, the congress also created a state-sponsored mortgage bank, the *Caja de Crédito Hipotecario*, to accompany the new mortgage law.[15] The property registries helped to mitigate the asymmetric information problem facing lenders. Equally important, the *Caja* became a delegated monitor that could reduce the costs of lending by adhering to legally mandated collateral requirements, by holding a diversified portfolio of loans, and by economies of scale in monitoring. The new mortgage law gave clear authority to the *Caja* to enforce bankruptcy proceedings (i.e., a closure rule) if a landholder fell sufficiently behind in making mortgage payments. The reform of mortgage laws and the creation of the *Caja* solved the "lemons" problem, thereby permitting some risk shifting from landowners to the *Caja* and to purchasers of the *Caja's* securities. The accompanying financial deepening propelled the expansion of irrigation and other land improvements by landholders.

Although the rapid five-year credit expansion permitted landowners to undertake capital improvements to their land, it also exposed them to macroeconomic shocks. Many landowners became unable to make their mortgage payments at the end of the 1850s, when the Californian and Australian export markets collapsed. Responding to intense pressure to prevent a generalized foreclosure of landholdings, the government in 1858 and 1859 clandestinely channeled to landholders about 2 million pesos of a 7 million peso railroad loan that had been financed in the London bond market by the government. This government action caused risk-shifting to taxpayers that was not envisioned by the *Caja Hipotecaria's* institutional structure. Pressures by foreign investors in the railroad loan, as well as the installation of a new government, led to an attempt to recover the clandestine loans in 1860. The resulting economic contraction of 1861 and 1862, which produced the liquidation of a large number of landholdings, was Chile's first financial crisis and one of its most severe economic contractions of the nineteenth century.[16]

The example highlights features common to the dynamics of many implicit financial safety nets. The *Caja Hipotecaria* and the accompanying legal reforms were created to promote financial deepening. Prudential lending practices were legally mandated, so that risk-shifting to the *Caja* was carefully controlled in theory. In practice, the *Caja* expanded its mortgage lending so quickly that it became overly exposed to the risk of a mass default by landowners in response to an external shock. The threat of massive foreclosures of landholdings initially created pressure for an ex post safety net financed by the government and then contributed to a severe economic downturn, as liquidation of properties finally took place.

The Creation of Central Banks without Ex Ante Safety Nets

The introduction of central banks into Latin America in the mid-1920s had far-reaching consequences for financial deepening and for incentives to shift risk onto the governments. The Central Bank of Chile—like most other central banks in Pacific-Rim countries—was the outcome of a mission led by Edwin Kemmerer, invited to establish a set of organizations that would allow Chile to return to the gold standard and eliminate the inflation that began in 1878. The Kemmerer Commission made recommendations to establish a central bank and a superintendency of banks that would jointly watch over the financial system.

The new legislation and institutional structure did not directly create an explicit safety net for banks. It did set up capital requirements, provisions for monitoring, and authority to close banks. Thus, the Chilean system in the late 1920s operated with capital/asset ratios of 20 to 30 percent (very high by current standards), monitoring by the *Superindencia de Bancos* was rigorous, and closure was enforced—in fact, Chile closed its second largest bank in the first year of the operation of the new institutions. By normal standards, the financial apparatus erected in the mid-1920s was sufficient to render moral hazard and adverse selection unimportant. At the same time, it facilitated financial deepening by lowering the cost of financial intermediation, as depositors required a lower premium and borrowers paid lower loan rates.[17]

While excluding an explicit safety net in the ex ante rules of the game, the new institutional framework provided for another form of guarantee, one that was inconsistent with a safety net based on unchecked access to central bank liquidity. The legislation created a guarantee that domestic currency would be convertible into foreign exchange at a fixed rate. The sustainability of such guarantee hinged on a strict money-issuance rule—namely, that high-powered money (domestic currency plus a bank's deposits in the central bank) could not exceed a certain multiple (normally less than two) of the central bank's holdings of gold and foreign exchange. The combination of a fixed exchange rate with the newly instituted environment of oversight of the banking system favored capital inflows and, hence, further fostered financial deepening. However, this combination also entailed risk-shifting to the government inasmuch as foreign exchange liabilities of banks enjoyed an implicit guarantee on account of the fixed peg.

Ad Hoc Safety Nets and Externalities

Safety nets emerged in Latin America just as in the United States—as an ad hoc response to the Great Depression. The strain this event put on the newly established institutional arrangements mentioned in the previous section eventually led to the abandonment of the exchange-rate peg. As in current episodes of financial crises, the process followed a fairly typical sequence. Orthodox authorities initially reaffirmed the commitment to the peg in the face of capital outflows and massive deposit withdrawals. But at the same time, the central bank was forced into a progressive departure from the strict money-issuance rules, as its liquidity assistance to distressed banks grew. Such departure increasingly eroded the viability of the convertible fixed peg, which eventually was abandoned. Thus, in much of Latin America, ad hoc safety nets emerged ex post, as governments could not guarantee the functioning of the banking system under the rules of the gold-linked fixed exchange rate system. The ad hoc bank safety nets created in response to the shock of the Great Depression saved the banks, typically at the cost of emergency loans from the central bank, inflation/devaluation spirals that reduced the real value of deposits, and moratoriums on foreign debt.

The pressure for ex post safety nets is related to the negative externalities that could result from a failing bank.[18] Bank failures (especially in the case of big banks) can have spillover, or "domino" effects in the form of a price race (high interest rates on deposits initiated by weak banks and followed by the rest in a fight for market share) and a generalized run on deposits. Depositors will rush to withdraw to avoid being the last one in line.[19] Depositors may find themselves increasingly unable to distinguish between individual bank problems and system-wide problems, which would induce them to withdraw their funds from otherwise sound banks, leading to failure by self-fulfilling prophecy. This would be exacerbated by a fire sale of assets by distressed banks, as these would further reduce the banks' net worth. The distribution of losses among bank creditors, governed only by the sequential-service constraint on deposit withdrawals, may be socially inefficient. Individual incentives to seek immediate liquidity would be incompatible with social preferences for systemic stability. Failures to service deposit withdrawals can cause a disruptive chain reaction on the payments system, with potentially high costs to the real economy. If massive deposit withdrawals are associated with capital outflows—as they are likely to be in the midst of a sharp erosion of confidence in the domestic banking system—an excessive contraction in credit would ensue, with prolonged adverse consequences on output and employment.

These externalities are a serious concern that governs much of the authorities' actions in banking system turbulence. Ensuring safety at all costs could lead to a sharp reduction in financial deepening, as was the case under financial repression, or lead the state to stand behind the entirety of the banking system's liabilities, as has often been the case of ex post safety nets unveiled under a crisis.

Financial Repression

Financial repression is an interesting historical episode that illustrates the trade-off involved between risk-shifting and financial deepening (or the lack of thereof). With the closing of Latin American economies and the advent of import-substitution industrialization, many financial systems became instruments of government policy. This led to severe distortions in resource allocation and "repressed" the development of financial systems (McKinnon 1973). Financial repression, however, created banking-system stability in the sense that under that regime banks rarely failed. Asymmetric information became less of a problem for banks and bank supervisors because much of banks' portfolio assets were held as central bank reserves, treasury

bonds, and low-risk directed credit to highly protected import-substituting firms. Bank capital was allowed to erode.[20] Government institutional capacity in monitoring eroded. Thus, the stability of the financial system came at a price: From the 1930s to the 1970s financial deepening did not take place in Latin America.

Such stable but atrophied systems implied a sort of safety net consisting of low-yielding loans and investments, and negative real deposit rates within a context of capital controls and high trade barriers. A wider, but latent, safety net was also maintained in the form of a broader role for the central bank as the lender of last resort. In the aftermath of the economic disorder caused by the Great Depression, legal frameworks were amended in several Latin American countries to relax or eliminate the money-issuance rules typical of the gold-linked fixed exchange rates, thereby enabling central banks to provide liquidity more broadly and for longer maturities, not only against the collateral of government securities and commercial paper but also against loan portfolios. In some Latin American countries, in the 1960s and 1970s, central banks became the main source of funds to banks. As a counterpart to these developments, exchange rates generally became fixed-but-adjustable, within the broader Bretton Woods architecture. Hence, as governments reduced exposure to the risk embedded in a hard commitment to the exchange-rate peg, their exposure to risk increased via the latent safety net implied by the greater lending powers for central banks. This latent safety net was to surface in the midst of the subsequent liberalization-driven crisis.

Financial Liberalization

Attempts at financial liberalization in Latin America— beginning in the Southern Cone in the 1970s and spreading through much of the rest of the region during the 1980s and 1990s—have not been painless. In most countries financial regulatory schemes had not changed appreciably since the 1940s. But information problems during liberalization became more severe than in the preceding 40 years as banks' portfolios switched from low-risk, low-yield government paper to much higher-yield and higher-risk loans to companies, construction, and consumers.

In the rapidly changing circumstances fueled by financial liberalization and the associated rapid credit growth, monitoring of borrowers by banks was difficult, and there was much incompetence among bankers regarding both initial and ongoing evaluations. There was equally great incompetence by bank examiners whose skills had been blunted by the rather boring situation of atrophied systems under financial repression. Modernization of supervisory agencies often got off to a slow start and, given the natural complexities and typical delays of institutional reform, could not keep up with the fast-acting, stroke-of-the-pen liberalization reforms.[21] Additionally, banks hired away many of the best bank examiners at high salaries, and the remaining examiners were too few and too powerless to engage in prudential supervision. During liberalization, bank capital was inadequate vis-à-vis the new and more complex risks, and even published capital/asset ratios were frequently overstated by concealing, or simply not reporting, bad loans and by double gearing within an economic group.[22]

Compared with the Chile of the 1920s, the Chile of the 1970s felt that it could not afford to follow orthodox banking rules for fear that the liberalization process would be derailed. This and an apparent growing concern among authorities about systemic and contagion risks in an economy open to capital flows eroded the political will to implement bank closures when needed. The relaxation of rules governing central bank provision of liquidity contributed to that erosion, as deep-seated bank problems could be temporarily masked by the use and abuse of central bank lender-of-last-resort facilities.

When banking crises erupted in Latin American countries, beginning with Chile in the late 1970s, governments tended to bail out banks and implicitly guarantee bank liabilities. In Chile, for instance, the rescue of Banco Osorno in early 1977 saved foreign creditors from losses that would have put an end to capital inflows that were helping to fuel the economic recovery. The implicit government guarantee meant that after 1977 bank spreads—the difference between loan interest rates and deposit interest rates—were much lower than they would have been. The lower bank spreads encouraged further financial deepening accompanied by excessive risk-taking. The ratio of private sector domestic credit to GDP rose from 8.8 percent in 1977 to 39.3 percent in 1981. But the implicit insurance—in the context of severe problems of asymmetric information, poor monitoring capacity, and low bank capital—also caused excessive risk-shifting to the government.

Thus, although the Chilean financial liberalization and many other liberalizations in Latin America appeared orthodox on the surface, the apparent initial success of the liberalization process was held together by the strength of an implicit government guarantee for bank liabilities. This was the case in Argentina, Uruguay, and Chile at the beginning of 1980s, Colombia in 1985, Venezuela in 1994, and Mexico in 1995. In each case the true bank safety net was only unveiled ex post and in an ad hoc manner as the financial crisis began.[23]

Crises

The improvised unveiling of ex post safety nets has reflected authorities' attempts to prevent a financial meltdown, characterized by failures in the payments system and a collapse in credit with deleterious and long-lasting effects on economic activity. Typically, ex post safety nets have taken the form of an implicit or explicit blanket protection of bank liabilities. The implicit ex post case has tended to apply more to weak or near-crisis situations, with agents perceiving an increasing willingness of governments not to allow bank failures, at least for banks considered to be "too big to fail," and acting in accordance with such perception. Often this type of implicit ex post safety net also has included widespread regulatory forbearance and abuse of access to central bank liquidity facilities, which have disguised the large and growing undercapitalization or insolvency in banks, with the illusory expectation that an upturn in the economic cycle would restore viability to troubled banks and their debtors.[24] If and when a major banking crisis has begun, and as part of the emergency containment efforts, ex post safety nets covering all banking system liabilities have in a number of cases been made explicit by governments (e.g., Mexico in 1995 and Southeast Asian countries over the past year).

Regardless of their specific form, such ex post and often universal safety nets for bank liabilities, while preventing a financial meltdown, have implied massive risk-shifting toward the government. They also have introduced substantial social costs through severe incentive distortions in financial markets, particularly in the form of runaway moral hazard. As ex post safety net protection in a number of cases extended beyond bank depositors toward bank debtors and bank owners and managers (e.g., Mexico in 1995), perverse incentives have tended to proliferate even more rapidly, eroding efficiency in financial intermediation. Experience has widely shown that the only way to extract the good out of these major distortions is for governments boldly to seize the occasion to restore banking system soundness through well-designed and executed crisis management and resolution programs. The Chilean systemic bank recapitalization and restructuring process in the early 1980s and the Argentine post-Tequila program in the mid-1990s provide regional illustrations of certain "best practice" elements in this connection.[25]

As "best practices" in resolving banking crises are being identified in an increasingly systematic way,[26] one important challenge is the need to design well-functioning regulatory and safety-net arrangements. This need arises in part from stylized facts that show how ex post safety nets emerge regardless of precommitments, which sometimes involves excessive risk-shifting to the government. The design of well-functioning safety nets is clearly a very complicated task, not the least because experience has shown that the excessive risk-shifting to the government and the incentive distortions created by ex post safety nets are very difficult to dismantle.

The Safety-Net Tripod: Capital, Monitoring, and Closure

One recurrent theme of the foregoing discussion is the ex post emergence of ad hoc safety nets, which causes ex ante rules to be abandoned. This suggests that credible efforts to "outlaw" risk-shifting to governments are unrealistic in the case of banking systems, except perhaps in a very narrow set of cases.[27] Hence, it becomes crucial to concentrate on the design of ex ante regulatory and safety-net arrangements that could better align the incentives of agents.

Well-functioning safety nets would promote sustainable financial deepening by strengthening market-originated discipline, while carefully minimizing and controlling risk-shifting to the government. This would ensure greater resiliency vis-à-vis systemic disturbances and, thus, minimize the probability of abandoning ex ante rules under bad states of the world. To this end, the design of functional safety nets should ensure that they reinforce rather than supplant the tripod of private capital, monitoring, and closure mechanisms. As will be explained later, an explicit deposit-insurance scheme may play a useful role in insuring safety-net functionality, particularly regarding the most difficult to enforce element of the tripod: closure.

The feasibility of establishing functional safety nets is not independent of initial conditions and raises important sequencing issues. For instance, in countries where signifi-

cant segments of the banking system remain undercapitalized or insolvent, the formalisms of an apparently well-designed safety net will not reduce risk-taking, because the behavior of banks without net worth would be dominated by incentives to "gamble for resurrection" or to loot the bank at depositors' or taxpayers' expense. In those circumstances, the first order of business, which must be accomplished prior to recasting a new and functional safety net, would be to root out insolvency through recapitalization, merger, or liquidation (Garber 1997).

Capital

Capital is the first leg of the tripod of a well-functioning safety net. Capital is the difference between assets and liabilities; it represents the ownership interest in a firm. Because bank owners have a residual claim on the bank cash flows, capital helps reduce the problems associated with information asymmetry by reducing incentives for excessive risk-taking: Other things being equal, as more of their own wealth is at stake, bank owners would have greater incentive to monitor the activities of bank managers, pressuring for improved internal controls, and less incentive to "milk" the bank for their benefit at the expense of depositors. Capital aligns incentives much as collateral does in the loan side. In addition, capital provides a cushion for losses: the greater the amount of capital, the greater the amount of assets that can default before the bank is technically insolvent, lowering the bank's risk (Koch 1992).

While from the point of view of regulators more capital is sure to align incentives better than less capital, it also increases lending rates and reduces financial deepening.[28] So, beyond a certain threshold, there can be "too much" capital in light of other financial-sector policy objectives.[29] At the same time, competitive forces in increasingly internationalized markets create pressure on regulators to make capital requirements lower, but this can erode incentive compatibility. In this context, the best international practice has been to establish minimum standards, leaving countries free to set their individual requirements above such minimums.

There is no simple formula to ascertain the appropriate minimum level of capital for a bank. This depends on a host of factors, including the degree of macroeconomic volatility, the quality and frequency of bank examinations, the reliability of published information, the quality of private monitoring (through internal controls, external auditors, risk-rating agencies, large depositors, etc.), and the riskiness of bank activities, whether they are on or off the balance sheets. Liberalization of financial markets confronts banks with more varied and increasingly complex risks to manage. In addition to credit risk, banks must increasingly manage liquidity risk, interest rates, exchange rates, and other market risks, as well as risks associated with conglomerate structures, derivative products, and other off-balance sheet items (Koch 1992). In this context, the simple Basle ratios of capital to risk-weighted assets, which initially focused on credit risk, are being complemented by more sophisticated risk-assessment and risk-management models.

In a number of Latin American countries the regulatory authorities have set capital-to-risky-asset requirements at levels higher than the 8 percent Basle minimum, principally in recognition that the relatively more volatile environment calls for greater capital cushions. For instance, recent changes in supervision have set them at 11.5 percent in Argentina, 9 percent in Ecuador, and 11 percent in Peru. However, relative to industrial countries, much effort is still needed in many Latin American countries to improve both the measure and quality of capital. Reliable capital measures hinge on appropriate accounting standards (including rules for asset-classification, loan-loss provisions, and income recognition on non-performing loans), information and disclosure requirements, limits on loan-concentration and loans to related parties, and enforcement.[30]

Even where accounting and disclosure standards appear adequate, the quality of capital can be undermined by a combination of shallow markets for bank stock and the concentration of wealth (Rojas-Suárez 1997). This is because interconnected balance sheets, which are typical of wealth-concentration, make it easier to offset capital increases with increased debt contracted directly or indirectly through related parties. These conditions also facilitate "creative accounting," making it difficult for supervisors to verify that the capital is real, that it does not consist of borrowed funds, and that it is actually paid up in liquid form. Also, the absence of a liquid market for bank stock leaves private and official supervisors without a key price signal to ascertain the true value of a bank's capital.[31]

Monitoring

Monitoring is the second leg of the tripod that sustains a well-functioning safety net. Lindgren, García, and Saal (1996) usefully distinguish three mutually reinforcing and interlinked levels of monitoring in banking systems: **internal governance**, **external governance**, and **international governance**.[32] The functionality of these forms of governance requires a sound broader legal and institutional environment, including, crucially, a reliable judiciary and adequate and enforceable corporate, bankruptcy, contract, and private-property laws. Also, these levels of monitoring work to the extent that bank shareholders and at least the large and sophisticated bank creditors have their funds truly at risk. Transparency—particularly through reliable (timely, consistent, and accurate) information and adequate disclosure standards—is a necessary condition for effective monitoring at any level. Conversely, good governance would itself improve the reliability, depth, and coverage of information and disclosure.

The entry of reputable foreign banks, particularly in the form of branches, into the domestic system could significantly improve overall governance in banking. Foreign banks accelerate the strengthening of developing countries' financial systems by "importing" good banking practices—including high-quality internal controls to monitor, evaluate, and manage risks; access to extra liquidity in crisis times; and the services of home-country regulation and supervision (Gavin and Hausmann 1997). However, in the absence of effective exit policies, foreign bank entry would put downward pressures on the franchise value of weak domestic banks, distorting incentives and leading to excessive risk-taking in an environment of unhealthy competition—e.g., distressed borrowing at high interest rates that forces general rates up in a disorderly fight for market share (Garber 1997).

Internal Governance

Internal governance succeeds in reducing informational asymmetries and conflicts of interest to the extent that bank shareholders, with their own money at risk, have incentives (a) to appoint able directors and managers and (b) to ensure, through those directors, that managers strive to increase the value of the bank and do not divert net earnings away from shareholders through excessive salaries, purchase of overvalued assets, and other forms of wasteful expenditures or imprudent investments. The reduction of agency problems via sound internal governance requires that bank licensing be based on appropriate "fit and proper" tests for bank owners, directors, and managers.[33] Internal governance would fail from the outset if the regulatory environment does not normally prevent unscrupulous bank owners and administrators, whose main goal is to loot the bank, from getting into the business.

External Governance: Market Discipline

External governance encompasses market discipline as well as official regulation and supervision.[34] To the extent that relevant bank creditors (large depositors, subordinated debt holders, and interbank creditors) have their funds at risk, they have incentives to monitor the bank's data—and they can respond to problems by withdrawing their resources, which could force the bank to close unless it promptly corrects its deficiencies. These creditors also can require a higher interest rate, although only up to a point, because the adverse selection problem accentuates incentive incompatibilities between agents. Responses to the perception of weaknesses in a bank are quickest in well-functioning interbank markets, where weak banks often are forced out of the market—hence the relevance of interbank market signals for supervisory systems aimed at early detection of problems (Rojas-Suárez 1998). Appropriately defined responsibilities for external auditors can substantially enhance overall governance, while credit-rating agencies can play an important role in strengthening market discipline. Recent reforms in Latin America have started to implement these practices.

External Governance: Official Regulation and Supervision

Official regulation and supervision is a crucial form of external monitoring. While there are no substitutes for internal governance and market discipline, there are also limits to these two forms of monitoring. The fundamental rule of a well-functioning system of official prudential oversight is that it should be complementary to private-sector monitoring and market discipline. To reinforce the operating environment for banks, official regulation should include procedures for the granting and revocation of licenses; a definition of the scope of banks' permissible activities; and a clear layout of the industrial structure of banking, which includes specifying the nature of its connection to other financial businesses (particularly securities and insurance) and to non-financial activities.

To reinforce internal governance, the focus of official regulation and supervision should be on fostering adequate capitalization of banks; restricting insider lending; ensur-

ing appropriate rules for loan-loss provisioning, asset-classification, and income-recognition; and promoting risk diversification and prudence in risk-taking (not only as regards credit risk, but also liquidity, exchange-rate, interest-rate, and concentration risks, as well as risks associated with conglomerate structures). To reinforce market discipline, official regulation and supervision should emphasize information disclosure of consolidated financial statements, and it should enhance the role of credit bureaus and credit-rating agencies, and provide for smooth exit of non-viable banks (see below).

Bank supervision, through off-site monitoring and on-site inspection, seeks to ensure compliance with prudential regulations, enhance the quantity and quality of information available to the market, and provide a second line of defense to complement internal governance and market discipline. Official prudential regulation without supervision will be worthless. The rapid pace of financial innovation and globalization, and the presence of complex financial and mixed conglomerate structures give rise to difficult challenges for official supervisory capacity.

Supervisory agencies in many Latin American countries are still in a process of transition from the rule-oriented, mechanistic practices brewed under the era of financial repression, toward more sophisticated and forward-looking methodologies to evaluate a bank's risks and prospects in an integrated manner. This transition is also toward a more dynamic assessment of the quality of management and the adequacy of the internal systems used to evaluate, control, and report on risk. External auditors—with their backward-looking assessment of the quality and consistency of accounting practices, accuracy of financial statements, and adequacy of internal risk-management systems—can complement official supervision. Indeed, the trend is toward increasing reliance on external auditors by supervisory authorities.

To perform its functions properly, the bank supervisory agency must have sufficient human and financial resources, which implies budgetary autonomy and the capacity to attract and retain high-quality professionals through adequate salary policies and merit-based career paths. Supervision must also be empowered with clear legal authority to act without delay in dealing with troubled banks and against managerial incompetence and non-compliance with prudential norms. Supervisors need to be legally protected against personal lawsuits for actions they take as

BOX 3.1

Market Discipline, Lender-of-Last-Resort Facilities, and Exchange Rate Systems

Central bank lender-of-last-resort facilities could undermine market discipline unless they are strictly short-term and incorporate provisions to minimize adverse selection and moral hazard. Bank runs are an unequivocal form of market discipline, but they can also be destabilizing and entail socially costly externalities (contagion and unwarranted panic, payments system disruption, excessive credit compression, etc.). To curb undesirable externalities while not blunting market discipline, "best practice" provisions for lender-of-last-resort (LOLR) facilities include strict standards for access (e.g., representations that the bank is solvent); overcollateralization and high-quality collateral requirements; restrictions on the uses of the liquidity provided by the central bank (e.g., prohibition of increasing risky assets, so as to avoid a de facto subordination of depositors in case the bank turns out to be insolvent); covenants allowing for intensified monitoring of the bank and its activities; and well-specified penalties in case of noncompliance with such covenants. This type of provision would effectively support market discipline if the lender of last resort yields a credible threat that it can precipitate, rather than delay, the closure of a non-viable bank where warranted.

LOLR facilities are often confused with open-market operations (OMOs), but they are conceptually and operationally different. OMOs normally include short-term repos and reverse repos with government or central bank paper. They aim at controlling the growth of monetary aggregates. As a derivative effect, OMOs give access to immediate liquidity to banks holding government or central bank paper. LOLR facilities, in contrast, do not aim at controlling growth in monetary aggregates (although they affect it), but rather seek to avoid externalities. In most Latin American countries, the maturities of LOLR facilities are in the 30-90 day range, whereas repos and reverse repos tend to be in the 1-7 day range. LOLR facilities tend to be structured as overcollateralized "loans," where acceptable collateral normally consists of top-grade loan portfolio.

The feasibility of LOLR facilities is inversely related to the degree of commitment to a nominal exchange rate. At the extreme of this commitment is a currency board, where the fixed nominal exchange rate is backed by a rigid money issuance rule, according to which the change in high-powered money must be exactly matched by an equivalent change in central bank international reserves. Under a strict currency board, LOLR facilities are ruled out. A currency board rules out LOLR facilities *and* OMOs. Argentina approaches this case, but it displays three important departures from it. First, the convertibility law allows for up to one-third percent of central bank international reserves to be constituted by dollar-denominated government securities, which delinks the automatic connection between changes in "true" foreign exchange reserves and changes in high-powered money; it also leaves room for the central bank to engage in operations formally equivalent to LOLR facilities. Second, the convertibility law enables a delinking of the connection between changes in monetary aggregates and changes in bank credit by allowing the central bank to change, at its discretion and for prudential reasons, liquidity (reserve) requirements (which are all invested in safe and liquid external, dollar-denominated instruments). And third, the Argentine authorities have "orchestrated" the involvement of the foreign banks as lenders of last resort by setting up, and paying a commitment fee for, a contingency repo line equivalent to about 10 percent of the system's deposits. This contingent repo line seeks to give immediate dollar liquidity to government bonds held by banks, during times of deposit withdrawal and capital flight.

part of the proper discharge of their official duties. All of this requires that the supervisory process be insulated from political interference and from the pressures of powerful bank lobbies. Many Latin American countries have a long way to go in achieving the type of institutional capacity, authority, and independence described here.

International Governance

International governance is a level of monitoring that is receiving increasing attention as financial markets become more international. Such a process can complicate information asymmetries and weaken monitoring, promoting excessive risk-taking on an international level. Typical concerns have to do with the cross-jurisdictional nature of operations; the potential for international regulatory arbitrage; and the growing linkages between banking systems across borders, which magnifies spillover effects of what were initially localized crises. In addition, the recent financial crisis in Southeast Asia and the associated international rescue packages have accentuated concerns about international moral hazard in at least two dimensions. First, emergency lending by the IMF and other multilateral agencies, aimed primarily at stabilizing capital accounts and exchange rates in order to prevent large and undesirable externalities, also has the unintended consequence of bailing out large portfolio investors, thereby eroding monitoring incentives and market discipline. Second, banks in industrial countries, as they experience competitive pressures in their home markets, may ride on their home-provided safety net so they can "gamble" in emerging markets whose risks they do not sufficiently understand.

Furthermore, the very process of increasing the presence of foreign banks in domestic markets stimulates the improvement of national supervisory systems and their convergence toward international standards, quickening the pace of cross-country coordination. Given asymmetric information, if depositors have a choice between domestic and foreign banks they would tend to choose the bank whose supervisor is considered to be more effective. This will create an incentive for national banks and supervisory authorities to improve supervision to attract or keep depositors.

Up to now, the main vehicle to improve international governance in banking has been international coordination. In general, arrangements and mechanisms to enhance international governance are at an embryonic stage. Fail-

---

BOX 3.2

International Harmonization of Regulatory and Supervisory Standards

Efforts toward international coordination have been led by the Basle Committee, with a main focus on achieving greater international harmonization of regulatory and supervisory standards. Milestones in the process include the issuance and subsequent efforts at encouraging implementation of the Basle Accord on Minimum Capital Standards and the Core Principles of Effective Banking Supervision. Important guidelines have been issued on the Evaluation of Internal Control Systems and Supervision of Cross-Border Banking. Extensive work has also been done on the development of payments systems, particularly through the Committee of Payment and Settlement Systems of the Central Banks of the Group of Ten Countries (G-10).[63] More recently, the Joint Forum of the Basle Committee, composed of bank, insurance, and securities supervisors, has promulgated recommendations for the Supervision of Financial Conglomerates.[64] In the developed world, the most ambitious and comprehensive process of regulatory and supervisory cooperation and coordination is taking place within the European Monetary Union.

International coordination efforts have been complemented by bilateral and multilateral initiatives to strengthen supervisory capacity in emerging economies through technical assistance and training programs. While the Basle Committee and the Joint Forum constitute mainly a locus for cooperation between the G-10, their recommendations are increasingly seen as setting global standards that countries outside the G-10, including those in the Latin American region, endeavor to adopt. In this context, regional groups of supervisors have been organized in Latin America and elsewhere to facilitate the sharing of experiences and provide impetus to the harmonization of practices and adoption (or adaptation) of international standards to regional milieus.

Substantial obstacles remain in the road toward implementation of international standards in supervision in the developing world. These obstacles include restrictions to information-sharing associated with legal confidentiality provisions. In addition, full harmonization of prudential norms is not always appropriate; factors such as the degree of macroeconomic volatility, the quality of accounting rules and information disclosure, differences in operating environment and in legal traditions, etc., call for either stricter standards than the international ones (e.g., capital requirements) or substantial adaptations of standards (e.g., supervision in the absence of liquid markets for bank stock).

ures in cross-border coordination between supervisors abound, as illustrated by such well known bank failures as that of the BCCI, Barings, and Daiwa, and the lesser-known Latin American cases, such as Banco Latino in Venezuela. Additionally, little has been done to avoid spillovers and systemic risks arising from bank failures. In particular, there has been no international harmonization of exit policies and standards for early intervention and bank-failure resolution. And the broader issue of a "new international financial architecture" looms large in the agenda for the future.[35]

Closure and the Complexities of Exit Policies

Compared with capital and monitoring, the third leg in the tripod that supports a functional safety net, closure, has been much less analyzed in the academic literature and has not been systematically dealt with in ongoing international coordination efforts. As a result, there is much less consensus as to what constitutes best international practices in this area. However, it is logical that capital and monitoring alone, no matter how well designed, can fail to sufficiently resolve the problems associated with informational asymmetries without closure, which is the disciplining event par excellence. Severe misalignment of incentives between participants in the banking system occurs if bank shareholders and bank creditors (other than small depositors) do not really have resources at risk. Exit policies give full meaning to "having resources at risk."[36]

However, bank closures caused by pure market forces—essentially by a run on the bank—and liquidation carried out without an appropriate framework can produce sizable negative externalities (see *ad hoc safety nets and externalities*, above). Consequently, countries typically do not rely on the unfettered operation of market forces when it comes to bank closure. Regulated exit is the norm. Exit policies and procedures are typically put in place with a view to handling failures of individual banks while minimizing negative externalities. The efficacy of these policies and procedures, however, varies widely across countries.

Exit in banking systems is a more complicated affair than closures in the non-financial sector. This is due to a host of factors. Problems of asymmetric information are relatively more pronounced in the case of banking, and even more acute as banks approach insolvency. Banks are at the heart of the complex web of payments-clearance and settlement systems, and they are highly levered relative to

non-financial firms. Both conditions tend to magnify the real or perceived systemic risk implications of badly handled bank failures. The "too big to fail" phenomenon not only implies erosion of monitoring but may also deter supervisory authorities from applying stiff penalties, weakening enforcement. Political economy constraints abound, not the least because bank owners typically have substantial political connections and lobbying powers—indeed, as Garber (1997; p. 184) puts it, "Closing down or stringently disciplining a bank is inherently a political act in all countries." Supervisors may fall prey to "regulatory capture," partly due to corruption or to a perception that the supervisors' main role lies in preventing bank failures; as a result, regulation may be manipulated so as to favor those that it was intended to constrain (Stigler 1971). Finally, the absence of adequate legal and institutional framework for the orderly resolution of failing banks undermines the authorities' willingness and capacity to take non-viable banks and unfit bankers out of the market.

Ineffective bank exit policies lead to a frequently observed bad equilibrium that, in the absence of shocks, can be fairly durable. This equilibrium may be labeled "the walking dead bank syndrome," and is characterized by insolvency and undercapitalization in important segments of the system, disguised by some form of regulatory forbearance that enables window-dressing accounting and postpones corrective action. In this type of situation, authorities and bankers tend to join in a speech of denial while hoping that an upturn in the business cycle will cure the problem over time. In reality, however, the insolvency "hole" only grows bigger, and the viability prospects for troubled banks only deteriorates, as a result of the associated dramatic exacerbation of perverse incentives. Reckless risk-taking by weak and unsound banks force sound banks into short-term strategies that are unsustainable in the longer term and end up weakening sound banks, adding to systemic unsoundness. Bank owners and managers of troubled banks tend to be driven by a "heads I win, tails you lose" attitude, and face an escalating temptation to loot the bank, as they move from "management by window dressing" to "desperate management" (de Juan 1987). Bank creditors tend to act under the perception of a universal safety net, with the attendant erosion of monitoring incentives. Bank debtors tend to organize themselves to lobby for protection (debt forgiveness) from the government.[37] In these circumstances, efficiency in the intermediation process suffers severe erosion and systemic vulnerability to shocks rises dramatically.

Fire Protection and Fire Fighting: Designing Exit Policies

The key elements of effective bank exit policies are analogous to good fire protection and fire fighting: There is a premium on prevention, but there also is the wherewithal to deal with fires that do occur. In order to ensure that buildings are safe against fire hazards, fire-resistant materials are promoted and building codes and other regulations are enforced. Building inspectors ensure compliance with these regulations and minimum building standards. Smoke alarms and fire-detection devices are installed. Fire extinguishers prevent small fires from getting out of hand. There are carefully designed fire escape routes and regularly conducted fire drills to avoid disorderly evacuation and unnecessary panic if the worst comes to pass. Fire departments and firefighters can be quickly summoned through emergency phone numbers or automatic fire alarms. They have well-rehearsed procedures to deal with large fires and, when in action, seek to contain the fire from spreading to neighboring homes or buildings. Poorly constructed buildings or those severely affected by fires can be "condemned" and demolished if they are not fit to be occupied.

For a city to be safe from fires, it must rely not only on good building codes and their enforcement through inspections but also on its fire department to fight those occasional fires that do occur. Similarly, for a banking system to be safe and sound, it not only needs risk-based capital standards and integrated internal, external, and international monitoring; it also needs effective exit policies. Exit policies include some basic components to function well. *Early-warning systems* (smoke alarms) help detect deterioration of a bank and identify banks that require intensified monitoring. *Rules for prompt corrective action* (fire extinguishers) try to reverse bank deterioration through increasingly more stringent enforcement measures. *Intervention and resolution processes* (fire escapes, firefighters) deal with, and dispose of, problem banks in a manner that is expeditious and least disruptive to the system. Basic exit policies, if well-designed, should deal well with a broad range of bank troubles and failures, while credibly ensuring that non-viable banks, even if large, would not remain in operation.

Early Warnings, Prompt Correction, and Intervention
Early-warning systems suitable for Latin American countries have to integrate macroeconomic, sectoral, and microeconomic aspects. While systems developed in industrial countries typically emphasize CAMEL-type microeconomic variables (an acronym for quantifiable indicators of Capital, Asset quality, Management, Earnings, and Liquidity), a recent trend in the literature on early-warning systems for developing countries has sought to combine macro and micro aspects, while endeavoring to identify microeconomic variables that could have greater predictive power than the traditional CAMEL variables. For instance, Rojas-Suárez (1998) shows the usefulness of alternative indicators such as fast growth in loan portfolio, relatively higher deposit rates, low financial spreads, and decreased access to interbank markets in predicting banking crises in some Latin American countries (Mexico, Venezuela, and Colombia).

The approach based on early-warning indicators should be complemented by forward looking, dynamic simulations or "stress tests" of the performance of banks under different scenarios. Early-warning systems are off-site tools of supervision that help identify banks that should be subject to special, intensified on-site monitoring. Such closer scrutiny is justified given that, as has been already mentioned, incompatibility of the incentives facing bank owners, managers, bank creditors, and debtors increases exponentially as the economic value of the bank decreases toward insolvency.

Prompt corrective actions aim at automatically curbing risk-taking by owners and managers of a bank that falls into increasing capital shortages relative to the required level, and at reversing the capital deficiency quickly. The key purpose is to leave little or no room for discretion, thereby avoiding the rarely effective and usually detrimental delays in addressing risky practices. Under these rules, as soon as a capital shortage is detected, restrictions are automatically triggered, while pre-specified deadlines come into effect to secure the needed capital injection. Initial restrictions tend to prohibit the payment of dividends or any increase in risky assets, together with the obligation to invest new deposits in highly liquid and safe instruments. As capital shortages increase, so do the restrictions, which tend to move from limits on growth toward forced shrinkage, as supervisory authorities become increasingly proactive in selecting assets to sell.[38] The main object of prompt corrective actions is to try to secure recapitalization of the troubled bank by the private sector, without exposing public funds. To this end, certain laws, such as Chile's, have an explicit range of recapitalization options.[39]

Enforcement of restrictions within the prompt corrective action process normally requires a stepped-up form of on-site monitoring that, under certain pre-specified conditions, may reach its strongest version: **intervention**. Intervention often implies the removal of the bank's management, even for reasons other than criminal activities if deemed necessary, and the appointment of a "conservator" or a "temporary administrator" to manage the bank.

In principle, intervention may serve a number of useful purposes. The threat of intervention, if credible, will encourage compliance with prompt corrective actions required from bank owners and managers. Once in effect, intervention can allow unfettered room for the supervisors to determine the true condition of the bank. It can also help "conserve" the franchise value of the bank, protecting depositors from the harm that could be caused by bank owners and managers bent on "gambling for resurrection" or "looting." And it can provide unhindered room for specialized personnel to evaluate alternative ways to resolve the bank and make recommendations on the best course of action. To achieve these purposes, the intervention authority must be firmly and unambiguously established in the law, and it should provide for the suspension of the rights of shareholders to interfere with the process.

In practice, however, the execution of an intervention faces a number of difficulties, particularly in emerging economies. Due to legal constraints or human resource shortages, often the "temporary administrator" is not the senior banker who is needed under the circumstances, but a bureaucrat with little managerial and banking experience who stifles the bank's operations and loses, rather than conserves, franchise value. This situation tends to be accentuated where the legal ground for intervention is weak, exposing the authorities to the risk of being personally sued by disgruntled bank owners.[40] Also, intervention may fuel, rather than curb, the run on the bank, if depositors interpret that it has just been placed on a faster track toward liquidation, which can be a serious problem where confidence in the banking system is fragile and contagion risk high.

Bank-Failure Resolution

Bank-failure resolution procedures are analogous to bankruptcy proceedings for non-financial firms, but to be effective they must contain elements specifically designed to address typical complexities of "exit" in banking systems, including the potentially destabilizing effects of disorderly failures. Resolution is the most complicated component of exit policies—legally and politically. As with any bankruptcy process, a key element of the needed legal infrastructure for bank-failure resolution consists of clear and enforceable priority of claim rules. These establish the position in the queue of the various classes of claims over the assets of the failed bank, with depositors' claims at or very near the beginning of the queue, and shareholders' claims always at the end.

A failing bank is considered to have been "resolved" when the following conditions have been met: (a) its insured deposits have been paid off in cash or transferred to another, sound financial institution and (b) its assets have been disposed of and its non-insured creditors have been paid according to well-defined rules that set the priority of claims. From the point of view of systemic stability, accomplishing the first condition in an orderly and rapid manner is of utmost importance, with some analysts and practitioners limiting the definition of resolution to it. While the "plain vanilla" form of resolving a failed bank is closure cum liquidation, resolution encompasses a broad range of alternatives. In fact, traditional liquidation (where *all* creditors are paid off according to the priority of their claims but only to the extent that the assets of the failed bank are collected or sold) tends to be a suboptimal form of resolution.[41] Well-designed exit policies should leave flexibility for alternative resolution structures, so long as the chosen alternative meets the least-cost criterion and there is adequate governance and transparency in its execution. In principle alternative resolution schemes are possible in the absence of explicit deposit insurance, although in practice they tend to presuppose its existence.

Basic alternatives in bank-failure resolution[42] include the following: First, the immediate cash payment of insured deposits, leaving the rest of the claims in the liquidation ("receivership"), including those of the deposit insurer, to paid off over time as assets are disposed of. Second, the transfer of insured deposits to an existing sound bank, with uninsured creditors paid off over time out of the liquidation of all the assets of the failed bank. This transfer can be accomplished, for instance, through a "negative bid," where the deposit insurer pays cash to the bank that asks for the least amount of compensation in order to take the insured deposits. And third, the transfer of insured deposits and other liabilities, together with enough "good" assets, to an existing sound bank, with liquidation of the remaining assets and payment of remaining liabilities over time.[43] If existing banks are unable to absorb good assets and liabilities (e.g., because the failed bank is large and existing banks do not have sufficient excess capital), a "bridge bank" could be created (with "good" assets at least equal to liabilities), which could be sold or merged with another institution later. This third alternative can be efficient given that the liquidation value of assets is significantly lower that their going-concern value. Its complications lie, however, in the need for the acquiring bank to examine the assets of the failed bank, which takes time, leads to strategic negotiating, and often requires complex contractual contingency clauses (e.g., stop-loss, loss-sharing, and profit-sharing clauses).[44]

The resolution phase may follow intervention if the latter does not solve the situation of a troubled bank. But this sequence is neither necessary nor always advisable, given the problems in intervention mentioned earlier. What is essential, however, is for the legal and regulatory framework to specify clearly the threshold at which resolution is formally activated, i.e., the point at which the shareholders are deemed to have lost their property rights over the troubled bank.[45] In addition, it is crucial to the effectiveness of resolution to substantially minimize or eliminate the capacity of shareholders to interfere through legal means with the resolution process, circumscribing their rights only to pecuniary compensation if they were to prevail in a lawsuit.[46] Without this, the authorities would not have full control of the resolution process and would be hesitant to act for fear of personal entanglement in legal proceedings.

The Role of Deposit Insurance in Bank-Failure Resolution

The literature has emphasized a dual role of deposit insurance—protecting depositors from losses in the event of a bank failure and avoiding the undesirable externalities of panic deposit withdrawals (Chandavarkar 1996)—while focusing concerns on its moral hazard implications (e.g., Calomiris 1996, 1997).[47] Only recently has there been an increasing recognition that well-designed, limited, and explicit deposit insurance can significantly improve market discipline by facilitating early closure without adding moral hazard, provided that capital and monitoring are adequate.[48]

Equity considerations normally make the protection of small depositors a politically noncontroversial issue.[49] As small depositors are not likely to monitor a bank systematically due to the free-rider problem, explicit deposit insurance for them is also noncontroversial from the point of view of incentive compatibility. Furthermore, uninsured creditors will indeed have greater incentives to monitor their bank—and to discipline it by withdrawing their deposits or requiring a premium in interest rates—if well-designed deposit insurance enhances exit policies, because these creditors will perceive a higher probability of having to share in the losses in the event of the bank's failure.[50] And bank owners and managers are sure to behave more prudently to the extent that they perceive that the probability of being bailed out has been virtually banished.[51] While consistent with monitoring and market discipline, a limited and explicit deposit insurance is unlikely to significantly deter contagious runs: the "hot" money is in large deposits and non-deposit bank liabilities, and it is their withdrawal that can bring a bank quickly to its knees, posing a risk of systemic instability.

If the goal is not so much to avoid large deposit runs but mainly to facilitate the prompt resolution of unviable banks, then a case can be made in favor of a deposit-insurance scheme that is explicit, limited in coverage, funded by premiums paid by the industry, and organized into an agency that would be publicly managed, endowed with intervention and failure resolution authority, and given access to a contingent line of credit from the ministry of finance.[52] In addition, to ensure compatibility between the various components of the safety net, the functionality of deposit insurance with the mentioned traits requires that every precaution be taken to circumscribe the lender-of-last-resort facilities of the central bank to liquidity (rather than solvency) problems. Otherwise, there would be incentives to abuse those facilities to artificially delay bank closures, undermining overall governance in the system. What follows in this section discusses the mentioned characteristics in some detail.

Some of the arguments in favor of an **explicit** scheme that would confine its coverage to small depositors have been advanced in previous paragraphs. In addition, compared with implicit schemes or to ex post safety nets, explicit and limited deposit insurance would imply clearer ex ante rules. These would provide greater insulation vis-à-vis political pressures to bail out all bank creditors and/or shareholders in difficult times and would also increase the likelihood of consistent results over the long run. Moreover, such a scheme would limit and help control risk-shifting to the government, making it a cheaper alternative for taxpayers, particularly if capital and monitoring are well designed and consistently enforced.

Funding via premiums assessed on the banking industry reduces the adverse selection problem to the extent that membership is compulsory; if membership were voluntary, there would be an adverse selection ("lemons") problem as weaker banks would be more willing to pay the premiums than prudent banks (Mishkin 1996; Stiglitz 1993). However, when both risky and prudent banks pay the same premium, there would be an incentive to become a risky bank. And if the established premium agrees with the risk of the riskier banks, prudent banks may engage in risky practices since they would already be paying to incur such risk. Hence, in addition to compulsory membership, the deposit-insurance premiums should be allowed to vary according to the riskiness of individual banks—rewarding prudent banks. Variable premiums make it easier to avoid underpricing the safety net. Some form of coercive power is needed to enforce compulsory membership and variable risk-based premiums and this suggests that, in one way or another, an explicit deposit-insurance scheme would need to be an instrumentality of the state.

There appear to be other advantages to organizing deposit insurance into a **publicly administered agency**, different from the supervisory agency, provided that such agency is independent from political interference, has budgetary autonomy and high professional standards, and possesses well-designed governance structures to enhance accountability and transparency. It could be advantageous to empower the deposit-insurance agency with authority to execute early intervention and to carry out the bank-failure resolution processes. An agency of this type may be more likely to provide the right incentives to perform intervention and resolution responsibilities efficiently because, by legal statute, it would have the mandate to protect the interests of insured depositors and the integrity of the accumulated insurance fund. In the absence of a publicly managed deposit-insurance agency, both bank supervision and closure would have to be in the hands of the supervisory authorities. But bank supervisors and inspectors do not typically have the skills needed for bank intervention and failure resolution. Furthermore, bank supervisors may

be less likely to close an insolvent bank, because they—and the public—tend to perceive their role as one of preventing banks from going insolvent in the first place, which makes the closing of a bank appear as an admission of failure (Lindgren, García, and Saal 1996). The organizational setup described here, which allows for appropriate division of labor and improving incentives,[53] may be more compatible with well-functioning exit policies than alternative organizational arrangements, and may more likely reduce the probability of the "walking dead bank syndrome" mentioned earlier.[54]

Finally, the **access to a contingent line of credit from the ministry of finance** is needed for the scheme to be credible. Otherwise, market participants would anticipate the abandonment of the rules of the game under difficult circumstances—e.g., if a large bank or a significant number of small banks were to become insolvent. In fact, purely "private deposit insurance schemes have a long and fairly uniform history—they eventually fail" (Garber 1997; p. 198); therefore, purely private schemes are unlikely to help in exorcising the ghost of ex post, improvised safety nets. It would be convenient for the ministry of finance to back its contingent obligation to the deposit insurance with a contingent liability to international creditors exclusively dedicated to this purpose. This would help avoid inflationary pressures and strengthen the exchange rate, thereby preventing the deterioration of the balance sheets of debtors who hold foreign-denominated liabilities.

Furthermore, if a contingency line to foreign creditors is involved—particularly if they are multilateral organizations—it could enhance governance if it is accompanied by appropriate conditionality. In order to reduce the attendant moral hazard, this conditionality should focus on improvements in banking laws, the legal environment, and governance for the corporate sector, as well as on strengthening the supervisory and regulatory environment for the financial sector.[55]

The risk-shifting implied in the contingent access to public-sector resources, however, must be counterbalanced by giving "hard control rights" to official supervision (to ensure appropriate prudential oversight over banks) and to the deposit-insurance agency (by endowing it with powerful tools for early intervention and effective bank-failure resolution).

If activated, the contingent line should be payable through future premiums; this would help clarify the way in which the burden is to be distributed over time and among different groups in society.[56] However, a sudden large use of the contingent line would likely run into the constraints posed by shallow domestic capital markets for long-term government debt typical of many Latin American countries. This suggests two possible solutions: First, to allow room for the central bank to purchase government debt (which should carry market-related interest rates) from the deposit-insurance agency—this would be feasible as long as a flexible exchange-rate system is in place. Second, to enable the government to contract a contingent long-term line of credit from international sources—this would be the only choice if there is a hard commitment to a nominal exchange-rate peg that rules out the central bank's purchases of government debt securities.

Safety Nets, Systemic Risk, and Catastrophe Insurance

A well-designed safety net—one that carefully controls risk-shifting to the government while promoting sustainable financial deepening—requires a sound tripod of capital, monitoring, and closure. The desirable design features that have emerged throughout the previous sections, including, importantly, the elements of functional exit policies described in *fire protection and fire fighting: designing exit policies*, should lead to an ex ante safety net that limits incentive incompatibility substantially, thereby enhancing banking system safety and soundness. These features should also lead to a resilient safety net—that is, one that is able to withstand a broad range of states of the world, without altering ex ante rules and without exposing taxpayers to losses. However, under extreme circumstances involving aggregate (systemic) risk rather than idiosyncratic (loan or bank-specific) risk, even the best designed ex ante rules may be overwhelmed and abandoned in favor of ad hoc safety-net rules, which under certain circumstances could be the optimal thing to do.[57] This raises the complex issue of when and how to override ex ante rules and whether the ex ante design should make provision for catastrophe-type states of the world, so as to minimize improvisation and enhance the effectiveness of emergency responses.

True systemic risk in banking can be likened to catastrophe situations, and catastrophes tend to be uninsurable by the private sector.[58] Governments have a comparative advantage in handling catastrophe risks, but to the extent that they make explicit their willingness to provide insurance against catastrophes, risk-shifting to taxpayers becomes unavoidable, and tougher monitoring and enforcement rules become necessary to limit moral hazard.[59] In the case of banking systems, historical experience has repeatedly shown that risk-shifting to the government cannot be avoided in the face of systemic crises, and market participants know it.[60] While the complexity of this matter goes beyond the scope of this chapter, it seems useful, for illustrative purposes, to classify into three groups the stylized government approaches to deal with the problem of safety nets under catastrophe-type circumstances.

The "never-ever" approach. In this case, governments are prevented by legislation from bailing out bank creditors, owners, or debtors, except for the limited coverage of an explicit deposit protection, if any. Any bailout beyond explicitly insured deposits would require the approval of legislative changes. The credibility of this precommitment not to abandon the ex ante rules of the game would be a positive function of the soundness of the tripod of capital, monitoring, and closure, and a negative function of the degree of the economy's exposure to macroeconomic shocks. If this tripod is poorly designed and enforced, the legal, regulatory, and policy framework will burst sooner rather than later, even under the pressures of idiosyncratic risk, let alone the pressures of macroeconomic shocks. In fact, the costs associated with not knowing when to relax ex ante rules and not knowing how to implement rescue packages are large (Caprio and Klingebiel 1996). In practice, some form of bailout beyond the limits of explicit deposit protection can be carried out in most countries within their existing legal frameworks, which puts us into the second category of stylized approaches.

The "maybe-maybe not" approach. In this case, bank bailouts can occur in some fashion without legislative changes. Approaches in this group allow for "constructive ambiguity" because the authorities can maintain a "no bailout" discourse (whose credibility depends on the same factors mentioned for the first case) but are known to have the discretion to decide when to unfold a wider safety net than that contained in the discourse. Often discretion is allowed in the use of instruments that are inappropriate to the task; for instance, the law may allow the use of lender-of-last-resort facilities without appropriate safeguards, opening the room for its misuse in dealing with insolvency. By contrast, if lender-of-last-resort facilities are well designed and if capital, monitoring, and closure are sound, then "constructive ambiguity" may have the advantage of keeping market participants guessing while giving flexibility to the authorities. In particular, if closure contains effective early intervention and bank-failure resolution policies and procedures, then a banking crisis probably would be managed much better than otherwise.[61] At the other extreme, however, the "maybe-maybe not" approach would lead to acute incentive incompatibility if the discretion it provides lives in the context of an undercapitalized banking system, with weak governance and poorly designed exit policies.

The **"only if" approach.** Under this approach, the legal framework would contain explicit contingency clauses, according to which, if a relevant set of authorities were to determine the existence of systemic risk, then the coverage of bank liabilities could extend beyond the explicitly insured amount. This approach has the advantage of reducing discretion while not ruling out the need to extend the safety net if systemic considerations warrant it. This "only if" approach also allows for "constructive ambiguity": Market participants do not have certainty as to when the authorities would determine that there is systemic risk. As in the previous case, the potential superiority of the "only if" approach hinges on the quality and strength of the tripod of capital, monitoring, and closure, and it presupposes that lender-of-last-resort facilities are appropriately designed and implemented.[62]

The "only if" and "maybe-maybe not" approaches imply that in managing a systemic crisis, there may be compelling reasons to protect depositors and other bank creditors beyond the explicitly insured amounts. However, even under these extraordinary circumstances, there does not seem to be a compelling reason for bank owners not to be the first to absorb the losses. In other words, systemic crises may call for bailing out depositors and other bank creditors but not for bailing out bank owners and administrators.

Summary and Conclusions

Drawing from historical experience as well from the analysis of incentive problems under asymmetric information, this chapter has explored issues in banking system safety nets. Even if not envisioned in regulatory arrangements, safety nets, which imply risk-shifting to the government, have emerged ex post and in improvised fashion under financial crisis situations. The pressures for safety nets are related to the substantial negative externalities that could result from disorderly bank failures. But bankers, borrowers, and depositors each have their own reasons for wanting to be covered by a safety net that have nothing to do with negative externalities. Bank owners, especially, may be powerful politically. In addition, if the government relies upon the banking system as a substantial holder of government debt, then the government may be reluctant to let banks go bankrupt. Efforts to "outlaw" safety nets are normally unrealistic in the case of banking, and market participants know it. Hence, it becomes crucial to concentrate on the design of ex ante regulatory and safety-net arrangements that could better align incentives.

A well-functioning safety net must balance its institutional components—lender-of-last-resort facilities, deposit insurance, capital requirements, prudential oversight, and exit (closure) policies—so as to control risk-shifting to the government, while promoting sustainable financial deepening by supporting, rather than blunting, market-originated discipline. A well-designed safety net would ensure greater resiliency vis-à-vis systemic disturbances, thereby minimizing the probability of abandonment of ex ante rules under bad states of the world, and ultimately improving social welfare. When a safety net's institutional components are poorly designed or inadequately implemented, it becomes dysfunctional and exacerbates moral hazard problems, which, if sufficiently severe, increase systemic instability, thereby undermining the safety net's raison d'être.

It has been argued throughout the chapter that well-functioning safety nets need to be adequately supported by a tripod of capital, monitoring, and closure. All of these three legs of the tripod are equally important and mutually reinforcing: the effectiveness of each one depends on the effectiveness of the other two. However, closure (exit policies), arguably the most difficult to implement of the three, legally and politically, has also been much less analyzed in the academic literature and has not been systematically dealt with in ongoing international coordination efforts. As a result, there is much less consensus as to what constitutes best international practices in exit policies.

Well-designed exit policies need to involve effective early-warning systems, prompt corrective actions, intervention, and bank-failure resolution. There is a good argument that a very useful tool in facilitating prompt and orderly bank-failure resolution is explicit deposit insurance—insurance with limited coverage that is funded through variable premium assessments on the industry, backed by a contingent line of credit from the fiscal authority, and endowed with intervention and failure-resolution powers. While this type of deposit-insurance setup seems to be consistent with the needed incentive structure, the jury is still out on this issue, and other institutional and organizational arrangements may serve equally well in complementing effective exit policies.

The design of a well-functioning safety net should not be confused with the design and implementation of banking crisis resolution and bank restructuring programs. In countries where significant segments of the banking system remain undercapitalized or insolvent, the formalisms of an apparently well-designed safety net will not reduce risk-taking, because the behavior of banks without net worth would be dominated by incentives to "gamble for resurrection" or to loot the bank at depositors' or taxpayers' expense. In those circumstances, the first order of business, which must be accomplished *prior to* recasting a new and functional safety net, would be to root out insolvency through a comprehensive bank restructuring program. Hence, the design of a functional safety net is not independent of initial conditions and gives rise to important sequencing issues.

A resilient safety net should be able to withstand a broad range of states of the world, without altering ex ante rules and without exposing taxpayers to losses. However, under extreme circumstances involving aggregate (systemic) risk rather than idiosyncratic (loan- or bank-specific) risk, even the best designed ex ante rules may be overwhelmed and abandoned in favor of ad hoc safety-net rules. This raises the complex subject of when and how to override ex ante rules, and of whether the ex ante design should make provision for catastrophes, so as to minimize improvisation and enhance the effectiveness of emergency responses. The issues involved can be in large part analyzed from the viewpoint of catastrophe insurance and involve the discussion on rules versus discretion. "Constructive ambiguity" and contingent clauses in the legal framework are two interesting ways of handling the eventuality of systemic—that is, catastrophe—risk.

A necessary word of caution: Mechanically exporting safety-net arrangements from one country to another is very likely to run into problems. The cultural, historical, political, legal, and institutional setup of each country has to be taken into account if a safety-net design is to be viable.

Notes

1. Much as been written in the last decade on financial safety nets, including Benston et al. (1986); Brock (1992a); Dewatripont and Tirole (1993); Hausmann and Rojas-Suárez (1996); Rojas-Suárez (1997); Alexander, Davis, Ebrill, and Lindgren (1996); Lindgren, García, and Saal (1996); Garber and Weisbrod (1992); Sheng (1996); and Chandavarkar (1996). Papers by Calomiris (1997), Mishkin (1996), and Garber (1997) are particularly valuable contributions to the safety-net literature for developing countries. The most researched aspect related to safety nets has been deposit insurance (Talley and Mas 1992; Cull 1998). Against the background of recent financial crises in Latin America and in Southeast Asia, the literature has started to deal more systematically with such difficult issues as resolution of bank insolvency (Caprio and Klingebiel 1996; Caprio and Keefer 1998; drafts for World Bank 1998b).

2. Although many of the concepts described below apply to broadly defined financial markets, the discussion concentrates on the banking sector, because the focus of the chapter is to analyze issues for the provision of safety nets for depository institutions (banks).

3. The agency literature deals with a principal and an agent. Typically, there is asymmetry in the information that each one holds; the agent has access to information not available to the principal, and information-gathering and analysis is costly. Even if information is equally shared between the principal and the agent, their incentives may not align if contracts are too costly to enforce.

4. Tradability of loan contracts is enhanced by such things as the bank's reputation and the degree of standardization of loan-underwriting practices.

5. The "lemons problem" was first introduced by Akerlof (1970). The main argument is that in the market for used cars, sellers and buyers have different knowledge about the quality of a given used car. Since the buyer does not know with certainty if a used car is of low quality (a "lemon"), she will be unwilling to pay beyond the price of a "lemon." The seller of a good-quality used car, in turn, would be unwilling to accept only a lemon's price. This gives rise to conditions where the market for used cars tends to be a market for lemons, and good-quality cars are not traded.

6. These solutions tend to arise even in the absence of government intervention. Information problems hurt firms by limiting the willingness of banks to lend and by raising the cost of loans that are made. Banks, in turn, are hurt by a loss of profits. Thus, both debtor firms and creditor banks have an incentive to promote institutions that reduce selection and moral hazard problems, facilitating the flow of credit.

7. A leverage index, which can be created by finding the ratio of a firm's debt financing to its equity financing, also is a measure of potential earnings volatility. The greater the leverage, the more volatile the firm's net profit or loss (Koch 1992).

8. North (1990) defines property rights as the exclusive rights for individuals to appropriate their own labor and the goods and services they posses.

9. Levine (1997b) shows that financial market development is positively and significantly related to legal heritage, again with common law performing better than civil law.

10. As in the case of loan contracts, the price mechanism alone may not work, because the increase in interest rate required by depositors would tend to exacerbate the adverse selection problem.

11. Broadly speaking, an externality entails that the cost or benefit of a certain activity is borne by someone other than the person undertaking the activity (Carlton and Perloff 1990). Externalities arise when property rights are not clearly defined. Positive externalities occur when someone undertakes an action that benefits others who do not pay for these benefits. The externality is negative if agents do not bear the full cost of their actions.

12. In addition to prudential regulation, government intervention can result in financial repression, which occurs when the government distorts incentives in the financial system, typically with the hope of achieving certain social objectives. Interest-rate ceilings (frequently resulting in negative real interest rates), high non-interest bearing reserve requirements, and targeted credit are examples of the instruments of financial repression widely used in developing countries before the 1980s, with perverse consequences for growth and development (McKinnon 1973).

13. The argument that a good safety net enables agents to act as if there were no net could be interpreted as pointing to the need for prudential regulation to mimic the market to the extent possible, thus aligning agents' incentives to reduce divergence between the pursuit of private and social benefits.

14. New York's 1838 Free Bank Law stated: "...nothing in this act contained shall be considered as implying any pledge on the part of the state for the payment of said bills or notes beyond the proper application of the securities pledged to the comptroller for their redemption." See Brock (1992a, p. 431).

15. The *Caja* was authorized to lend up to 50 percent of the assessed value of the real estate and was given legal precedence in the collection of its loans. In exchange for the mortgages the *Caja* issued *letras de crédito* with maturities of 21–25 years and coupon rates of 5–8 percent. Borrowers could then sell the *letras* on a secondary market for cash. When landholders went to sell the *letras* on the secondary market, they received a higher price because purchasers demanded a smaller insurance premium knowing that the *Caja*, via its capital and reserves, was the primary insurer of the mortgages.

16. See Brock (1992b) and Fetter (1931).

17. Deepening, however, was not automatic in all countries with new central banks. For instance, in Mexico the public continued to rely heavily on the Banco de Mexico as a depository institution as a result of continued distrust of commercial banks.

18. While from the point of view of regulators the pressure mainly arises from externalities, there are internal pressures, too, because bankers, borrowers, and depositors each have their own reasons for wanting to be covered by a safety net that have nothing to do with externalities. In particular, bank owners may be powerful politically, which enables them to exert significant pressure over regulators.

19. Depositors may run even when there is a deposit-insurance scheme, if they fear that in the event of a failure the payment from the insurer would take a long time. For an individual depositor, while the risk from the withdrawal of deposits by another depositor is very small, the cost is smaller still if she withdraws her own deposits.

20. For example, in Chile, bank capital as a fraction of assets fell from 27 percent in 1932 to 20 percent in 1940, 14 percent in 1948, 9 percent in 1955, and 6 percent in 1962.

21. This is related to "regulatory dialectic" (Kane 1977). The underlying argument is that regulation affects the behavior of agents, leading to a different outcome than otherwise. This process induces innovation on the part of the financial agents to avoid regulation. These innovations tend to spread rapidly, while authorities tend to lag in adapting regulation to the innovations. Eventually, though, new regulation takes place and the process starts again.

22. Double gearing means using the same capital to support additional assets.

23. Recent research has shown some evidence that financial liberalization has contributed to the eruption of financial crises (Demirgüç-Kunt and Detragiache 1998).

24. A bank is insolvent if the economic value of its assets is not enough to pay its debtors. An insolvent bank has negative equity in economic terms. In principle, a bank may be insolvent but liquid, or solvent but illiquid. Contrary to an insolvent bank, a solvent but illiquid bank has the assets to meet its debt obligations over time, but not immediately due to the illiquidity of the assets (i.e., the assets cannot be transformed into cash fast enough). In the absence of central bank lender-of-last-resort facilities, this raises the possibility of runs on banks, even if they are solvent. The disposal of assets at "fire sale" prices could turn a solvent into an insolvent bank. In fact, illiquidity and insolvency interact and may reinforce each other (Gavin and Hausmann 1997).

25. Important elements of best practices outside the Latin American region include the phase of the U.S. savings-and-loan crisis that started after 1988, once Congress appropriated needed funds for the deposit insurance agency and created the Resolution Trust Corporation, and the resolution of Spain's banking crisis during the 1980s.

26. See, for instance, the book edited by W. E. Alexander et al. (1997) and Rojas-Suárez (1997).

27. One possible case is where the entire domestic banking system is small and fully dominated by first-rate foreign banks. However, during the Latin American debt crisis of the 1980s, banks were bailed out in Uruguay, a small open economy dominated by first-rate foreign banks, because foreign banks threatened to leave the system (Brock 1992a).

28. While regulators prefer more capital because of their concern for systemic stability and safety, bankers generally prefer less capital and higher leverage ratios (Koch 1992; Jensen and Meckling 1976).

29. Narrow banking involves the same trade-off of higher stability but lower financial deepening.

30. Lending to related parties and underprovision of reserves against loan losses have been common causes of vulnerability in the banking system in Latin America. The former affects the true stake of owners in the bank, and the latter overstates the book value of capital relative to its true economic value.

31. This adds an argument in favor of promoting bank monitoring through price revelation in the markets for bank liabilities,

which are well-developed markets relative to equity markets in Latin America. This approach can work to the extent that there is no explicit or implicit government backing of *all* bank liabilities and could be accomplished by requiring banks to issue subordinated debt to comply with part of their regulatory capital (Rojas-Suárez 1997 and Calomiris 1997), as is done currently in Argentina.

32. This subsection draws heavily on Lindgren, García, and Saal (1996).

33. In addition, the criminal history of owners and managers can be taken into account in the licensing process of banks, as has been the case in a number of Latin American countries (e.g., Argentina and Peru).

34. Market discipline can be undermined by poorly designed lender-of-last-resort facilities (see Box 3.1).

35. For a recent discussion of international lenders of last resort for emerging markets, see Mishkin (1998).

36. The term "exit policies" is better than "closure," as it conveys better the complexity and breath of this key third leg of the safety-net tripod.

37. For instance, the Barzón in Mexico, which is a debtors' organization.

38. Prompt corrective action rules in the FDIC Improvement Act of 1991 (section 131) of the United States are considered to be an example of "best practice." Lindgren, García, and Saal (1996, Table 24, p. 198) summarize these rules. A significant number of banking laws in Latin America contain specific clauses in this area, although enforcement varies widely.

39. About one-fourth of the 1986 Chilean bank law is devoted to the precise specification of alternative closure and recapitalization mechanisms for troubled banks. The recapitalization mechanisms include recapitalization by the bank's owners or outside capital injections, interbank loans that turn into preferred stock if the borrowing bank does not regain solvency, and a recapitalization process that turns a fraction of a bank's noninsured liabilities into preferred stock.

40. In comparison with the legal protection afforded in the United States for supervisory and FDIC officials (no private right of action can be leveled against them for actions performed in the discharge of their official duties), virtually all Latin American countries fail to offer sufficient immunity, a situation that is aggravated by unreliable judicial systems. This is a key factor in explaining why there are often delays in taking decisive action on bank closures in various countries in the region.

41. In most Latin American countries, bank liquidation processes tend to be legally cumbersome and potentially destabilizing, with depositors typically getting paid several months after the liquidation has been decreed. This is in large part because deposit insurance schemes do not exist, or, if they do, they lack well-designed policies and procedures, are underfunded, or are poorly managed.

42. For a more complete description of alternative resolution structures see Talley and Mas (1992) and Federal Deposit Insurance Corporation (1997).

43. This alternative is known as a "purchase and assumption"— i.e., the existing bank purchases assets of the failed institutions and assumes its liabilities. It is also a variant of the so-called "good bank/bad bank approach," where good assets and as much bank liabilities as possible are carved out to be transferred to an existing bank, or bad assets are taken out to permit the sale of the "good" bank.

44. Supervisory and intervention authorities can also pressure owners into a merger or a sale of their troubled bank—typically during the prompt corrective action and intervention stages. "Induced" mergers and acquisitions are also a form of "resolution," with the difference that shareholders still have some net worth at stake. "Assisted mergers" (where public funds are used to enable a merger) are not uncommon, especially in crisis situations, but they run the risk of upsetting basic priority-of-claim principles by benefiting shareholders ahead of depositors.

45. This often involves constitutionally defined property rights. To ensure that no property is "taken," the U.S. failure resolution process (which formally starts when a troubled bank is placed in "receivership") is triggered when the bank's regulatory capital is non-positive. In some Latin American countries, resolution (frequently limited to traditional liquidation) is triggered before regulatory capital reaches zero, in order to maximize the probability that shareholders still have something at risk at time of closure. For instance, in Peru a bank is considered "insolvent" when its ratio of capital to risk-weighted assets is less than 5 percent. Under most banking legislation in Latin America, deficiencies in loan loss provisions are subtracted from capital in order to arrive at the measure of regulatory capital.

46. The receivership figure in the United States seems to achieve this objective well. Labor and corporate laws, as well as the broader civil code, seem to complicate matters in this regard for Latin American countries. In this connection, the case of Spain (with a similar legal heritage) may be a useful reference. It provides for an expeditious route to translate the loss of regulatory capital of a failing bank into a *legal* extinction of capital, thereby enabling the resolution agency (the Spanish *Fondo de Garantía de Depósitos*) to subscribe common stock and become the sole owner in full control of the bank.

47. Based on econometric results, Demirgüç-Kunt and Detragiache (1997) argued that although the presence of explicit insurance may have reduced the incidence of self-fulfilling bank runs, it appears to have worsened banking sector fragility. They suggested that this could be attributable to moral hazard or to weaknesses in the design and implementation of deposit insurance schemes. Their sample of countries included 31 systemic crises (six in Latin America) between 1980 and 1994.

48. This is suggested, for instance, by Lindgren, García, and Saal (1996).

49. However, from a historical perspective, explicit deposit insurance does not seem to have been politically popular; rather, it is a relatively recent and untested institutional innovation. Since 1981, the number of countries in the world with explicit deposit insurance programs has risen from 15 to 45 (Lindgren, García, and Saal 1996). Until the last decade, depositors were not generally included in explicit safety nets in Latin America; indeed, depositors' interests

tended to be sacrificed to save bank shareholders through implicit or ex post safety nets—a bad habit that lingers on in several present-day Latin American countries.

50. Benston et al. (1986) and Calomiris (1996, 1997) have persuasively argued in favor of obligating banks to issue subordinated debt as a way to improve monitoring.

51. De Juan (1995) notes that discipline increased in the Spanish banking industry after 1980, as bankers realized that the government had come to posses powerful and effective instruments to root out bad bankers, particularly as regards intervention and failure resolution.

52. Talley and Mas (1992) discuss extensively the different design alternatives for deposit insurance, although they would not necessarily endorse the combination suggested here.

53. To avoid the risk of stifling bureaucratization, the deposit insurance agency could, by statute, be forced to rely heavily on subcontracting of professional expertise as needed.

54. Having intervention and failure-resolution powers in the deposit insurance agency may create problems of coordination and information-flow with the supervisory agency that would need to be appropriately solved.

55. This line of reasoning, albeit limited to a deposit-insurance scheme, is consistent with Mishkin's (1998) thoughts on potential international lender-of-last-resort arrangements.

56. Variable, risk-based deposit insurance premiums pose an added burden on already fragile individual banks, exacerbating their rate of deterioration. This is not an argument against variable premiums; it rather is an argument in favor of intensified monitoring and, if necessary, of early intervention and resolution. Onerous premiums, however, would be counterproductive if the entire banking system or a large segment of it is fragile.

57. As discussed in Sheng (1996), even the most sophisticated bank supervisors in advanced OECD countries have not been able to prevent bank failures completely. Besides adequate supervision, greater attention is needed to sector and national imbalances that may destabilize the banking sector and to the creation of an overall national risk management system.

58. For instance, because of the Northridge earthquake in 1994 and Hurricane Andrew in the Miami area in 1995, private catastrophe insurance came close to drying up in the United States. In the case of catastrophe insurance, the law of large numbers does not apply. Hence, insurance companies cannot predict accurately the level of claims and cannot adjust insurance premiums so as to reduce the mismatch between premiums collected and claims paid out in a given year. Catastrophe insurance requires a large point-in-time payout after a catastrophe occurs, but can be funded only by collecting premiums over a long time period. This mismatch between the time claims are paid and the time premium are collected could be solved by accumulating large pools of liquid capital, but these are difficult to maintain due to tax disincentives or because they attract hostile takeovers, among other reasons. Reinsurance is limited in availability: The international reinsurance catastrophe capacity is only $15 billion. Catastrophe futures and options are only lightly traded on the Chicago Board of Trade, partly due to the lack of any options pricing formula, like the Black-Scholes, for catastrophe losses.

59. For instance, where governments are committed to assist homeowners whose homes in oceanfront areas have been damaged by hurricanes, strict rules must be enforced to prevent home builders from building too close to the ocean or building with too flimsy construction materials.

60. Efforts to avoid the unavoidable can often lead to higher costs than otherwise. For instance, Chile's decision in the early 1930s to stand by the gold standard and to enforce prudential regulation and bank closures was eventually followed by a military coup and the adoption of a series of ad hoc economic policies that later formed the basis for the import substitution strategy in that country.

61. The framework in place in Spain since the crisis management period of the 1980s would seem to fall under the second stylized case: "Constructive ambiguity" is allowed in the context of strong capital, monitoring, and closure, and the *Fondo de Garantía de Depósitos* has remarkably effective early intervention and bank-failure resolution capacities.

62. The framework in place in the United States since the FDIC Improvement Act of 1991 may be considered as a "best practice" referent in regard to the "only if" approach. Under this Act, when handling a troubled bank, the FDIC can extend coverage to bank liabilities beyond the insured amounts if there is a joint determination by the board of governors of the Federal Reserve, the FDIC board, and the treasury secretary (after consulting with the president of the United States) that the failure of such bank would entail systemic risk. To curb the attendant adverse selection, limit risk-shifting to the government, and avoid underpricing of the safety net, the FDIC is authorized not only to assess risk-based premiums, but also to assess premiums on the basis of total bank liabilities, and not just deposits, as banks whose failure could pose systemic risk normally have a relatively low ratio of deposits to total liabilities.

63. Currently, the so-called Group of Ten (G-10) actually has 11 members: Belgium, Canada, France, Germany, Italy, Japan, the Netherlands, Sweden, Switzerland, the United Kingdom, and the United States.

64. The relevant publications are listed in the Bank for International Settlements (BIS) website (http://www.bis.org/publ/publist.htm).

CHAPTER 4

Capital Markets and Legal Institutions

I
N THIS CHAPTER WE FOCUS ON THE INSTITUTIONS REQUIRED TO SUPPORT LARGE CAPITAL MARkets and survey the empirical evidence on the link between legal institutions and financial markets. Specifically, we are interested in providing an answer to why we observe such large differences in the size, breadth, and valuation of capital markets. Why, for example, are equity markets so much larger in South Africa than in Mexico or Peru? Why did many companies go public in India and Hong Kong in 1995, while no company went public in Brazil or Uruguay or Venezuela in the same year? Why do countries like New Zealand have large credit markets while Argentina and Colombia do not have them?

In a simple Modigliani-Miller (M&M) framework (Modigliani and Miller 1958) the size of capital markets is determined only by the cash flows that accrue to investors. Therefore, roughly speaking, the size of capital markets should be proportional to GNP. To explain the large discrepancies in the size of financial markets across countries with similar GNP, we need to recognize that securities are more than the cash flows they represent, since they entitle investors to exercise certain rights. Shares not only entitle investors to dividend payments, but also to exercise control over management through the voting process. Similarly, debt not only entitles creditors to receive interest payments, but also to regain their collateral in the event of bankruptcy of the firm.

The separation between ownership and control can have a large effect on the size of capital markets once we depart from the M&M assumptions and allow for the existence of agency costs. To take an extreme view, outside equity would have no value if shareholders did not have control rights to force managers to pay out dividends. In the same vein, creditors would be unwilling to lend money at any interest rate if their control rights did not allow them to punish debtors who default on their financial obligations. Both financiers and management would benefit from the elimination of the agency conflict if they could write a complete contract that specified what the manager should do with the funds and how he would give them back to investors in all states of the world. Of course, a complete contract cannot be implemented in practice, making it necessary for management to have a level of discretion

(Grossman and Hart 1986). Management discretion, although a cost-effective way of dealing with the separation of ownership and control, can unfortunately be used to expropriate financiers through outright expropriation, transfer-pricing, or asset-stripping.

The agency model could, in principle, explain why some countries have much larger capital markets than others, since it is apparent that countries differ enormously in the extent to which they afford legal protection to investors. Not only does a shareholder in Mexico, for example, have a very different bundle of rights from one in the United States, but his recourse to redress is likely to be significantly weaker. The agency model predicts larger capital markets in countries where agency costs are reined in by the law and the institutions built to support their enforcement. La Porta et al. (1998a) systematically assess the rights of investors as well as the quality of their enforcement for 49 countries. La Porta et al. (1997a, 1998a, and 1998b) relate legal institutions to the size and breadth of external capital markets as well as to corporate ownership concentration around the world.

In this chapter, we review and summarize the cross-country evidence on the influence of institutions on capital markets' development. The chapter is divided into four sections. *Legal protection to investors*, the first section, describes the differences in legal protection for shareholders and creditors in a cross-section of 49 countries. Because investor rights are not only determined by laws, *Enforcement of laws* compares the quality of the legal enforcement and accounting standards across nations. The ultimate question is whether countries with poor investor protections actually do suffer. If laws and their enforcement matter, then countries that offer entrepreneurs better terms of external finance would have both higher-valued and broader capital markets. We also predict that countries that offer entrepreneurs better terms would have widely held corporations. Consequently, *External finance and legal institutions* compares external finance and ownership concentration across countries as a function of the origin of their laws, the quality of legal investor protections, and the quality of law enforcement. *Conclusion and policy implications* concludes the chapter and discusses policy implications of the results.

Legal Protection to Investors

La Porta et al. (1998a) assembled a data set covering legal rules pertaining to the rights of investors, and to the quality of enforcement of these rules, for 49 countries with publicly traded companies. Naturally, laws in different countries are typically not written from scratch, but rather transplanted—voluntarily or coincidentally—from a few legal families or traditions. In general, *commercial* laws come from two broad traditions: common law and civil law. Most English-speaking countries belong to the common-law tradition based on the British Company Act. The rest of the world belongs to the civil-law tradition, derivative of Roman law, which has three main families: the French family based on the Napoleonic Code of 1804, the German family based on Bismarck's Code of 1896, and the Scandinavian family, which legal scholars describe as less derivative of Roman law but "distinct" from the other two civil families.

The common-law family includes former British colonies and other nations like Thailand and Israel who modeled their initial corporate laws on the laws of England. There are 18 common-law countries in the sample. The French legal family includes France, Spain, Portugal, and their colonies. There are 21 French legal origin countries in our sample, including nine in Latin America. The German tradition has had less influence, and we have only six in this family: Austria, Germany, Japan, the Republic of Korea, Switzerland, and Taiwan, China. Finally, the Scandinavian family includes the four Nordic countries of Denmark, Finland, Norway, and Sweden.

There are numerous potentially measurable differences among countries in their company and bankruptcy laws. We focus exclusively on those basic rules that scholars (e.g., Paul Vishny 1994, White 1993, American Bar Association 1989 and 1993) and observers (e.g., Investor Responsibility Research Center 1994, Institutional Shareholder Services 1994) believe to be essential to corporate governance. Furthermore, we restrict our attention to those basic rules that easily can be interpretable as either pro-investor or pro-management.

Shareholder Rights

Shareholders have residual rights over the cash flows of the firm. The right to vote is the shareholders' main source of power. This right to vote in the general assembly for the election of directors and on major corporate decisions guarantees shareholders that management will disgorge the firm's cash flows to shareholders through the payment of dividends rather than divert the funds to pay themselves higher compensation or undertake poor acquisitions, for example. Therefore, voting rights and the rights that support voting mechanisms are the defining features of equity.

Table 4.1 provides a detailed description of all the variables that we use in this chapter, and Table 4.2 presents the evidence on shareholder rights for the cross-section of 49 countries. A useful way to begin the discussion of shareholder rights is by first assuming the role of an investor in a U.K. firm and then switching identity to become an investor in a Mexican corporation. (We do this not to praise the United Kingdom, nor to single out Mexico for criticism, but rather merely to illustrate differences between a legal system based on English common law and one based on French civil law.)

The first column of Table 4.2 shows that not all U.K. shareholders have the right to vote. That is probably a bad thing, because when votes are tightly linked to dividends,

TABLE 4.1

The Variables

This table describes the variables collected for the 49 countries included in our study. The first column gives the name of the variable. The second column describes the variable and gives the range of possible values. The third column provides the sources from which the variable was collected.

VARIABLE	DESCRIPTION	SOURCES
Origin	Identifies the legal origin of the Company Law or Commercial Code of each country.	Foreign Law Encyclopedia Commercial Laws of the World
One share–one vote	Equals 1 if the Company Law or Commercial Code of the country requires that ordinary shares carry one vote per share, and zero otherwise. Equivalently, this variable equals 1 when the law prohibits the existence of both multiple-voting and non-voting ordinary shares and does not allow firms to set a maximum number of votes per shareholder irrespective of the number of shares owned, and 0 otherwise.	Company Law or Commercial Code
Proxy by mail	Equals 1 if the Company Law or Commercial Code allows shareholders to mail their proxy vote to the firm, and 0 otherwise.	Company Law or Commercial Code
Shares not blocked before meeting	Equals 1 if the Company Law or Commercial Code does not allow firms to require that shareholders deposit their shares prior to a General Shareholders Meeting thus preventing them from selling those shares for a number of days, and 0 otherwise.	Company Law or Commercial Code
Cumulative voting or proportional representation	Equals 1 if the Company Law or Commercial Code allows shareholders to cast all of their votes for one candidate standing for election to the board of directors (cumulative voting) or if the Company Law or Commercial Code allows a mechanism of proportional representation in the board by which minority interests may name a proportional number of directors to the board, and 0 otherwise.	Company Law or Commercial Code
Oppressed minorities mechanism	Equals 1 if the Company Law or Commercial Code grants minority shareholders either a judicial venue to challenge the decisions of management or of the assembly or the right to step out of the company by requiring the company to purchase their shares when they object to certain fundamental changes, such as mergers, assets dispositions, and changes in the articles of incorporation. The variable equals 0 otherwise. Minority shareholders are defined as those shareholders who own 10 percent of share capital or less.	Company Law or Commercial Code
Preemptive rights	Equals 1 when the Company Law or Commercial Code grants shareholders the first opportunity to buy new issues of stock and this right can only be waved by a shareholders' vote, and 0 otherwise.	Company Law or Commercial Code
Percentage of share capital to call an extraordinary shareholders' meeting	It is the minimum percentage of ownership of share capital that entitles a shareholder to call for an Extraordinary Shareholders' Meeting. It ranges from 1 to 33 percent.	Company Law or Commercial Code
Anti-director rights	An index aggregating the shareholder rights, which we labeled as "anti-director rights." The index is formed by adding 1 when: (1) the country allows shareholders to mail their proxy vote to the firm; (2) shareholders are not required to deposit their shares prior to the General Shareholders' Meeting; (3) cumulative voting or proportional representation of minorities in the board of directors is allowed; (4) an oppressed minorities mechanism is in place; (5) the minimum percentage of share capital that entitles a shareholder to call for an Extraordinary Shareholders' Meeting is less than or equal to 10 percent (the sample median); or (6) shareholders have preemptive rights that can only be waived by a shareholders' vote. The index ranges from 0 to 6.	Company Law or Commercial Code
Restrictions for going into reorganization.	Equals 1 if the reorganization procedure imposes restrictions, such as creditors' consent, to file for reorganization. It equals 0 if there are no such restrictions.	Bankruptcy and Reorganization Laws
No automatic stay on secured assets	Equals 1 if the reorganization procedure does not impose an automatic stay on the assets of the firm upon filing the reorganization petition. Automatic stay prevents secured creditors to gain possession of their security. It equals 0 if such restriction does exist in the law.	Bankruptcy and Reorganization Laws
Secured creditors first	Equals 1 if secured creditors are ranked first in the distribution of the proceeds that result from the disposition of the assets of a bankrupt firm. Equals 0 if non-secured creditors, such as the government and workers, are given absolute priority.	Bankruptcy and Reorganization Laws
Management does not stay	Equals 1 when an official appointed by the court, or by the creditors, is responsible for the operation of the business during reorganization. Equivalently, this variable equals 1 if the debtor does not keep the administration of its property pending the resolution of the reorganization process, and 0 otherwise.	Bankruptcy and Reorganization Laws

(Table continues on the following page.)

TABLE 4.1

(Continued)

VARIABLE	DESCRIPTION	SOURCES
Creditor rights	An index aggregating different creditor rights. The index is formed by adding 1 when: (1) the country imposes restrictions, such as creditors' consent or minimum dividends to file for reorganization; (2) secured creditors are able to gain possession of their security once the reorganization petition has been approved (no automatic stay); (3) secured creditors are ranked first in the distribution of the proceeds that result from the disposition of the assets of a bankrupt firm; and (4) the debtor does not retain the administration of its property pending the resolution of the reorganization. The index ranges from 0 to 4.	Bankruptcy and Reorganization Laws
Efficiency of judicial system	Assessment of the "efficiency and integrity of the legal environment as it affects business, particularly foreign firms" produced by the country-risk rating agency Business International Corporation. It "may be taken to represent investors' assessments of conditions in the country in question." Average between 1980–83. Scale from 0 to 10, with lower scores lower efficiency levels.	Business International Corporation
Rule of law	Assessment of the law and order tradition in the country produced by the country-risk rating agency International Country Risk (ICR). Average of the months of April and October of the monthly index between 1982 and 1995. Scale from 0 to 10, with lower scores for less tradition for law and order. (We changed the scale from its original range of 0 to 6.)	International Country Risk Guide
Corruption	ICR's assessment of corruption in government. Lower scores indicate "high government officials are likely to demand special payments" and "illegal payments are generally expected throughout lower levels of government" in the form of "bribes connected with import and export licenses, exchange controls, tax assessment, policy protection, or loans." Average of the months of April and October of the monthly index between 1982 and 1995. Scale from 0 to 10, with lower scores for higher levels of corruption. (We changed the scale from its original range of 0 to 6.)	International Country Risk Guide
Accounting standards	Index created by examining and rating companies' 1990 annual reports on their inclusion or omission of 90 items. These items fall into seven categories (general information, income statements, balance sheets, funds flow statement, accounting standards, stock data and special items). A minimum of 3 companies in each country were studied. The companies represent a cross-section of various industry groups where industrial companies numbered 70 percent while financial companies represented the remaining 30 percent.	International Accounting and Auditing Trends, Center for International Financial Analysis & Research, Inc.
Ownership, 10 largest private firms	The average percentage of common shares owned by the three largest shareholders in the 10 largest non-financial, privately owned domestic firms in a given country. A firm is considered privately owned if the state is not a known shareholder in it.	Moodys International, CIFAR, EXTEL, WorldScope, 20-Fs, Price-Waterhouse, and various country sources
External cap / GNP	The ratio of the stock market capitalization held by minorities to gross national product for 1994. The stock market capitalization held by minorities is computed as the product of the aggregate stock market capitalization and the average percentage of common shares not owned by the top three shareholders in the 10 largest non-financial, privately owned domestic firms in a given country. A firm is considered privately owned if the state is not a known shareholder in it.	Moodys International, CIFAR, EXTEL, WorldScope, 20-Fs, Price Waterhouse, and various country sources
Domestic firms / Pop	Ratio of the number of domestic firms listed in a given country to its population (in millions) in 1994.	Emerging Market Factbook and World Development Report 1996
IPOs / Pop	Ratio of the number of initial public offerings of equity in a given country to its population (in millions) for the period July 1995 to June 1996.	Securities Data Corporation, AsiaMoney, LatinFinance, GT Guide to World Equity Markets, and World Development Report 1996
Debt / GNP	Ratio of the sum of bank debt of the private sector and outstanding non-financial bonds to GNP in 1994, or last available.	International Financial Statistics, World Bondmarket Factbook
GDP growth	Average annual percent growth of per capita gross domestic product for the period 1970–93.	World Development Report 1995
Log GNP	Logarithm of the Gross National Product in 1994.	World Development Report 1996

it is more difficult to control a company by having a small fraction of the equity. Yet, as it turns out, one share–one vote rules are uncommon everywhere—including Mexico.

The next six columns of Table 4.2 provide different measures of how strongly the corporate law protects minority shareholders against expropriation of managers or dominant shareholders. We label these rights as "anti-director" rights. The first four anti-director rights measure how easy it is for an investor to exercise any voting rights that he may have. Shareholders in the United Kingdom will receive proxy statements two weeks in advance of the shareholders' meeting with detailed information on the items that are going to be discussed at the meeting. Should they wish to vote, they do not need to show up in person at the meeting—they can mail their proxy vote instead. The shares of investors who have indicated that they will participate in the shareholders' meeting will not be blocked in the days that surround the meeting; the freedom to trade shares around shareholders' meetings is an important right for people who may want to form alliances to challenge management proposals. Directors are chosen one at a time through a majority vote, and thus shareholders are not entitled to have proportional representation or cumulative voting for directors. Our hypothetical investor may have a resolution that he would like to be considered by an extraordinary shareholders' meeting (ESM). If that is the case, he has the right to call an ESM if he owns 10 percent of the share capital.

The next right in Table 4.2 measures the protection of minority shareholders against a particular type of expropriation: issuing shares at favorable prices to, for example, associates of the controlling shareholders. In the United Kingdom, shareholders have a preemptive right to buy new issues of stock of their holdings, and that right can be waived only by a shareholder vote. Finally, U.K. investors who feel they have been hurt by the decisions of the majority can seek redress through the courts. When the court believes that oppression has indeed taken place, it may order that the oppressed members' shares be bought out at a fair price or that the firm remedy the matters at issue. More generally, best-practice countries provide legal mechanisms for the protection of oppressed minorities. To give just another example, a dissenting investor in Chile has the right to request—at the meeting—that the firm buy back his shares at the market price prevailing before the meeting.

Suppose that the shareholders' meeting took place not in London but in Mexico City. As in the United Kingdom, not all shares are endowed with the same right to vote. However, unlike in the United Kingdom, investors in Mexico will be notified of the forthcoming shareholders' meeting but will not typically receive detailed information on the items to be discussed. Only by going to the meeting will they know what is discussed. In fact, attending the meeting—or designating someone to do so in their place—is the only way in which they can vote; proxy by mail is not allowed. Furthermore, announcing that they intend to vote their shares will cause them to be blocked, making it impossible for them to trade the shares in the days surrounding the meeting. At the meeting, shareholders vote on the slate of directors proposed by management and are not allowed proportional representation on the board. Investors in Mexican firms must have at least 33 percent of share capital to have a resolution considered by the ESM. Fortunately, investors in Mexico do have a preemptive right that prevents dilution. Regrettably, this is the only right (of those that we collect) that shareholders in Mexico have, since they do not have any legal recourse against the decisions of the majority. To summarize, Table 4.2 paints a very bleak picture of shareholder rights in Mexico.

A convenient way of summarizing shareholder rights is to aggregate anti-director rights into an index adding 1 if the corporate law protects minority shareholders, and a zero otherwise. For the case of the percentage of share capital needed to call an ESM, we give a 1 to those countries where this percentage is at or below the world median of 10 percent. When we add up these six anti-director rights scores, the United Kingdom has a score of 5 while Mexico's score is only 1.

The comparison between Mexico and the United Kingdom illustrates the broad findings of Table 4.2: Shareholder protection in common-law countries is significantly better than in French civil-law countries. While the incidence of one-share-one-vote rules, cumulative voting for directors, and preemptive rights are not statistically different across English and French legal origins, the remaining four measures show marked differences. Common-law countries more frequently allow shareholders to exercise their vote by mail than French-origin countries (39 percent vs. 5 percent). No common-law country blocks shares before shareholders' meetings, while 57 percent of French civil-law countries do. On average, 9 percent of the share

TABLE 4.2

Shareholder Rights around the World

This table classifies countries by legal origin. Definitions for each of the variables can be found in Table 4.1. Panel B reports the test of means for the different legal origins.

PANEL A: SHAREHOLDER RIGHTS (1 = INVESTOR PROTECTION IS IN THE LAW)

COUNTRY	ONE SHARE – ONE VOTE	PROXY BY MAIL ALLOWED	SHARES NOT BLOCKED BEFORE MEETING	CUMULATIVE VOTING/ PROPORTIONAL REPTN.	% OF SHARE CAPITAL TO CALL AN ESM	PREEMPTIVE RIGHT TO NEW ISSUES	OPPRESSED MINORITY	ANTI-DIRECTOR RIGHTS
Australia	0	1	1	0	0.05[d]	0	1	4
Canada	0	1	1	1	0.05	0	1	5
Hong Kong, China	0	1	1	0	0.10	1	1	5
India	0	0	1	1	0.10	1	1	5
Ireland	0	0	1	0	0.10	1	1	4
Israel	0	0	1	0	0.10	0	1	3
Kenya	0	0	1	0	0.10	0	1	3
Malaysia	1	0	1	0	0.10	1	1	4
New Zealand	0	1	1	0	0.05	0	1	4
Nigeria	0	0	1	0	0.10	0	1	3
Pakistan	1	0	1	1	0.10	1	1	5
Singapore	1	0	1	0	0.10	1	1	4
South Africa	0	1	1	0	0.05	1	1	5
Sri Lanka	0	0	1	0	0.10	0	1	3
Thailand	0	0	1	1	0.20[e]	0	0	2
United Kingdom	0	1	1	0	0.10	1	1	5
United States	0	1	1	1	0.10	0	1	5
Zimbabwe	0	0	1	0	0.05	0	1	3
English origin avg.	0.17	0.39	1.00	0.28	0.09	0.44	0.94	4.00
Argentina	0	0	0	1	0.05	1	1	4
Belgium	0	0	0	0	0.20	0	0	0
Brazil	1	0	1	0	0.05	0	1	3
Chile	1	0	1	1	0.10	1	1	5
Colombia	0	0	1	1	0.25	1	0	3
Ecuador	0	0	1	0	0.25	1	0	2
Egypt, Arab Rep.	0	0	1	0	0.10	0	0	2
France	0	1	0	0	0.10	1	0	3
Greece	1	0	0	0	0.05	1	0	2
Indonesia	0	0	1	0	0.10	0	0	2
Italy	0	0	0	0	0.20	1	0	1
Jordan	1	0	1	0	0.25	0	0	1
Mexico	0	0	0	0	0.33	1	0	1
Netherlands	0	0	0	0	0.10	1	0	2
Peru	1	0	1	1	0.20	1	0	3
Philippines	0	0	1	1	open	0	1	3
Portugal	0	0	1	0	0.05	1	0	3
Spain	0	0	0	1	0.05	1	1	4
Turkey	0	0	1	0	0.10	0	0	2
Uruguay	1	0	0	0	0.20	1	1	2
Venezuela	0	0	1	0	0.20	0	0	1
Latin American avg.	0.44	0.00	0.67	0.44	0.18	0.78	0.44	2.67
Rest of French origin avg.	0.17	0.08	0.50	0.17	0.12	0.50	0.17	2.08
French origin avg.	0.29	0.05	0.57	0.29	0.15	0.62	0.29	2.33

TABLE 4.2

(Continued)

			PANEL A: SHAREHOLDER RIGHTS (1 = INVESTOR PROTECTION IS IN THE LAW)					
COUNTRY	ONE SHARE – ONE VOTE	PROXY BY MAIL ALLOWED	SHARES NOT BLOCKED BEFORE MEETING	CUMULATIVE VOTING/ PROPORTIONAL REPTN.	% OF SHARE CAPITAL TO CALL AN ESM	PREEMPTIVE RIGHT TO NEW ISSUES	OPPRESSED MINORITY	ANTI-DIRECTOR RIGHTS
Austria	0	0	0	0	0.05	1	0	2
Germany	0	0	0	0	0.05	0	0	1
Japan	1	0	1	1	0.03	0	1	4
Korea, Rep. of	1	0	0	0	0.05	0	1	2
Switzerland	0	0	0	0	0.10	1	0	2
Taiwan, China	0	0	0	1	0.03	0	1	3
German origin avg.	0.33	0.00	0.17	0.33	0.05	0.33	0.50	2.33
Denmark	0	0	1	0	0.10	0	0	2
Finland	0	0	1	0	0.10	1	0	3
Norway	0	1	1	0	0.10	1	0	4
Sweden	0	0	1	0	0.10 [e]	1	0	3
Scandinavian origin avg.	0.00	0.25	1.00	0.00	0.10	0.75	0.00	3.00
Sample average	0.22	0.18	0.71	0.27	0.11	0.53	0.53	3.00
			PANEL B: TESTS OF MEANS (T-STATISTICS)					
Common vs. civil law	-0.72	3.03 [a]	4.97 [a]	0.15	1.48	-0.91	5.59 [a]	5.00 [a]
English vs. French origin	-0.87	2.82 [a]	3.87 [a]	-0.05	-2.53 [b]	-1.08	5.45 [a]	4.73 [a]
English origin vs. Latin America	-1.57	3.29 [a]	2.00 [c]	-0.85	-3.56 [a]	-1.67	3.44 [a]	2.98 [a]
French vs. German origin	-0.22	1.00	-1.78 [c]	-0.22	2.64 [b]	1.23	-0.96	0.00
French vs. Scandinavian origin	2.83 [b]	-1.37	-3.87 [a]	2.82 [b]	2.43 [b]	-0.48	2.83	-1.06
Rest of French origin vs. Latin America	-1.39	1.00	-0.74	-1.39	-1.71	-1.29	-1.39	-1.11

a = Significant at 1% level; b = Significant at 5% level; c = Significant at 10% level; d = as a percentage of votes; e = as a percentage of the number of shares

capital is sufficient to call an ESM in common-law countries, whereas 15 percent of share capital is required in French civil-law nations. Finally, 94 percent of common-law countries have an oppressed minority mechanism in place, while only 29 percent of French-origin countries do. The differences between English- and French-origin countries are captured in the anti-director's index, which has an average of 4.00 for common-law countries and only 2.33 for French civil-law nations (t-statistic of 4.73).

It is important to note that Mexico actually scores lower than the rest of Latin America when it comes to shareholder rights, so our choice of Mexico for this example does not mean that Mexico is typical of Latin America. In fact, Latin America generally scores a little higher than the average of the rest of the French-origin countries in many shareholder rights. Latin America has a higher incidence of

one-share-one-vote (44 percent vs. 17 percent), is less likely to block shares (67 percent vs. 50 percent), has a higher incidence of proportional representation (44 percent vs. 17 percent), is more likely to grant preemptive rights (78 percent vs. 50 percent), and has a higher incidence of oppressed minority remedies (44 percent vs. 17 percent). On the other hand, Latin America never allows proxy by mail (vs. 8 percent for the rest of French origin) and requires a higher fraction of the share capital to call for an ESM (18 percent vs. 12 percent). With the exception of the percentage needed to call an ESM, these differences are not statistically significant when taken in isolation. Although not statistically significant, differences add up to marginally better shareholder rights in Latin America than in the rest of the French civil origin when rights are aggregated in the anti-director index (2.67 vs. 2.08). However, Latin

America's anti-director rights index is statistically significantly lower than that of common-law countries.

German civil-law countries share the French origin lack of protection of shareholder rights. Although German-origin countries have a significantly higher incidence of oppressed minority mechanisms, they block shares more often than French countries do. The average anti-director scores for the German and French families are the same (2.33). Finally, Scandinavian-origin countries, although clearly inferior to common-law countries in shareholder protection, are the best within the civil-law tradition. The average Scandinavian anti-director rights score is 3. In short, relative to the rest of the world, common-law countries have the package of laws most protective of shareholders.

Creditor Rights

In principle we would like to measure the ability of creditors to use the law to force companies to meet their credit commitments. In practice, creditor rights are difficult to assess for two main reasons. First, most countries have in place both reorganization and liquidation procedures that are used with varying frequency and may confer different levels of protections to creditors. Therefore, a country may be very protective of creditors if it offers, for example, strong rights in liquidation and weak protection in reorganization, provided that the reorganization procedure is seldom used. Second, creditors, unlike shareholders, do not have a homogeneous claim against the firm—i.e., they differ in the priority of their claim. As a result, it is possible that measures that favor some creditors (e.g., unsecured creditors) may hurt others (e.g., secured creditors).

To undertake a cross-country analysis of creditor rights, we score creditor rights in both reorganization and liquidation, and add up the scores to create a creditor rights index, in part because almost all countries rely to some extent on both procedures. In assessing creditor rights below, we also take the perspective of senior secured creditors, in part for concreteness, and in part because much of the debt in the world has that character. Creditor rights for the cross-section of 49 countries in the sample can be found in Table 4.3. Once again, to illustrate differences between English common-law countries and French civil-law countries, we describe the data by comparing the rights of an investor who has a credit against a firm incorporated in the United Kingdom versus the rights of an investor with a credit against a firm incorporated in Mexico.

Suppose that a debtor to whom the creditor has lent money files a petition for reorganization in a London court. The court will then notify the creditor, who will have two weeks to oppose reorganization. A secured creditor who chooses to oppose a reorganization petition has the right to appoint a so-called *trustee* to decide what will happen to the firm. The important thing is that the debtor does not have the right to unilaterally file for reorganization. Even if the borrower has his petition for reorganization accepted, there is not an "automatic stay" that prevents secured creditors from gaining access to their collateral. In addition, secured creditors who choose not to withdraw their collateral are paid first in the event that reorganization fails and liquidation ensues. Finally, the bargaining position of creditors is strengthened by the fact that pending the resolution of the bankruptcy procedure, the old management team will not continue to run the firm. Rather, a trustee appointed by the creditors would be in charge of the firm's day-to-day operations.

Now suppose that a debtor to whom the creditor has lent money files a petition for reorganization in a Mexico City court. Creditors have no say in whether the firm's reorganization petition is accepted or declined. But if the petition is accepted, secured creditors are not able to pull their collateral out of the firm; an "automatic stay" is triggered by the acceptance of the reorganization petition. Secured creditors have additional worries, because if liquidation takes place, they are not paid first. Rather the state and the firm's employees take priority. The creditors' predicament is aggravated by the fact that the debtor not only will write the reorganization proposal, but will continue to run the firm pending the resolution of the bankruptcy procedure, which may take several years.

As with shareholders, one way to summarize the difference in creditor rights across countries is to create an index that adds 1 when the pro-investor right is granted by law, and zero otherwise. This index is shown in the last column of Table 4.3 and takes a value of 4 for the United Kingdom and zero for Mexico. Again, as with shareholder rights, the picture for creditor rights in Mexico is substantially bleaker than in the United Kingdom.

Although the Mexico-U.K. comparison is extreme, common-law countries in general offer creditors stronger legal protections against managers. Table 4.3 shows that all four measures of creditor rights are weaker for countries of French legal origin by an amount that is statistically significant. A total of 72 percent of common-law countries place restrictions on managers seeking court protection from creditors, while only 42 percent of French civil-law nations do. The incidence of having no automatic stay on assets is 72 percent in common-law countries versus only 26 percent in French civil-law nations. Relatively fewer countries of French legal origin (65 percent) assure that secured creditors are paid first than do countries of English legal origin (89 percent). Finally, only 26 percent of French civil-law countries remove managers in reorganization, compared with 78 percent of countries of the common-law family. In brief, the average aggregate creditor rights score is 3.11 for English origin and a mere 1.58 for French origin.

Unlike the case of shareholder rights, Latin America offers considerably *less* legal protection to creditors than the rest of the French civil-law countries. When compared with the other countries of French civil-law origin, countries in Latin America are less likely to place restrictions for going into reorganization (38 percent vs. 45 percent), have no-automatic-stay policies (13 percent vs. 36 percent), pay secured creditors first (56 percent vs. 73 percent), and prevent management from remaining in office (25 percent vs. 27 percent). However, these differences are not statistically significant even when aggregated in the creditor-rights index (1.25 vs. 1.81).

Latin America also scores lower than the other two civil-law families. German legal origin countries are relatively more pro-creditor than Latin American and French civil-law countries, averaging an aggregate score of 2.33. The differences between German- and French-origin countries are particularly significant in liquidation measures: 67 percent of German civil-law countries have no automatic stay and always pay secured creditors first.

Finally, countries of Scandinavian origin always pay secured creditors first, but always allow management to stay pending reorganization. In three out of four cases they impose an automatic stay on assets and place restrictions to go into reorganization. As a result, the aggregate creditor-rights index for countries of Scandinavian legal origin has a value of 2.00—a difference that is not statistically significant from the 1.58 value for countries of French legal origin.

To summarize the results thus far, bankruptcy laws differ a great deal across countries. In particular, they differ because they come from different legal families. Relatively speaking, common-law countries protect creditors the most, and French civil-law countries protect them the least. German and Scandinavian civil-law countries are in the middle. The one exception is the strong protections that German civil-law countries afford secured creditors.

Enforcement of Laws

Legal rules are only one element of investor protection; the enforcement of these rules may be equally or even more important. If good laws are not enforced, they cannot be effective. Likewise, investors may enjoy high levels of protection despite bad laws if an efficient judiciary system can redress expropriations by management. In this way, strong legal enforcement may serve as a substitute for weak rules.

Table 4.4 presents several proxies for the quality of enforcement of laws in different countries. These measures are collected by private credit-risk agencies for the use of foreign investors interested in doing business in the respective countries (Business International Corporation, Political Risk Services). We use three measures: efficiency of the judicial system, rule of law, and corruption. The first two of these proxies pertain to law enforcement, while the last one captures the government's general attitude toward business. In addition to these measures, we also collected data on the quality of accounting standards of publicly traded firms in different countries. Accounting is central to corporate governance, as it may be difficult to assess management performance without reliable accounting standards. More broadly, cash flows may be very difficult to verify in countries with poor accounting standards; consequently, the menu of financial contracts available to investors may be substantially narrower in such countries. The index of accounting standards in Table 4.4 is provided by the Center for International Financial Analysis and Research based on examination of company reports of firms in each country. It is available for 41 of the 49 countries in our sample.

We can begin the discussion of this data by focusing on the Latin American average. Compared with the English-origin average, Latin America has very weak legal institutions and accounting standards. A corrupt or inefficient legal system coupled with poor disclosure standards could render legal rules ineffective.

While the Latin American average across all enforcement variables is below the French-origin average, it turns out that the French civil-law family shares Latin America's weak legal-enforcement mechanisms. The French family has the weakest quality of legal enforcement and account-

TABLE 4.3

Creditor Rights around the World

This table classifies countries by legal origin. Definitions for each variable can be found in Table 4.1. Panel B reports tests of means for the different legal origins.

PANEL A: CREDITOR RIGHTS (1 = CREDITOR PROTECTION IS IN THE LAW)

COUNTRY	RESTRICTIONS FOR GOING INTO REORGANIZATION	NO AUTOMATIC STAY ON ASSETS	SECURED CREDITORS FIRST PAID	MANAGEMENT DOES NOT STAY IN REORGANIZATION	CREDITOR RIGHTS
Australia	0	0	1	0	1
Canada	0	0	1	0	1
Hong Kong, China	1	1	1	1	4
India	1	1	1	1	4
Ireland	0	0	1	0	1
Israel	1	1	1	1	4
Kenya	1	1	1	1	4
Malaysia	1	1	1	1	4
New Zealand	1	1	0	1	3
Nigeria	1	1	1	1	4
Pakistan	1	1	1	1	4
Singapore	1	1	1	1	4
South Africa	1	0	1	1	3
Sri Lanka	1	1	0	1	3
Thailand	0	1	1	1	3
United Kingdom	1	1	1	1	4
United States	0	0	1	0	1
Zimbabwe	1	1	1	1	4
English origin avg.	**0.72**	**0.72**	**0.89**	**0.78**	**3.11**
Argentina	0	0	1	0	1
Belgium	0	1	1	0	2
Brazil	1	0	0	0	1
Chile	1	0	1	0	2
Colombia	0	0	0	0	0
Ecuador	1	1	1	1	4
Egypt, Arab Rep.	1	1	1	1	4
France	0	0	0	0	0
Greece	0	0	0	1	1
Indonesia	1	1	1	1	4
Italy	1	0	1	0	2
Jordan	n.a.	n.a.	n.a.	n.a.	n.a.
Mexico	0	0	0	0	0
Netherlands	1	0	1	0	2
Peru	0	0	0	0	0
Philippines	0	0	0	0	0
Portugal	0	0	1	0	1
Spain	0	1	1	0	2
Turkey	1	0	1	0	2
Uruguay	0	0	1	1	2
Venezuela	n.a.	n.a.	1	n.a.	n.a.
Latin American avg.	**0.38**	**0.13**	**0.56**	**0.25**	**1.25**
Rest of French origin avg.	**0.45**	**0.36**	**0.73**	**0.27**	**1.81**
French origin avg.	**0.42**	**0.26**	**0.65**	**0.26**	**1.58**

TABLE 4.3
(Continued)

	PANEL A: CREDITOR RIGHTS (1 = CREDITOR PROTECTION IS IN THE LAW)				
COUNTRY	RESTRICTIONS FOR GOING INTO REORGANIZATION	NO AUTOMATIC STAY ON ASSETS	SECURED CREDITORS FIRST PAID	MANAGEMENT DOES NOT STAY IN REORGANIZATION	CREDITOR RIGHTS
Austria	1	1	1	0	3
Germany	1	1	1	0	3
Japan	0	0	1	1	2
Korea, Rep. of	0	1	1	1	3
Switzerland	0	0	1	0	1
Taiwan, China	0	1	1	0	2
German origin avg.	0.33	0.67	1.00	0.33	2.33
Denmark	1	1	1	0	3
Finland	0	0	1	0	1
Norway	1	0	1	0	2
Sweden	1	0	1	0	2
Scandinavian origin avg.	0.75	0.25	1.00	0.00	2.00
Sample average	0.55	0.49	0.81	0.45	2.30
	PANEL B: TESTS OF MEANS (T-STATISTICS)				
Common vs. civil law	1.86 [c]	2.65 [a]	1.04	4.13 [a]	3.61 [a]
English vs. French origin	1.89 [c]	3.06 [a]	1.75 [b]	3.55 [a]	3.61 [a]
English origin vs. Latin America	1.71 [c]	3.25 [a]	2.04 [b]	2.83 [a]	3.42 [a]
French vs. German origin	0.37	-1.85 [c]	-3.20 [a]	-0.32	-1.29
French vs. Scandinavian origin	-1.18	0.05	-3.20 [a]	2.54 [b]	-0.60
Rest of French origin vs. Latin America	0.33	1.14	0.77	0.11	0.90

a = Significant at 1% level; b = Significant at 5% level; c = Significant at 10% level.

ing standards. Scandinavian countries have the strongest enforcement mechanisms, with German civil-law and common-law countries close behind. Common-law countries, although behind Scandinavian nations, are still ahead of the French civil-law countries. Note that rule of law is the only measure where differences in means between common law and French legal origin are not statistically significant.

These results do not support the conclusion that the quality of law enforcement substitutes or compensates for the quality of laws. An investor in Latin America—and more generally in a French civil-law country—is poorly protected by both the laws and the system that enforces them. The converse is true for an investor in a common-law country, on average. Poor enforcement and accounting standards aggravate, rather than cure, the difficulties faced by investors in French civil-law countries.[1] The weak scores obtained by Latin America in shareholder and cred-

itor rights may actually understate the severity of the corporate governance problem in the region.

External Finance and Legal Institutions

There are at least two reasons why legal institutions may have no effect on the pattern of external financing of firms. First, laws may not be necessary to support external financing if, for example, companies deliver on their promises not because they are forced to but because they want to build a good reputation to facilitate their access to capital markets (Diamond 1989, 1991; Gomes 1996). Reputation unravels if there is ever a time when the gains from cheating exceed the value of keeping external financing open, since investors, through backward induction, would never extend financing to such a firm to begin with.

Second, poor laws and their enforcement may have no real consequences if firms can easily opt out of the laws of

TABLE 4.4

Enforcement of Laws

This table classifies countries by legal origin. Definitions for each of the variables can be found in Table 4.1. Panel B reports the tests of means for the different legal origins.

	PANEL A				
	ENFORCEMENT VARIABLES			ACCOUNTING	GNP PER CAPITA
COUNTRY	EFFICIENCY OF JUDICIAL SYSTEM	RULE OF LAW	CORRUPTION	RATING ON ACCOUNTING STANDARDS	(U.S.$)
English origin avg.[a]	8.15	6.46	7.06	69.62	9,353
French origin avg.[b]	6.56	6.05	5.84	51.17	7,102
Latin American avg.	6.47	5.18	5.22	46.25	3,077
Rest of French origin avg.	6.62	6.70	6.30	55.10	10,121
German origin avg.[c]	8.54	8.68	8.03	62.67	22,067
Scandinavian origin avg.[d]	10.00	10.00	10.00	74.00	24,185
Sample average	7.67	6.85	6.90	60.93	11,156

a=Countries surveyed: Australia, Canada, Hong Kong (China), India, Ireland, Israel, Kenya, Malaysia, New Zealand, Nigeria, Pakistan, Singapore, South Africa, Sri Lanka, Thailand, United Kingdom, United States, Zimbabwe.

b=Countries surveyed: Argentina, Belgium, Brazil, Chile, Colombia, Ecuador, Arab Republic of Egypt, France, Greece, Indonesia, Italy, Jordan, Mexico, Netherlands, Peru, Philippines, Portugal, Spain, Turkey, Uruguay, Venezuela.

c=Countries surveyed: Austria, Germany, Japan, Republic of Korea, Switzerland, Taiwan (China).

d=Countries surveyed: Denmark, Finland, Norway, Sweden.

PANEL B: TESTS OF MEANS (T-STATISTICS)					
Common vs. civil law	1.27	-0.77	0.39	3.12 [a]	-0.94
English vs. French origin	2.65 [a]	0.51	1.79 [c]	4.66 [a]	0.85
English origin vs. Latin America	2.37 [b]	1.25	2.33 [b]	6.53 [a]	2.08 [b]
French vs. German origin	-2.53 [a]	-2.55 [a]	-2.49 [a]	-2.10 [b]	-3.79 [a]
French vs. Scandinavian origin	-9.34 [a]	-20.80 [a]	-9.77 [a]	-3.32 [a]	-4.28 [a]
Rest of French origin vs. Latin America	0.19	1.52	1.28	1.49	2.27 [b]

a = Significant at 1% level; b = Significant at 5% level; c = Significant at 10% level.

their legal jurisdictions. Easterbrook and Fischel (1991) are skeptical that legal rules are binding in most instances, since entrepreneurs can offer better investor rights, when it is optimal to do so, through corporate charters that effectively serve as contracts between entrepreneurs and investors. In practice, however, opting out may be costly both for firms that need to write non-standard contracts and for investors who need to study them. In addition, courts may be unwilling or unable to enforce non-standard contracts, further limiting the scope for opting out.

Alternatively, if legal institutions matter, ownership concentration should be higher in countries with poor investor protection than in countries with strong protections for investors for at least two reasons: First, agency problems may call for large shareholders to monitor managers and thus prevent or minimize expropriation. Second, minority shareholders may be unwilling to pay high prices for securities in countries with weak legal protection. At the same time, entrepreneurs are going to be more reluctant to offer shares at discounted prices, thus resulting in higher ownership concentration as well as smaller and narrower markets for external equity.[2] Similarly, bad creditor rights may have analogous price and quantity effects on debt markets. In other words, if laws do not protect the rights of creditors, debt markets may be small since creditors may demand high interest rates and firms may be reluctant to borrow from arm's-length sources in such conditions.

Ultimately, the question of whether legal institutions matter is fundamentally empirical: If opting out were cheap and simple, the patterns of ownership and external finance of firms would not be affected by differences in legal institutions across countries.[3] Accordingly, in this section, we examine two types of evidence regarding the influence of legal institutions on external finance: ownership concentration, and the size and breadth of capital markets. Table 4.5 summarizes the results.

Data

We describe sequentially our measures of ownership concentration, external equity financing, and debt markets. First, to measure ownership concentration, La Porta et al. (1998a) assembled data for the 10 largest publicly traded, non-financial private domestic firms in each of 45 countries. For each country we measure ownership concentration as the median percentage owned by the three largest shareholders in each of these 10 firms.

Second, as in La Porta et al. (1997a), we also use three measures of equity finance. The first measure is the 1994 ratio of external equity finance to GNP in each country. To compute a rough proxy of external equity finance, we multiply the total market value of common stock of all publicly traded firms by the average fraction of the equity not held by the largest three investors (i.e., the complement of the ownership variable just described). We scale the total market value of common stock by the fraction of equity held by minority shareholders to avoid overestimating the availability of external financing. For example, when 90 percent of a firm's equity is held by insiders, looking at the market capitalization of the whole firm gives a tenfold overestimate of how much has actually been raised externally. The procedure we follow may still overestimate the level of external financing, because our ownership concentration figures are based on the largest firms and because they ignore cross-holdings. Still, this procedure is conceptually better than looking at the ratio of market capitalization to GNP.[4]

The remaining two measures of external equity finance capture market breadth. The first is the number of domestic firms listed in the stock exchange of each country relative to its population. The second is the number of initial public offerings of shares in each country between mid-1995 and mid-1996 (the period for which we have been able to obtain the data), also relative to the population. We look at both the stock and flow of new companies obtaining equity financing since the development of financial markets has accelerated greatly in the last decade, and hence the IPO data provides a more recent picture of external equity financing.

Finally, also as in La Porta et al. (1997a), we measure the availability of debt financing in each country as the ratio of the sum of private-sector bank debt and corporate bonds outstanding to GNP. Our choice of debt variable is partly determined by data availability, because the analogue of the stock market data that we use to measure external equity financing does not exist for debt markets. However, the fact that our debt measure includes not only corporations but the whole private sector may actually be an advantage, because in many countries entrepreneurs raise money on their personal accounts to finance their firms (for example, by mortgaging their properties).

Results

The first striking result of Table 4.5 is that in the world as a whole, dispersed ownership is a myth: In an average median firm 45 percent of the common shares are held by the largest three shareholders. The second result is that those countries with weaker investor protections have larger share ownership concentration. In particular, countries of the French legal family have an average ownership concentration of 55 percent. Statistically this number is significantly higher than the mean of the rest of the world and of each of the other three legal families individually.

Like the rest of the French origin, Latin America has highly concentrated ownership. With the exception of Chile, which has strong shareholder rights, all Latin American countries in the sample have higher ownership concentration than the world mean. After Greece (68 percent), the three largest ownership concentration levels in the world are found in Colombia (68 percent), Mexico (67 percent), and Brazil (63 percent). In sum, these data indicate that Latin American countries—and the French civil-law countries in general—have unusually high ownership concentration, possibly as an adaptation to weak legal protection.

Several interesting patterns emerge from looking at our proxies for external equity finance on Table 4.5. First, access to external equity financing is most limited in French civil-law countries. Specifically, both the ratio of external capital to GNP and the ratio of domestic firms to population are roughly half the world mean, whereas the ratio of IPOs to population is roughly one-fifth of the world mean. Equity markets are particularly narrow in Latin America; the ratio of the number of firms to population is roughly one-third of the world mean, whereas the ratio of the number of IPOs to population is more than 10 times smaller than the world mean. In contrast, all three equity measures indicate that, on average, access to external equity is easiest in common-law countries: The ratio of outsider-held stock market to GNP is 60 percent, vs. 40 percent for the world mean; the number of listed firms per

TABLE 4.5

External Finance and Legal Institutions

This table classifies countries by legal origin. Definitions for each of the variables can be found in Table 4.1. Panel B reports tests of means for the different legal origins.

PANEL A

COUNTRY	OWNERSHIP CONCENTRATION (10 LARGE FIRMS) (MEDIAN)	EXTERNAL CAP / GNP (MEAN)	DOMESTIC FIRMS / POP	IPOS / POP	DEBT / GNP	GDP GROWTH	LOG GNP
Australia	0.28	0.49	63.55	–	0.76	3.06	12.64
Canada	0.24	0.39	40.86	4.93	0.72	3.36	13.26
Hong Kong, China	0.54	1.18	88.16	5.16	–	7.57	11.56
India	0.43	0.31	7.79	1.24	0.29	4.34	12.50
Ireland	0.36	0.27	20.00	0.75	0.38	4.25	10.73
Israel	0.55	0.25	127.60	1.80	0.66	4.39	11.19
Kenya	–	–	2.24	–	–	4.79	8.83
Malaysia	0.52	1.48	25.15	2.89	0.84	6.90	11.00
New Zealand	0.51	0.28	69.00	0.66	0.90	1.67	10.69
Nigeria	0.45	0.27	1.68	–	–	3.43	10.36
Pakistan	0.41	0.18	5.88	–	0.27	5.50	10.88
Singapore	0.53	1.18	80.00	5.67	0.60	1.68	11.68
South Africa	0.52	1.45	16.00	0.05	0.93	7.48	10.92
Sri Lanka	0.61	0.11	11.94	0.11	0.25	4.04	9.28
Thailand	0.48	0.56	6.70	0.56	0.93	7.70	11.72
United Kingdom	0.15	1.00	35.68	2.01	1.13	2.27	13.86
United States	0.12	0.58	30.11	3.11	0.81	2.74	15.67
Zimbabwe	0.51	0.18	5.81	–	–	2.17	8.63
English origin avg.	**0.42**	**0.60**	**35.45**	**2.23**	**0.68**	**4.30**	**11.41**
French origin							
Argentina	0.55	0.07	4.58	0.20	0.19	1.40	12.40
Belgium	0.62	0.17	15.50	0.30	0.38	2.46	12.29
Brazil	0.63	0.18	3.48	0.00	0.39	3.95	13.03
Chile	0.38	0.80	19.92	0.35	0.63	3.35	10.69
Colombia	0.68	0.14	3.13	0.05	0.19	4.38	10.82
Ecuador	–	–	13.18	0.09	–	4.55	9.49
Egypt, Arab Rep.	0.62	0.08	3.48	–	–	6.13	10.53
France	0.24	0.23	8.05	0.17	0.96	2.54	14.07
Greece	0.68	0.07	21.60	0.30	0.23	2.46	11.25
Indonesia	0.62	0.15	1.15	0.10	0.42	6.38	11.84
Italy	0.60	0.08	3.91	0.31	0.55	2.82	13.94
Jordan	–	–	23.75	–	0.70	1.20	8.49
Mexico	0.67	0.22	2.28	0.03	0.47	3.07	12.69
Netherlands	0.31	0.52	21.13	0.66	1.08	2.55	12.68
Peru	0.57	0.40	9.47	0.13	0.27	2.82	10.92
Philippines	0.51	0.10	2.90	0.27	0.10	0.30	10.44
Portugal	0.59	0.08	19.50	0.50	0.64	3.52	11.41
Spain	0.50	0.17	9.71	0.07	0.75	3.27	13.19
Turkey	0.58	0.18	2.93	0.05	0.15	5.05	12.08
Uruguay	–	–	7.00	0.00	0.26	1.96	9.40
Venezuela	0.49	0.08	4.28	0.00	0.10	2.65	10.99
Latin American avg.	**0.57**	**0.23**	**7.49**	**0.10**	**0.29**	**2.84**	**11.11**
Rest of French origin avg.	**0.53**	**0.19**	**11.89**	**0.28**	**0.56**	**3.43**	**11.89**
French origin avg.	**0.55**	**0.21**	**10.00**	**0.19**	**0.45**	**3.18**	**11.55**

TABLE 4.5

(Continued)

	PANEL A						
COUNTRY	OWNERSHIP CONCENTRATION (10 LARGE FIRMS) (MEDIAN)	EXTERNAL CAP / GNP (MEAN)	DOMESTIC FIRMS / POP	IPOS / POP	DEBT / GNP	GDP GROWTH	LOG GNP
Austria	0.51	0.06	13.87	0.25	0.79	2.74	12.13
Germany	0.50	0.13	5.14	0.08	1.12	2.60	14.46
Japan	0.13	0.62	17.78	0.26	1.22	4.13	15.18
Korea, Rep. of	0.20	0.44	15.88	0.02	0.74	9.52	12.73
Switzerland	0.48	0.62	33.85	–	–	1.18	12.44
Taiwan, China	0.14	0.88	14.22	0.00	–	11.56	12.34
German origin avg.	0.33	0.46	16.79	0.12	0.97	5.29	13.21
Scandinavian origin							
Denmark	0.40	0.21	50.40	1.80	0.34	2.09	11.84
Finland	0.34	0.25	13.00	0.60	0.75	2.40	11.49
Norway	0.31	0.22	33.00	4.50	0.64	3.43	11.62
Sweden	0.28	0.51	12.66	1.66	0.55	1.79	12.28
Scandinavian origin avg.	0.33	0.30	27.26	2.14	0.57	2.42	11.80
Sample average	0.45	0.40	21.59	1.02	0.59	3.79	11.72

	PANEL B: TESTS OF MEANS (T-STATISTICS)						
Common vs. civil law	-0.91	3.12[a]	3.16[a]	3.97[a]	1.33	1.23	-1.06
English vs. French origin	-2.68[a]	3.29[a]	3.16[a]	4.50[a]	2.29[b]	1.97[c]	-0.28
English origin vs. Latin America	-2.34[b]	1.97[c]	2.29[b]	3.21[a]	3.42[a]	1.93[b]	0.46
French vs. German origin	3.29[a]	-2.38[b]	-1.85	0.78	-3.39[a]	-1.96[c]	-2.48
French vs. Scand. origin	3.32[a]	-0.91	-3.31[a]	-5.45[a]	0.82	0.97	-0.33
Rest of French origin vs. Latin America	-0.54	-0.35	1.36	2.41[b]	2.20[b]	0.88	1.22

a = Significant at 1% level; b = Significant at 5% level; c = Significant at 10% level.

1 million people is 35, vs. 21.6 for the world mean; and the number of IPOs per million people is 2.2, vs. 1.02 for the world mean. Finally, equity markets in countries of Scandinavian origin are smaller but broader than in countries of German origin. To summarize, external equity markets line up pretty well with shareholder rights and legal institutions: They are smallest in French civil-law countries and largest in common-law countries.

The last column in Table 4.5 shows the aggregate debt measure. The ratio of total debt to GNP is 45 percent for French civil-law countries, 57 percent for Scandinavian countries, 68 percent for common-law countries, and 97 percent for German countries. It is also interesting to note that Latin America, with a ratio of total debt to GNP of only 29 percent, is an outlier even within the French civil-law family. Low creditor rights line up with small markets when we compare French, Scandinavian, and English ori-

gin. However, German civil-law countries are a mystery. We conjecture that a possible explanation of the German-origin anomaly is that firms in both Germany and Japan have large liquid assets and, therefore, our debt measure overstates their true liabilities (Rajan and Zingales 1995).

Regression Results

We present two sets of regressions on Tables 4.6 and 4.7 for each of our measures of ownership concentration, external equity finance, and debt markets. The first set of regressions (Table 4.6) includes legal-origin dummies, whereas the second one (Table 4.7) includes our measures of shareholder and creditor rights. In both specifications we regress our measures of capital markets on two control variables and on law enforcement. The first control is the growth of GDP on the theory that growth affects valuation and that in turn may affect ownership patterns as entrepreneurs are

TABLE 4.6

Regressions of External Finance and Legal Origin

Ordinary least squares regressions of the cross section of 49 countries around the world. The dependent variables are: (1) Ownership Concentration (the mean of each country); (2) External Cap / GNP; (3) Domestic Firms / Pop; (4) IPOs / Pop; and (5) Debt / GNP. The independent variables are (1) GDP growth; (2) Log GNP; (3) Rule of law; (4) French origin; (5) German origin; and (6) Scandinavian origin. Robust standard errors are shown in parentheses.

INDEPENDENT VARIABLES			DEPENDENT VARIABLES:		
	OWNERSHIP CONCENTRATION	EXTERNAL CAP / GNP	DOMESTIC FIRMS / POP	IPOS / POP	DEBT / GNP
GDP growth	-0.0077	0.0584[b]	1.0111	0.1938 [b]	0.0251 [b]
	(0.0084)	(0.0259)	(1.3676)	(0.1112)	(0.0148)
Log GNP	-0.0436[a]	0.0038	-2.9127	-0.0662	0.0370
	(0.0132)	(0.0420)	(1.9117)	(0.1193)	(0.0281)
Rule of law	-0.0031	0.0417	4.8422 [a]	0.2122 [b]	0.0698 [a]
	(0.0067)	(0.0272)	(1.4708)	(0.0926)	(0.0163)
French origin	0.1217 [a]	-0.3225 [a]	-21.9070 [a]	-1.5982 [a]	-0.1516 [b]
	(0.0317)	(0.1131)	(7.9944)	(0.3902)	(0.0817)
German origin	-0.0013	-0.2962 [c]	-25.1485 [a]	-2.8119 [a]	0.1080
	(0.0660)	(0.1629)	(9.1683)	(0.6257)	(0.1116)
Scandinavian origin	-0.0589	-0.3391 [b]	-22.2680 [b]	-0.3123	-0.2764 [b]
	(0.0434)	(0.1494)	(10.9897)	(0.9516)	(0.1145)
Intercept	0.9889 [a]	0.0336	33.0486	-0.9201	-0.3496
	(0.1314)	(0.4001)	(22.2848)	(1.4532)	(0.2786)
Observations	45	45	49	41	39
Adjusted R^2	0.5517	0.3840	0.3497	0.5671	0.6647

a = Significant at 1% level; b = Significant at 5% level; c = Significant at 10%

more willing to issue at attractive prices. We also control for the logarithm of total GNP on the theory that the creation of capital markets may be an activity subject to increasing returns to scale. If this theory is true, we should observe that larger economies have larger firms, which might therefore have lower ownership concentration.[5] As a measure of quality enforcement we chose the "rule of law" index, but the results we present are representative of other specifications with alternative enforcement measures.

The regression results in the first column of Table 4.6 show that larger economies have lower ownership concentration and that, although not significant in this specification, better enforcement leads to lower ownership concentration. In addition, this regression confirms the sharply higher concentration of ownership in the French civil-law countries: Controlling for other variables, the average country of French legal origin has 12 percentage points more concentrated ownership in the hands of the largest

three shareholders than the average country of English legal origin.

The first regression in Table 4.7 has the same controls and legal enforcement variables as Table 4.6, but instead of legal origin it tests for the significance of stronger shareholder protection in the form of more anti-director rights and the existence of one share–one vote rules. Looking at Table 4.7, the coefficient on the logarithm of GNP remains significant, showing that larger economies have less concentrated ownership. The results also show that legal enforcement significantly reduces the concentration of ownership in the regression. A 4.65 point increase in the rule-of-law score (roughly the distance between New Zealand and Argentina or Mexico) reduces average ownership concentration by 7 percentage points. Similarly, countries with stronger shareholder protection, measured by our aggregate score of anti-director rights, also have a statistically significantly lower concentration of ownership. A

TABLE 4.7

Regressions of External Finance and Shareholder and Creditor Rights

Ordinary least squares regressions of the cross section of 49 countries around the world. The dependent variables are: (1) Ownership Concentration (the mean of each country); (2) External Cap / GNP; (3) Domestic Firms / Pop; (4) IPOs / Pop; and (5) Debt / GNP. The independent variables are (1) GDP growth; (2) Log GNP; (3) Rule of law; (4) Anti-directors rights; (5) One share – One vote; and (6) Creditor rights. Robust standard errors are shown in parentheses.

INDEPENDENT VARIABLES	DEPENDENT VARIABLES:				
	OWNERSHIP CONCENTRATION	EXTERNAL CAP / GNP	DOMESTIC FIRMS / POP	IPOS / POP	DEBT / GNP
GDP growth	-0.0124	0.0604[a]	1.3926	0.1433	0.0311[c]
	(0.0097)	(0.0176)	(1.3976)	(0.1251)	(0.0184)
Log GNP	-0.0312[b]	-0.0205	-4.7687[a]	-0.1814	0.0667[b]
	(0.0116)	(0.0306)	(1.7815)	(0.1541)	(0.0270)
Rule of law	-0.0151[b]	0.0456[b]	4.8174[a]	0.2824[a]	0.0615[a]
	(0.0060)	(0.0214)	(1.4273)	(0.0887)	(0.0142)
Anti-director rights	-0.0385[a]	0.1244[a]	6.0688[a]	0.5761[a]	
	(0.0385)	(0.0378)	(1.6293)	(1.438))	
One share – One vote	0.0044	0.1433	0.4189	0.0226	
	(0.0461)	(0.1278)	(7.0938)	(0.5267)	
Creditor rights	–				0.0518[c]
					(0.0287)
Intercept	1.1041[a]	-0.3219	20.9494	-1.1172	-0.8622[a]
	(0.1304)	(0.2614)	(17.3374)	(1.4796)	(0.2763)
Observations	45	45	49	41	39
Adjusted R²	0.4862	0.4549	0.2671	0.4541	0.5993

a = Significant at 1% level; b = Significant at 5% level; c = Significant at 10%

1.6 point increase in the anti-director rights score (roughly the distance between common-law and French civil-law averages) reduces ownership concentration by 6 percentage points. Finally, the existence of a one share–one vote rule in the corporate law turns out not to be significant for ownership concentration. In sum, regression results confirm our previous finding that the protection of shareholders through legal institutions is an important determinant of ownership concentration.

As with ownership concentration, we present two sets of regressions for external equity markets on Tables 4.6 and 4.7. Two key results emerge from the analysis of the regressions that use legal origin (Table 4.6). First, rule of law has a large impact on all three variables: A move from the world mean of 6.85 to a perfect score of 10 is associated with an increase of 13.1 percentage points (the standard deviation of the variable is 37) in the ratio of external market capitalization to GNP, an additional 15.3 (the standard

deviation of the variable is 25) firms per million population, and a further 0.67 (the standard deviation of the variable is 1.5) IPOs per million population. However only the last two results are statistically significant. Second, legal origin matters. Relative to common-law countries, French civil-law countries have a ratio of external equity-to-GNP 32.2 percentage points lower, 21.9 fewer publicly traded firms per million population, and 1.6 fewer IPOs per million population. German and Scandinavian legal origin are also associated with smaller and more narrow stock markets than English origin but the effects are not as pronounced as with French legal origin. All estimates are statistically significant with the sole exception of the effect of Scandinavian origin on the number of IPOs per million population.

The results on anti-director rights and one share–one vote (Table 4.7) are easy to summarize. One share–one vote has the expected sign, but it is never significant. In contrast, anti-director rights has a large impact on equity financing both in statistical and economical terms: A move from the world mean of 2.5 to a perfect score of 6 is associated with an increase of 43.5 percentage points in the ratio of external market capitalization to GNP, an additional 21.2 publicly traded firms per million population, and 2.0 additional IPOs per million population. Finally, as in previous regressions, rule of law has a large impact on equity financing, and it is now statistically significant everywhere.

Overall, the results on external equity finance in Tables 4.6 and 4.7 show that rule of law and shareholder rights have a large impact on the availability of external equity financing. With the exception of the number of IPOs per million population in Scandinavia, the regressions also confirm our earlier results that the legal institutions of civil-law countries reduce the size and breadth of the stock markets.

As for the results on the size of debt markets, the last column on Table 4.6 shows that French civil-law countries have a ratio of debt-to-GNP 15 percentage points lower than common-law countries. Similarly, Scandinavian origin countries also have much lower (28 percentage points) debt-to-GNP ratios than common-law countries. In contrast, German origin countries have higher (11 percentage points) debt-to-GNP ratios than common-law countries. Finally, both regressions show that rule of law has, as in the case of equity financing, a large and statistically significant effect on the level of the debt-to-GNP ratio: The move from world mean (6.85) to a perfect 10 is associated with a 20 percentage point increase in the debt-to-GNP ratio.

The results using legal origin are confirmed in regressions that include creditor rights. In particular, Table 4.7 shows that the creditor-rights index is statistically significant at 10 percent. The point estimate implies that a move from the world mean (2.30) to a perfect score of 4 is associated with a 8.8 percentage point increase in the debt-to-GNP ratio, which is economically significant when compared with a world mean debt-to-GNP ratio of 59 percent. The size of the debt market does vary with rule of law, creditor rights, and legal origin. As a result, French and Scandinavian civil-law countries have narrower debt markets than common-law countries.

In sum, the results in this section show that the protection of investors through legal institutions is an important determinant of ownership concentration and the size and breadth of capital markets across nations.

Conclusion and Policy Implications

In this chapter we have surveyed the evidence on laws governing investor protection, the quality of enforcement of these laws, and their effect on the availability of external financing on a sample of 49 countries. The analysis suggests three broad conclusions.

First, investors in different legal jurisdictions have very different bundles of rights. Therefore, investor rights are not inherent to securities but rather are determined by laws. In particular, French civil-law countries protect investors the least and common-law countries the most. Countries of German and Scandinavian legal origin take an intermediate stance toward investor rights.

Second, law enforcement differs a great deal around the world. French civil-law countries have the worst quality of law enforcement, whereas German and Scandinavian civil-law countries have the best quality of law enforcement. Law enforcement is strong in common-law countries as well. These rankings also hold for one critical input into law enforcement in the area of investor protections: accounting standards.

Third, the evidence surveyed in this chapter suggests that large capital markets require that countries protect financiers against expropriation by entrepreneurs and provide them with good enforcement mechanisms to exercise such rights. In the absence of a good legal environment financiers are reluctant to surrender funds in exchange for securities, and hence the scope of capital markets is limited. Specifically, we see evidence that poor legal institutions result in high levels of ownership concentration, low availability of external equity financing, narrow equity markets, and small debt markets.

Latin America offers investors a rather unattractive legal environment. Both creditor rights as well as the quality of enforcement lag behind the rest of the French civil-law origin countries while shareholder rights are marginally better than the rest of the French legal origin average. As a result, credit markets are exceedingly small, and stock markets are both small and very narrow.

It is clear that improving corporate governance should be at the top of the policy agenda in Latin America. The immediate reaction to the evidence surveyed in this chapter is to call for wholesale legal reform. Clearly, minority shareholders would benefit from the existence of a mechanism to redress expropriation, and there is plenty of room to strengthen voting rights and to enhance disclosure requirements. Similar arguments can be made for creditor rights.

However, to the extent that improving the efficiency of the judicial system and asserting the rule of law are slow processes, it is important to incorporate those constraints in the policy design. For example, it may be particularly valuable to adopt an oppressed minority mechanism, perhaps similar to that of Chile, that minimizes the involvement of the courts even if its more mechanical nature results in less fair outcomes. Similarly, mandating enhanced disclosure requirements may not be sufficient in countries with weak legal institutions. In such instances it may be desirable, for example, to require that institutional investors only be allowed to invest in companies that meet minimum corporate-governance standards as determined by independent best-practice commissions.

Finally, in the area of creditor rights one may want to emphasize bankruptcy procedures that minimize the involvement of courts. The United Kingdom's administration procedure is an example of bankruptcy procedure that puts most of the discretion on the hands of commercial banks rather than on courts. Along the same lines, another departure from current practice would introduce market forces in the bankruptcy process by auctioning off bankrupt firms much the same way that state-owned enterprises are currently privatized (Hart et al. 1997).

Notes

1. By every single measure, richer countries have a higher quality of law enforcement. Nonetheless, even controlling for per capita income, French civil-law countries still score lower on every single measure, and statistically significantly lower for almost all measures, than the common-law countries do. The regression results continue to show that legal families with investor-friendlier laws are also the ones with stronger enforcement of laws. (See regression results in La Porta et al. 1998a.)

2. Ownership concentration per se may be efficient, because the existence of large shareholders monitoring management reduces the agency problem between management and shareholders (Jensen and Meckling 1976; Shleifer and Robert Vishny 1986). But large concentration comes at a cost as it creates another agency problem: the expropriation of minority shareholders by large ones. An additional cost of heavily concentrated ownership is that the core investors are not diversified.

3. La Porta et al. (1998c) find that, for a cross-section of countries around the world, various measures of dividend payout ratios are lower in countries with poor investor protection than in countries with high investor protection. This evidence suggests that companies in countries with poor laws and poor enforcement of those laws do not build reputations by paying high dividends to their shareholders.

4. The results presented below hold for that uncorrected ratio as well.

5. In alternative specifications presented in La Porta et al. (1998a) we also controlled for the Gini coefficient of each country on the theory that more egalitarian nations have lower ownership concentration; and for the logarithm of GDP per capita under the theory that richer countries may have different ownership patterns. The coefficients on these two variables are insignificant in most specifications, and their inclusion does not significantly affect the results presented here. In the case of GDP per capita, a further reason to eliminate this variable from the specifications is that its correlation with rule of law is quite high (0.87).

PART 3
Institutional Reform
in Hierarchies

CHAPTER 5

Reforming the School in Latin America and the Caribbean: An Institutional Analysis

THE EDUCATIONAL SYSTEM IN LAC CONTINUES TO BE UNSATISFACTORY, DESPITE RECENT efforts to improve the quality and equity of education, including new national education policies, sustained financial support to basic education, and the implementation of educational reforms. Achieving the goals of those initiatives depends largely on the institutional structure and capacity of the public sector, which is the main provider of basic education, and on the interaction of the people involved in providing education at the school, local, and national levels.

Persistent inequality and low quality characterize basic education systems in the LAC region. Education inequalities—in access to school, readiness, attendance, quality of teaching, and learning outcomes—perpetuate income and social inequalities and contribute to making Latin America and the Caribbean one of the most inequitable regions of the world. Figure 5.1 illustrates the patterns of differences in preschool enrollment for poor and non-poor children in rural and urban areas in Costa Rica and Chile. Similar patterns exist in secondary education participation; in Brazil, for example, 40 percent of non-poor urban children are enrolled in secondary school, but only 10 percent of rural poor children are.

Poor children attend poor schools, have fewer opportunities to complete their basic education, and perform below their counterparts in private schools. Figure 5.2, which compares rural public schools with elite private schools, shows typical differences in educational achievement between poor and non-poor children in LAC countries. Moreover, the level of attainment of the poor in several Latin American countries compares unfavorably with that of other regions of the world, such as East Asia or East Africa. For example, 46 percent of Brazil's poor complete Grade 5, compared with 89 percent of the poor in Zimbabwe (Filmer et al. 1998).

Most education experts of the region agree that the outcomes of school systems are disappointing. School attainment and completion rates continue to be low, and levels of student learning do not meet the expectations of educational reformers (Rama 1992; UNESCO 1994). Empirical evidence from national tests and international comparisons

of student learning confirms this observation. In science and mathematics, Colombian students consistently perform below their counterparts in other regions of the world (see Figure 5.3), and regional testing carried out by UNESCO (1995) demonstrated that Colombia's performance is typical of the region.

Many of the quality-related problems also apply to private schools, although there is evidence that elite private-school students in several Latin American countries score higher on achievement tests than their peers in public schools (UNESCO 1995)—see Figure 5.2. Privately managed schools in Chile perform better on national achievement tests than municipal schools in Chile (Larrañaga 1997). Privately managed schools (for example, *Fe y Alegría* schools in 12 Latin American countries) also show higher student retention and attendance rates than similar public schools (Swope and Latorre 1998).

FIGURE 5.1

Preschool Gross Enrollment Rates in Costa Rica and Chile, Poor vs. Non-poor

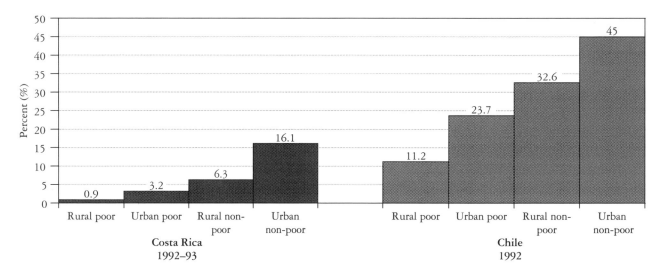

Source: World Bank estimates based on household survey data.

The limitations and challenges of LAC education systems were discussed and debated at the Summit of the Americas (OAS 1998 and PNUD 1998). There was general agreement about the symptoms of the problems of education in the region, and the region's political leaders agreed on the directions the required changes needed to take in the Summit Action Plan (Summit of the Americas 1998).

Many of the proposed changes, such as creation of mechanisms for evaluation and participation by civil society, require improvement of institutional frameworks that will lead to alteration of traditional social behaviors.

The patterns of behavior of the actors involved in education and the interaction among them—which are shaped by the rules of the game (both formal and informal)—have

FIGURE 5.2

Achievement Test Results, 1992

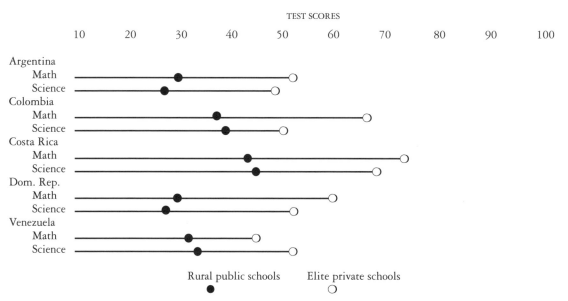

Source: UNESCO/OREALC in Schiefelbein (1995).

FIGURE 5.3

Average Mathematics Achievement Test Scores, Grade 8

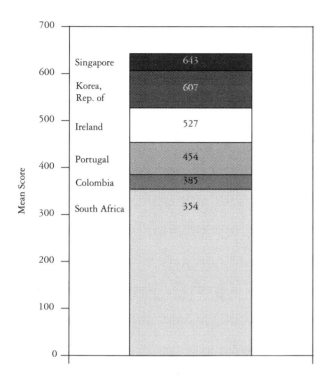

Source: Beaton et al. (1996).

not changed significantly with the initiation of educational reforms. Misallocation of resources, inefficiencies, and lack of accountability are still predominant attributes of the organizational structure of education in LAC. Parents are still not demanding better performance from public schools, schools lack capacity and resources to respond to new institutional environments, and clientelistic practices continue to dominate the decision-making in several countries (PNUD 1998).

A decade of educational reforms in LAC countries has achieved legal changes, placed education as an important theme in social policy, and demonstrated the possibility of radical change on a relatively small scale. Indeed, most LAC countries have developed new education policies, and some of them have adopted general education laws (e.g., Argentina, Brazil, Colombia, and Mexico). Nevertheless, the effect of the legal changes and their impact on the provision of education at the school level, and on the improvement of education nationally, remains to be seen. Few reforms are affecting schools and teachers at the local level, and there are difficulties in changing value systems and

behaviors of the main actors involved, despite the institutional changes on the national level. The question for the next generation of institutional reforms is how to facilitate change in values and behavior where it matters most—at the classroom and school level.

Educational Institutions and the School

The Latin American school has been a remarkably stable system. Not only have the key actors remained unchanged for centuries, but the shared values, expected behaviors, and rules of the game—the institutional framework—also have been remarkably stable. Only recently has a first generation of education reforms attempted change. A major challenge to implementation of these school reforms, in fact, has been the strength of the system and its resistance to change.

The traditional school and its principal actors are shown in Figure 5.4. The school includes a director, teachers, and students and is influenced by a number of external actors, including parents, supervisors, ministries of education, teacher associations, and politicians. The interactions between these actors, both within the school itself and between the school and the external actors, are very complex. What is important, however, is that in many cases the combined interactions and behaviors of these diverse actors are dysfunctional, so adequate learning does not take place, despite additional public spending and despite new education laws. In the pages that follow, we describe some of the major interactions, starting with those inside the school itself. Although the discussion focuses on public schools,

FIGURE 5.4

Principal Actors in the Traditional School

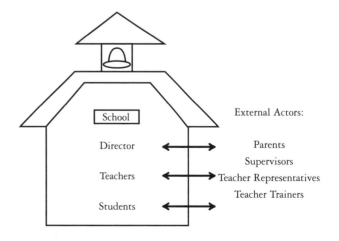

91

which enroll 80 percent or more of all primary-school students in LAC, the implications are also relevant for private schools, which are on the increase in several LAC countries. Private secondary-school enrollment in Bolivia, for example, increased from 17 percent in 1980 to 26 percent in 1990, and from 24 percent to 42 percent in Chile during the same period (UNESCO 1994).

Actors in the School

Students are the fundamental principals of the education system, but they have little power to influence the quantity and quality of services they receive. Nevertheless, they have considerable power to affect their own learning through personal decisions about how to use their time, including, for older students, whether to participate in the labor force. And student decisions about their own classroom behavior—which are, in turn, strongly influenced by the values and behaviors of peers, parents, and teachers—affect learning and schooling outcomes. While students clearly have some choice, research shows that negative expectations of teachers and parents about student achievement, which occur frequently, are often self-fulfilling. Thus, the very high probability of failure and repetition in many Latin American schools may in and of itself adversely affect learning.

Teachers are the fundamental agents of the school, and they are agents for multiple principals in addition to students, including the school director, parents, and the teacher associations. Research on learning shows the predominant influence of the teacher on learning in the classroom. Teachers have the problem of divided loyalties that all agents face: They have self-interests that may not coincide with the interests of their employers or bosses, yet they have strong professional interests that are consistent with those of the principals.

Most teachers first enter the classroom after graduating from teacher-training programs in universities or in specialized teacher-training institutions, or normal schools. These training programs inculcate values and behaviors, in addition to providing knowledge on subject content and pedagogy. Teachers make numerous decisions that affect learning in the classroom, including whether to be present or absent, to take training to improve teaching skills, to use their own time to develop lesson plans or to grade examinations, to carefully assess individual students and individualize teaching accordingly, to try new methods that may not succeed, to seek assistance from school supervisors, the director or peers, to spend time discussing student performance with parents, to collaborate with peers in assessing students, to collaborate with peers and the director in managing the school, and to allocate time to nonschool activities, including those of the teacher associations. Each of these decisions in and of itself is complex, but each is also heavily influenced by the behavioral norms and expectations of other actors. Excessive teacher absenteeism, for example, may be condoned by peers as "beating the system" rather than "violating the rights of the child." Teacher associations may protect the employment rights of the teacher as a matter of principle, even when students suffer. Teachers may view impoverished parents as too poorly educated to understand their children's learning problems.

Directors of the traditional public school are selected from the teaching faculty and sometimes return to the faculty after serving this administrative duty. Usually, directors retain membership in the teacher association. The responsibilities and authority of directors are severely constrained, especially regarding the recruitment and evaluation of teachers. Their principal duty is the administrative enforcement of basic employment rules. They usually are not expected to initiate change, evaluate staff, or provide support to teachers with performance problems, and they have very few ways to reward good performance or address special needs of individual teachers. Besides, directors typically receive no specialized training in school management that would equip them to carry out these responsibilities, so they seldom know the arcane and complex requirements for removing or disciplining teachers, even in cases of extreme cause. Like teachers, directors have divided allegiances. They are agents of the education ministry, but their day-to-day work cannot be carried out without the cooperation of the teaching faculty, whom they may one day rejoin.

Local External Actors

External to the school, but closely tied to it, are four extremely important actors—parents, locally elected representatives of the teacher association, the appointed local representatives of the education ministry, and the trainers of teachers.

Parents are by far the most important determinant of learning by children. Their own education (that of mothers, especially), the value they attach to doing well in school, and the interest they express in their children's performance—all affect the child's motivation and effort. On the other hand, parents have very little "voice" or "choice." If they are seriously unhappy with their child's education, they have little recourse—especially if they are poor—save lengthy appeals through the education bureaucracy. Since the costs of such action are high and the probability of a positive response low, parents seldom undertake it. Highly motivated parents may be active in their parents' association at the school; however, they quickly discover that most school authorities want them for their potential to contribute financially and not for their interest in the education of their child. Indeed, these parents may receive a hostile response from school staff if they are perceived to be questioning the work of trained professionals. In short, parents have learned to be passive actors in the system.

In the traditional school, parents depend heavily on the state to monitor and regulate education. Given the limited knowledge most parents have to evaluate pedagogic practices or the quality of instruction, they depend on the state to do this for them. Indeed, ensuring quality and information about quality is an essential role of the education ministry. But since parents rarely fight their battles up the education bureaucracy, the staff of education ministries seldom find out about their problems, making monitoring particularly difficult.

We should point out, however, that parents are not powerless. Those with adequate resources may elect to send their children to private schools or to move to neighborhoods where schools may have better reputations. Parents may also purchase additional instruction after school hours, and they may work with and encourage their children to engage in learning activities in the home. The home environment is a powerful factor in determining students' academic success (Kellaghan et al. 1993).

Local *teacher representatives*, elected by majority vote, generally reflect the perspective of the average teacher, although, as with all democratic systems, large numbers of teachers disagree with the positions taken by their association (Scobie 1998). Local leaders serve three main functions: They protect teachers from violations of their contractual rights; they communicate to teachers the association's perspective on educational policies and programs advocated by the education ministry; and they marshal vocal teacher support for the positions of the associa-

tion, especially, but not exclusively, around salary negotiations at the regional or national level. From the perspective of the individual teacher, the representative is available and responsive.

Local *ministry representatives* are typically former teachers. Often they have received little specialized training to prepare them for this role. These frontline representatives or supervisors are responsible, in principle, for ensuring quality by monitoring and assisting teachers and directors, and they communicate policy and regulatory changes to school staff; however, their primary role in fact is that of enforcement of government regulations and policies. In most countries of Latin America, their supervisory role is not taken seriously. There are few supervisors, and they generally make infrequent school visits; supervisors in rural areas, where the need is greatest, often lack transportation to school sites. In short, the local representatives of the ministry are not highly visible and are not viewed as sources of help.

Teacher trainers offer both pre-service and in-service training and are most commonly situated on university faculties and specialized teacher-training colleges. The trainers of teachers have heavy responsibilities. They must take the theory of pedagogy found in the textbooks and convert it into instruction on good teaching practices. This requires that the trainers themselves have extensive experience in the classroom and, perhaps more importantly, that they have continued intimate contact with actual classroom practice. The trainers have the responsibility for knowing classroom reality, identifying good teaching practices in light of that reality, and communicating those practices to their student teachers. They are, in effect, responsible for carrying out "action research" on teaching to permit the education system to "learn" from its experiences. In several respects, the typical teacher trainer in Latin America falls short of this model. Those who have studied the issue cite several problems, including failure to maintain close contact with practice in the schools; failure to effectively translate theory into practice; excessive emphasis on theory over practice in instruction; failure to carry out practical research and feed lessons learned back into teacher training; and failure to maintain contact with newly graduated teachers (Villegas-Reimers 1998). In short, the deficiencies in teacher training pose a major obstacle to raising the quality of learning in the classroom.

National External Actors

Also external to the school—but physically remote from it—are other important actors who directly affect the school. These include the national ministries of education and finance, the national teacher association, and political actors, including political parties, the church, non-governmental think tanks, and, increasingly, private business leaders concerned with the quality of skilled labor.

The national *ministry of education* is itself a highly complex organization with numerous principals and agents, some of whom are physically separated by great distances. The minister is the agent of the president and brings to the ministry a number of high-level appointed officials who are responsible for policy development and overall management of the sector. For typical ministers, the education ministry is a short-term step in their political career. Their major challenge is to balance the demands from the finance ministry to keep a lid on costs with demands from the teacher associations to increase wages and demands from politicians to provide political payoffs in the form of new schools or employment for political supporters. The single largest risk he faces is a prolonged teachers' strike, which probably would force him to resign. In short, the principal wants an agent who generates political benefits, not costs.

The minister is the principal to a group of appointed executive officials, who by and large have goals congruent with those of the minister. The difficulty arises in the relationship between the appointed officials and the ministry's civil-service bureaucracy, which has seen many ministers, which has dealt with many new, short-lived policy initiatives, and which has the power to defeat policy and management initiatives that threaten its own power. Venezuela's failure to decentralize education, for example, has been attributed to the resistance of the rank and file staff of the central ministry (Hanson 1995).

Public administrators often view the education ministry as being among the weakest of all government ministries in its capacity to manage its sector and to implement new programs and policy initiatives. It also tends to have poor capacity, relative to other ministries, to plan and implement its budget. This particular weakness puts the education ministry at a technical disadvantage relative to the finance ministry when it comes to justifying its budget request. However, the education ministry has a political advantage in the ever-present threat of a teachers' strike. In this sense, the teacher association is its political ally on budget decisions. However, the ministry has no equivalent ally when it comes to making the argument for non-salary expenditures. Thus, there is a persistent distortion in resource allocation in favor of salaries.

The weak capacity of education ministries to carry out rigorous analyses, to prepare well-justified budgets, and to manage itself reflects in part the dominance of the political over the educational goals of the ministry itself. The weak capacity of the education ministry, combined with its political role, constrains its ability to carry out two key responsibilities of the state—ensuring quality and ensuring equality of educational opportunity.

The *ministry of finance* is headed by someone who is as much a technical appointee as a political appointee. He is selected by the president of the country for his combination of political skills and credibility as the guardian of the treasury. The importance of maintaining a credible macroeconomic policy also results in the finance minister's having longer tenure in office than the education and other social-sector ministers. The seriousness of purpose of the finance ministry usually translates into a determined attempt to control the fiscal deficit by constraining increases in public spending, including that of the education ministry. Since salaries represent a very high percentage of total education spending, there is a natural conflict of objectives between the education minister, who needs to increase salaries to appease labor, and the finance minister, who needs to limit salaries to maintain an acceptable fiscal deficit.

The leadership of the *teacher association*[1] is democratically elected and usually has much longer tenure in office than the education ministry leadership. While the leadership of the association or union can guide its membership, the democratic nature of the organization means its positions never can deviate too far from those of the average teacher. The association has as its first and foremost objective protecting and enhancing teachers' employment rights. This translates into ensuring stable employment, adequate salaries, and satisfactory working conditions. The pursuit of employment stability means the association, and at least a majority of its member teachers, are steadfastly opposed to any political or management change that might threaten the employment or even location of employment of the teacher. Naturally, this translates into vehement opposition to market-oriented proposals to increase parental choice in the selection of schools.

The real power of the teacher association is its capacity to convince teachers to take to the streets.[2] Successful teacher associations recognize that constant and effective communications with the rank and file are critical to maintaining this capacity. Association leaders who fail to listen to their membership will find that eventually their call to strike will fail, and possibly will result in a demand for a change in union leadership. Highly successful associations, like FECODE in Colombia, publish sophisticated education news journals for their membership, sponsor educational conferences, and in other ways maintain constant and effective communications with teachers. The sophistication of this communication is in stark contrast with the communication programs and policies of most education ministries.

Teacher associations in Latin America have another characteristic that significantly influences their own behavior and complicates labor relations: They are highly politicized, with leaders who frequently aspire to political office. Indeed, many associations are so closely aligned with particular political parties that their leadership becomes a stepping-stone to an important party candidacy. These political aspirations sometimes result in the leadership's expressing positions on numerous issues unrelated to education.

Political parties have two main effects on education. First, some political parties depend on the political support of teachers and teacher associations. These parties, of course, are expected to deliver benefits to teachers if and when they take office—although they may not always be able to do so if the political benefits of increasing teacher pay are outweighed by the economic risks of an increased fiscal deficit. On the other hand, at least those parties are likely to consult with teacher associations when making major educational policy changes; parties not having the political support of teacher associations have no political obligations to pay and, therefore, no need to consult.

The second effect of political parties is their demand on the education ministers to deliver political benefits to loyal party members in the form of employment and contracts. In its extreme form, this political clientelism results in the familiar phenomenon called "ghost teachers," i.e., teachers who receive salaries but do not teach. These phantom teachers, who have traditionally been a significant share of the total teaching force in areas like Northeast Brazil, represent a significant loss of resources for the schools.

The church is a unique actor in education with two major concerns: One has to do with the values taught in the public school curriculum; the other is the desire for continued state support for church schools. Since church schools compete with public schools for students, there would appear to be a natural conflict with teacher associations, many of whose members are also supporters of the church. This conflict is avoided in most countries by giving public support to church schools in the form of school teachers who are recruited and paid by the government, thereby minimizing the employment risk to public-school teachers.

Problems with Educational Institutions

The traditional school as characterized here is an inefficient organization. The description given above of the various internal and external actors in the school illustrates a number of the concepts of institutional economics. For one thing, the *information asymmetries* between principals and agents are large. Both ministry staff and parents have little information about the performance of particular schools or teachers. Other more general information problems are also severe. Teachers have little information about the performance of individual students or even their own classroom relative to others; hence, their capacity to diagnose instructional problems is constrained. Educational policy analysts and budget analysts often do not have the information required to do good analyses, and ministry policy-makers lack the information to make good policy decisions.

The general problem of lack of information, however, is less important than the *shortage of incentives* to seek and use information. Teacher trainers are often criticized for not being sufficiently "connected" to the real world of school practice and school problems, but it is within their own capacity to obtain this information. Both education and finance ministry officials are keenly aware that budgets are distorted in favor of salaries, with serious, negative implications for the performance of schools and teachers, yet the distortion persists. When important educational policy decisions are made primarily on political grounds, good information and good analysis of education issues may be irrelevant.

Principal-agent problems abound inside and outside the school. If students are the fundamental principals, poorly informed and poorly educated parents may fail to adequately represent their interests. Even when parents think they know what constitutes a good education for their children, they have almost no voice to express their preferences. The transaction costs of expressing preferences to the ministry are extremely high. In addition, there is the moral hazard problem that parents depend on the ministry to regulate the schools their children attend and, hence, have little incentive to use their own time and energy to monitor school performance.

Other principal-agent problems are also evident. School directors have little power to manage resources, resulting in a high degree of autonomy among their agents. However, the problem is still more serious. Teachers and directors, who have the best information about the school, have little authority to act on that knowledge. They cannot change the curriculum, select different textbooks, or in other ways change production relationships within the school. While teachers do have control within their own classrooms, this control is constrained by what happens to students outside their classroom and by the low level of technical assistance and support provided to them by the representatives of the ministry.

These problems translate into a lack of incentives for school directors to set organizational goals and monitor the school educational outcomes. School principals do not posses the resources to motivate teachers and give them incentives to improve their teaching skills and innovate their classroom practices. Teachers are not rewarded for their teaching quality or their level of effort for helping students to learn. There are no standards for the teaching profession, nor evaluation mechanisms. Parents do not have incentives to participate in school management or the information to monitor school performance. In the majority of cases their choices are nonexistent.

The final and perhaps most important underlying

problem with the traditional educational organization is its *slow evolution* in the face of glaring and obvious problems. There are excellent schools and excellent teachers and excellent teacher trainers, supervisors, directors, etc., within any school system. There are also very bad examples of each. The richness of the range of educational experiences provides a fertile ground for learning and improving—in short, for evolving. Creating a learning organization will require changes in values and behaviors that go beyond solving information problems. It will require instilling a sense of personal responsibility and accountability among all the actors for the performance of the school.

The Theory and Practice of Education Reforms

Many of the problems analyzed above have been addressed in several education reforms undertaken in Latin America and the Caribbean over the last decade. These reforms have concentrated on:

- Increasing the emphasis on learning outcomes, over simply increasing inputs
- Providing opportunities for broader social and community participation
- Giving more management autonomy to individual schools
- Promoting the development of new curricula, and localizing some of the content
- Upgrading teacher competencies, and
- Raising the accountability and social responsibility of the system (Alvarez 1998).

The mechanisms employed by most reforms to carry out

FIGURE 5.5

LAC Education Reforms

	YEAR REFORM INITIATED	STUDENT EVALUATION	MANAGEMENT INFORMATION SYSTEMS	PARENT PARTICIPATION	DECENTRALIZED MANAGEMENT
Argentina	1994	X	X		X
Brazil					
Minas Gerais	1991	X	X	X	X
Paraná	1995	X	X	X	X
Chile	1991	X			X
Colombia	1989		X		X
Dominican Republic	1990	X	X	X	X
El Salvador (EDUCO)	1992	X		X	X
Mexico	1991	X	X	X	X
Nicaragua	1992	X	X	X	X
Paraguay	1995		X	X	X

Source: Based on data in AED (1996).

these goals are summarized in Figure 5.5. Most reforms have seriously addressed the information problem by piloting national student-evaluation systems. The magnitude and importance of this change is immense. A decade ago, only Chile had a national student-testing system, and even it failed to make local results available to the public. Today, most countries in the region have some kind of testing system, as shown by Figure 5.6. Although few of these systems have matured sufficiently to provide feedback to parents and teachers about the performance of individual schools and individual students, most countries now have the capacity to sample schools and students and to monitor national progress in learning (Rojas forthcoming). In short, the capacity of education ministries to monitor and provide information on quality has clearly improved in the past decade, and this improvement is widespread throughout the region.

Similarly, many countries in the region have made significant investments in modern management information systems that allow decision-makers and budget analysts and planners to carry out their work with more timely and more comprehensive and accurate information on student flows, educational costs, and expenditures. Advances in computer hardware and software have permitted more rapid improvements in these systems within shorter periods of time than was true with past investments in information. While the sustainability of these systems is still in doubt, the participation of countries like Mexico in OECD and the MERCOSUR countries in the World Education Indicators Project means there is now high-level demand for such information.

Perhaps the most common element of the last decade's reform is decentralization. Several countries (Argentina, Brazil, Colombia, Mexico) increased the education responsibilities of regional governments; in Argentina and Brazil, central government ministries now have very little responsibility for financing and managing primary and secondary education. In other countries, most notably Chile, the fiscal and administrative management of education has been largely turned over to the municipalities. Decentralization of education to subnational governments has moved the locus of much decision-making closer to parents, but it has not, in general, affected the school.

More important for the school than government decentralization has been the movement toward increased school autonomy and community participation in a few countries. In Chile this has taken the form of empowering teachers and school directors to develop school-specific development projects. In El Salvador, the EDUCO program has given parent councils the authority to employ teachers and allocate resources. In Minas Gerais, Brazil, school councils comprising parents and teachers have the authority to select the school director, who is required to present a school development strategy as part of the selection process (see Box 5.1).

Finally, decentralization and movements toward school

FIGURE 5.6

Assessment of Educational Quality: Latin American Testing Systems, 1986–97

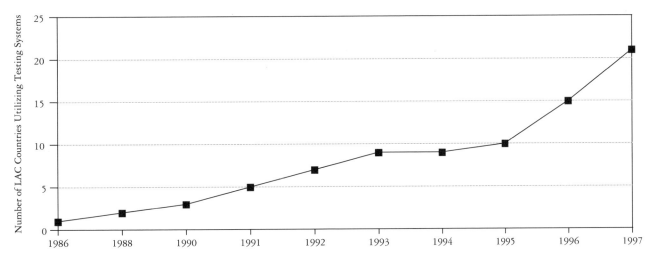

Source: Rojas (forthcoming).

BOX 5.1

Minas Gerais, Brazil: Building Capacity in Schools

Committed to improving education, the government of Minas Gerais embarked on a radical "silent revolution" in 1991. The government opted for transferring to school councils the authority, resources, and freedom to make decisions, so schools themselves could address the problems of high repetition rates, low student achievement, and low graduation rates. The process of education reform and decentralization was begun with the following strategic priorities:

- *Building capacity in school management and administration.* The way school administrators are selected has been revised. The new process includes testing the technical knowledge and management capacity of candidates, then dialogue with the community about the vision and plans for the school, followed by a vote by the community.
- *Promoting school autonomy.* The schools are self-directed in financial, administrative, and pedagogical matters, creating a sense of local-level ownership in the reform.
- *Creating opportunities and supporting professional development for teachers and administrators.* The process emphasizes both in-service and pre-service professional development. It offers courses in areas of spe-

cialization, and it provides basic training to all teachers of first through fourth grades. School principals are now trained in pedagogical knowledge and management techniques before assuming their posts.
- *Using evaluation and testing systems.* An evaluation system provides each school with feedback on its performance, allowing the school to determine which are its strong points and which areas require additional attention for improvement. The school, in conjunction with the community, then formulates a five-year development plan that includes teacher training and professional development.
- *Generating cooperation among the municipalities.* The entire decentralization process is reinforced by mechanisms to establish cooperation among the municipalities.

Within five years of its implementation, the new educational policies had produced promising results. Schools demonstrated that they could manage themselves and the resources when given the opportunity. In addition, students had become more interested in school activities and had improved academically.

Source: Machado in PNUD (1998).

autonomy have been accompanied by changes in financing arrangements. Several countries have introduced competitive financing mechanisms under which schools can compete to receive financing for special projects. Minas Gerais, Brazil, introduced capitation grants to schools, giving school councils a degree of budgetary authority and ensuring at least a minimum level of spending on non-personnel inputs. In the early 1980s, Chile introduced capitation grants to municipalities and privately managed schools, providing strong incentives for schools to compete for enrollment and retention of students. In 1997, Brazil reformed national revenue-sharing rules to ensure that all jurisdictions receive education revenues sufficient to guarantee a minimum level of spending per student ($350).

Second Phase of Education Reforms

The first phase of education reforms over the past decade set the stage for new large-scale social interventions that will more fundamentally attack the institutional and other problems of the school. The first generation of reforms emphasized decentralization, legal changes, development of pilot innovations, and creation of testing and evaluation systems. The second phase of reforms will need to broaden and deepen these reforms by focusing on changing rules and institutions that explicitly address the information and accountability problems that shape the behavior of actors at the school level. Table 5.1 illustrates this evolution.

First, the new phase of reforms needs to move from a focus on the national system to a focus on institutions at the school level. The reforms of the past decade have fre-

TABLE 5.1

Focus and Goals of Two Generations of Educational Reform in LAC

FIRST	SECOND
Focus on system	**Focus on school**
Decentralized decision-making	Teacher and parent empowerment
Pilot innovation projects	New roles in policy-making
	Large scale implementation of piloted projects
Changes in legal framework	**Changes in value systems and behavior**
Top-down reform efforts	Popular reforms
New educational policies	Behavioral changes in all actors
Priority given to education in social policy	
Development of management information systems	**Development of accountability mechanisms**
Creation of basic data bases	Broadening the use of information by all actors
Establishment of testing services	Using evaluation information at the school level
Changes in structures	**Changes in pedagogical practices**
New role of governments	Professional development of teachers
Emphasis on states	Use of advanced technologies
	Changes in classroom activities
	Emphasis on learning processes
Basic re-engineering	**Development of learning institutions**
Blueprint approach	Social learning approach
	Application and utilization of research findings

quently decentralized decision-making, improved information, and legally empowered parents with relatively little impact on the school. For example, the municipalization of primary and secondary schooling in Chile had relatively little impact on the municipal school (Espinola 1997). The extensive constitutional and legal reforms in Colombia have affected the school only very slowly (Montenegro 1995). In contrast with these legal reforms, the second generation of institutional reforms needs to empower parents and teachers or, where these actors have been legally empowered already, focus on the actual implementation of the law to ensure that parents and teachers begin to play out their new roles—that is, change their traditional behavior. In some cases, this will require giving school councils real, rather than advisory, powers, as is beginning to occur in the states of Minas Gerais and Paraná, Brazil, and in Nicaragua (Winkler 1997). The case of Chile demonstrates that real education reform can occur

in small slices in diverse areas. There need not be one grand, top-down education reform (see Box 5.2).

Second, with the legal framework often in place, the next set of reforms needs to focus on the much more difficult problem of making sure the legal framework leads to a change in the values and behaviors of the actors. This transformation will require navigating uncharted waters, and, to be successful, will require a systemic approach that reinforces change. It will be difficult to sustain change at the school level unless ministry officials, teacher-association officials, and parents also change their behaviors.

While the first generation of reforms has centered on the top, emphasizing legal changes, the second generation of reforms must start at the bottom, emphasizing behavioral changes. For example, for local decision-making to occur, there needs to be training to allow the school councils (or teachers) to exercise their new powers fully. The irony is that if grassroots efforts are to succeed, they need to be promoted by the educational leadership, at both the ministry level and in the teacher association. In short, top-down reforms need to be converted to popular reforms supported by a broad, national consensus. This will require, among other things, that ministries develop the capacity to effectively publicize and sell reform efforts. As the case of Colombia shows (see Box 5.3), grand education reform designs are not necessarily implemented if key actors, especially the teachers, do not buy into the reform. The implementation of Paraguay's 1990 second-phase educational reform followed an initial top-down reform effort. The top-down approach used in the first phase "delivered" the reforms to teachers via traditional in-service teacher training aimed at changing classroom behavior. The initial failure of this approach led to a radical change. Teachers were invited to participate in discussions and "learning circles." They took on ownership of the reform-implementation process and committed themselves as individuals and members of small groups to improve their teaching behavior (Hobbs and Rentel 1997).

However, not only the behavior of teachers needs to be changed. Parents need to be given voice so they can contribute to the second phase of reforms. One way of empowering parents is by expanding their choices and promoting competition among schools. Case studies on the provision of education and health services conducted in Chile, Costa Rica, and Venezuela suggest that competition improves efficiency, regardless of the public or private nature of the

BOX 5.2

Education Reform in Chile: The Whole Exceeds the Sum of Its Parts

Since the beginning of the 1990s, Chile has approached education reform with a strategy of continual and incremental changes initiated by schools rather than a comprehensive, linear action plan. Four basic factors explain the success of the reform process:

- A national consensus around the idea that education plays a strategic role in economic growth, social cohesion, and political development

- Continuous and consistent government support for and prioritizing of reform of the education system for over a decade, in spite of changes in national and ministerial administrations

- Macroeconomic stability and growth, making available the financial resources to sustain reform, and

- Widespread public acceptance of proposed policies, which focused on the need to modernize the education sector rather than on addressing issues of control and institutional power relationships (C. Cox 1998).

A decentralized strategy is being used for improving educational quality; the approach involves action at the school level, the establishment of incentive systems and competitive processes, the use of networks, and curricular reform. A national call for each school to generate "Projects for Educational Improvement" (called PMEs, by its Spanish abbreviation) opened the door for local-level innovation to become the engine for reform. In 1997, 80 percent of eligible primary schools were implementing PMEs that they had designed and that the government had approved and funded.

The projects are as diverse as the educational needs of the country and may involve more than a single school. The 900 Schools Program (P900) is biased in favor of the 900 lowest-achieving schools in rural and poor urban areas. It focuses on meeting the specific needs of the learners in those schools to increase achievement, improve teaching quality, provide books and other educational materials, and improve physical school infrastructure. *Enlaces* is a project that seeks to increase the use of computers in schools and create on-line learning communities, connecting secondary and primary schools to a national network and then to the Internet. Other projects focus on a variety of areas, including teacher training, specialized teaching methodology and curriculum for rural schools, installation of classroom libraries, and transferring functions of the ministry of education to the provincial departments.

In spite of the variety in project content and methodology, there are several commonalties among the PMEs, based on new criteria for education policy, both at the system level and at the level of the actors:

- A consensus must be built in the process of defining national education policies.

- Decentralization increases responsiveness to societal demand.

- Systems should be based on incentives, information sharing, and evaluation, and should demonstrate efficient use of resources.

- A new priority is placed on equity that responds to differences rather than providing homogenous educational services.

- Teachers and the school are now responsible for educational results rather than compliance with regulations.

- There is local-level participation in the design of the education process, generating a sense of ownership within communities.

- Teamwork and networking support the establishment of a culture of communication.

- Experimentation and incremental improvement are stressed, making the education reform a process of social learning (Cariola 1996).

These criteria serve to unify expectations, goals, and performance in the sector. This approach to education reform is, in its essence, an incremental, inductive process of system-wide transformation. The whole of the Chilean education reform far exceeds the sum of its parts.

BOX 5.3

Colombia: A Battle Between Giants

In the early 1990s, an educational reform started in Colombia with ambitious purposes: to decentralize education by empowering municipalities, increasing efficiency and accountability, expanding enrollment, improving quality of education, increasing public expenditure in education, and increasing the participation of the private sector. Three years of intensive political struggle resulted in an increase of public spending in education (from 2.7 percent of GDP in 1991 to 3.6 percent in 1994), legislation supporting decentralization, and the initiation of several reform projects, the majority of which were interrupted. Although it has achieved some success, the educational reform remains unfinished (Montenegro 1995).

The main actors of the struggle were the national government and the national teachers' union (FECODE)—not consumers of education services—resulting in a lack of civil society's ownership of the reform. Private-sector and local-government leaders were not active participants of the debate and negotiations, nor were parent representatives or non-governmental organizations included. The national government, represented by different agencies, did not present a coherent agenda through the debate, but FECODE was consistent and successful in impeding reforms that could affect its constituents' interests and power status. Thus, the battle for the reform was devel-

oped in a legal dimension with limited impact on the routine of education in the schools.

Although contextual factors influence educational change, the Colombian experience suggests the following:

- Educational reforms need to involve all the actors that affect or are being affected by the changes. A dialogue between the government and the teachers' union is insufficient and does not elicit ownership by critical actors such as parents, local-government officials, school administrators, and political parties.
- Reaching consensus for reform depends on the negotiation capacity of the government agencies leading the process; they need to have clear ideas and to be consistent to be able to negotiate with other interested parties.
- New approaches for improving education have to be developed to deal with teachers' unions.
- The reform process needs the active involvement of the private sector.

The battle for reforming education in Colombia continues. In 1994 a new general education law decentralized the management of the school system to departments, and school have been given tools, through the "Institutional Education Project," to develop their own pedagogical plans.

education services provided (Zuckerman and de Kadt 1997). Chile introduced a private provider system through government subsidies, allowing privately managed schools to compete with publicly managed municipal schools. Science-oriented schools in Costa Rica and charter schools in Nicaragua are setting high academic standards and promoting competition. School grants and awards in Paraná, Brazil, aim to motivate self-evaluation, teamwork, and a competitive attitude in public schools. Scholarships for poor students, competitive provision of additional resources and technical assistance, and publication of learning results are among the experiments underway to increase competitiveness in schools.

Other incentives have been used to promote teacher behavioral changes, besides the professional involvement in the planning and implementation of reform, such as finan-

cial incentives and recognition. Some of these are aimed at improving teachers' qualifications by establishing different salary scales; other incentive systems emphasize teamwork. In Colombia, for example, there was an attempt in 1995 to increase teachers' pay according to results attained on students' achievement tests. (Although the teacher association negotiated an initial agreement, political circumstances changed, and the association subsequently blocked the incentive program's implementation.)

Third, while the first phase of reforms often established a basic database, the second phase of reforms needs to ensure that this database is used by the actors to facilitate and ensure accountability. Two particular actions will be required for this to occur: First, the management information systems that have been designed and piloted need to be made accessible as tools for the public and parents to obtain usable information, and for education researchers to have access to the raw data. Second, the student assessment systems that have been piloted in most countries need to be made universal; they need to provide student-specific information that helps teachers diagnose learning problems, and they need to provide school-specific information that permits ministries to identify schools that need additional support. Such assessment systems also provide parents with the information they need to carry out their role in ensuring accountability. Critics of student testing claim that simply providing test results does not provide a good measure of the value-added of the school. New Zealand provides an example of how an independent audit agency can provide more comprehensive information to teachers and parents on school performance (see Box 5.4).

Fourth, the emphasis on changes in structures in the first phase of reforms needs to be shifted to an emphasis on classroom pedagogy and technology in the next wave of reforms. The impact on learning of increasing parental voice and

improving information and accountability are constrained by the pedagogical practices of teachers, which will not easily change. The speed of change can potentially be increased through the use of distance learning, both to deliver in-service teacher training and to complement teachers' work in the classroom. Changing pedagogical practices—from top-down teacher dictation to having the teacher as a learning resource and facilitator of individual exploration and group learning (sometimes called "learning to learn")—will, in turn, require the strong support of teacher trainers, both in-service and pre-service. The first generation of reforms has had little impact on pedagogy and the reform of teacher training; the second generation of reforms will not succeed if these two areas are not specifically and intensively addressed.

Finally, the second phase of reforms needs to pay specific attention to the design of incentives to facilitate the development of a "learning organization." If teachers, schools, and systems as a whole do not develop the capacity to learn from the successes and failures of past experience, the prob-

---

BOX 5.4

New Zealand's Education Review Office

To deal with the problem of information asymmetry and establish greater accountability, New Zealand has established the Education Review Office (ERO) as part of its education reform. The ERO is an independent body charged with assessing the performance of schools and reporting to the public its findings and recommendations.

The independence of the ERO is ensured by vesting the responsibility for assessing the performance of schools in a Minister for Education Review, who reports directly to parliament, rather than the minister of education. To carry out his responsibility, the Minister for Education Review works out a purchase agreement with ERO for a specific number and quality of individual school-accountability reviews, thematic national and regional evaluation reports, and publications to be delivered on agreed dates.

Under the law the ERO has the authority to enter and inspect schools as it deems necessary. The present practice, however, is for ERO to audit a school every three years and to conduct follow-up visits for schools with significant problems. In assessing school performance, trained ERO reviewers visit schools and see whether they are in compliance with relevant laws and their charters. Following

evaluative criteria prepared by the ERO, the reviewers observe classroom practices and interview members of the board of trustees, school directors, teachers, and students. The ERO does not set educational standards; it simply measures school performance against the ministry of education's best-practice guidelines on teaching, school governance, and management. It is, however, within the power of the ERO to measure student learning through standardized tests, although it is not currently doing so.

In New Zealand, the principal-agent relationship has been redefined and made effective in the education sector through a variety of mechanisms. Contractual agreements for the provision of services ensure the accomplishment of the ministry of education's work of providing quality schooling and having it appropriately and objectively evaluated. School boards of trustees empower parents to positively influence their children's schools. Independent and publicly available accountability reviews by the Education Review Office are keeping school authorities and teachers on their toes.

Source: Perris (1998).

lems that are solved today will reappear tomorrow. If the benefits of educational reform are to be sustained, teachers must learn to carry out their own action research to identify problems and seek solutions; school supervisors must play an important role in facilitating this kind of research by teachers; and teacher trainers must also actively support teachers and communicate to future teachers the lessons being learned. There are no hard-and-fast rules about how to create learning organizations, but the extensive research on successful organizations can provide clues. National ministries and regional secretariats of education will certainly play a key role in the creation and maintenance of learning, and this will require fundamental changes in the organization and functions of ministries, with a new focus on support rather than control.

The Political Economy of Reform

Latin America has by now acquired considerable experience in educational reform. These experiences, which have been reviewed in detail elsewhere (see Alvarez and Ruiz-Casares 1997), suggest that the political economy of reform needs to be divided into two distinct stages—design and implementation.

In the first stage, a reform is designed, legislated, and regulated. When reforms can be designed within the existing legal framework or when governments enjoy overwhelming majorities in the legislature, the first stage of reforms is not complicated. Reforms can be designed by technocrats inside or outside the education ministry and subsequently adopted and announced by the government. When governments do not enjoy majority representation in the legislature, or when proposed reforms would threaten the interests even of party members, sophisticated political strategies are needed. In cases such as the Dominican Republic (see Box 5.5), El Salvador (see Box 5.6), and Chile, a process of consensus building and participation accompanied the development of the reform framework. This process, however, does not guarantee the successful implementation of the reforms.

In the second stage, reforms are implemented. Regardless of the political power of the government, implementation is a complicated business. Latin American experience, however, suggests a few factors to consider in the implementation of an educational reform.

The Interests of Principal Actors. This involves opportunities as well as challenges for reform implementation. New actors could bring support and direction to the reforms. The private sector, for example, now understands the need for better education of the labor force for its own success in the global context. The first stage of the educational reform in Dominican Republic, initiated by the private sector, illustrates the possibilities of cooperation between the private and the public sectors. The ministers of finance, who traditionally had considered the social sector only as a source of expenditure, are now more committed to the development of human resources. The declaration of the Summit of the Americas is an expression of this new climate of political interest in education by all government agencies. On the other hand, teacher associations continue to resist the educational reforms that introduce accountability, decentralization, and performance-based pay.

Parental Voice and Choice. Parents may fear that local participatory school management will cause a decline in government financial commitment to schools. However, providing voice and choice to parents and communities helps balance the interests in favor of children, the ultimate principals in the educational organization, and introduces some degree of competition among schools. Various countries are trying out creative financial alternatives to respond to the new reform philosophy. Several countries, including Chile and Colombia, have experimented with voucher systems with varying results. Trinidad and Tobago schools have employed school donation schemes with in-kind local contributions, and Ecuador has tried competitive mechanisms for public-school improvement through the *Red de Apoyo Técnico*.

Incentives for Change. The negotiation process underlying reform efforts has varied from country to country with diverse results, given different political circumstances and reform packages. In some cases, compensation schemes for teachers, such as increasing their salaries or maintaining the purchasing power of their salaries (in Chile, for example) have been used to obtain their support. Other countries have provided bonuses for participating in reform activities, as in the Dominican Republic. Non-monetary incentives, such as participation in the reform planning, and professional development have worked in Paraguay (Hobbs and Rentel 1997). Appealing directly to teachers and generating community support were successful strategies to the *Escuelas Integrales* (Integrated Schools) reform program in Venezuela (Lowden 1996). However, linking incentives for educators to school performance, and align-

BOX 5.5

The Dominican Republic: Reform Captured by the Bureaucracy

Businessmen and -women in the Dominican Republic played a decisive role in shaping an educational reform at the beginning of this decade. Working with educators and NGOs, such as EDUCA and *Plan Educativo*, they presented a public declaration, *"Pacto por la Patria,"* the precursor to the Ten Year Education Plan in 1992. The Ten Year Plan resulted from a long process of discussion, negotiation, and consensus building, in which nearly 50,000 Dominicans participated. Building national consensus implied reorganizing school committees comprising teachers and parents; holding a national pedagogical congress attended by teachers, parents, university professors, and government officials; and establishing a common objective, the development of a national education plan. A special newspaper, *El Consenso,* served as a tool for communicating the vision of a national education plan in a broad social campaign. Incentives for teachers to participate in the dialogue included financial rewards, professional advancement, and recognition.

In addition to revitalizing education, the process of building a national consensus helped to strengthen the practice of participatory democracy in the country. Consensus was reached via a two-stage process, which included an assessment of the socioeconomic situation of the country and educational needs, and the development of a reform agenda for education. This consensus supported intensive activities on several fronts such as curriculum development, reinvention of school management, textbook production, and establishment of evaluation mechanisms of learning outcomes.

In 1994 the reform's momentum began to slow. The educational reform that had been initiated and promoted by the civil society became more centralized in its implementation and institutionalized within the ministry of education. The private sector participated less and lost control of the reform process when the ministry of education assumed leadership.

Several factors caused the paralysis of the reform and the decrease of social motivation and participation. Data obtained from interviews with main actors (Zaiter 1997) suggest the following:

- *Local political factors.* Changes occurred in political party strategies and leadership, and the initial strong process of social participation was abandoned.
- *Organizational factors.* Necessary changes were not made in the structure, operation, and competencies of organizations involved (the ministry of education, for example); the existing behavioral patterns continued to prevail.
- *Financial factors.* There was a lack of national resources to complement international funds

The lessons of the Dominican experience are relevant for other countries wishing to undertake participatory educational reforms. Educational reform is a long-term social learning process. Initial national consensus is critical, but not sufficient, to achieve necessary and fundamental changes in the role of the different agents involved in education.

ing performance with broader social goals still presents theoretical and practical difficulties. Incentives for teacher trainers are also critical in the implementation of long-term educational changes. School-reform implementation depends ultimately on the quality of the teaching force.

Organizational Capabilities of Rule-Setting Organizations. The implementation of reforms depends also on the attitudes and behaviors of bureaucrats. The political (negotiation skills) and technical capabilities (clarity of goals and of incentive strategies) of the reform leaders are critical ele-

ments for the successful implementation of reforms. A small group of highly professional educators in the ministry of education in Chile, with previous experience in project management and research, changed the organizational culture and provided national and international credibility to the reform efforts (Angell 1996). As a social learning enterprise, an educational reform requires evaluation and knowledge-development mechanisms in addition to incentives and motivation for those who lead the process.

BOX 5.6

The Case of El Salvador: Stability, Consensus Building, and Sustained Reform

After years of civil war and internal instability in El Salvador, the Chapultepec Accords were signed in 1992, and agreement was reached on the primary importance of national education reform. With the achievement of socioeconomic stability in the country, economic growth resumed. Steady commitment on the part of the government and especially the ministry of education (MINED) provided the appropriate political environment for implementation of the 1992 National Plan of Action for Education to begin, allowing the establishment of legal, administrative, and financial management mechanisms to enable the effective transformation of the education sector.

The principal component of the reform, Education with Community Participation (EDUCO), began as a pilot project in 1991 and focuses on preschool and primary-level education in rural areas. Through Community Education Associations (ACEs) with democratically elected directors, EDUCO involves the participation of parents and communities in the design and administration of formal education in rural areas. The ACEs assume responsibility for hiring teachers and monitoring their performance, management of school budgets, and maintenance of school libraries and classrooms. This transfer of resources shifts some responsibility for the quality of educational services to local communities, creating a sense of local ownership in the education process. EDUCO proved effective and became an inspiration and model for the 1995 Educational Reform, a 10-year plan for sectoral transformation.

Underscoring the government's commitment to and design of reform and mobilization of local participation is an ongoing dialogue between MINED and the population, which began in 1993 with the establishment of the Advisory Group. The Advisory Group—formed from researchers who undertook the baseline study of the education system and representatives from various governmental and nongovernmental organizations, including universities, teachers' organizations, and MINED—convened weekly to discuss observations, conclusions, and recommendations for action. This was a valuable process of consensus building that enabled a coherence between the various components of the reform and has continued throughout implementation, adding credibility to the process. In 1994, the Advisory Group became the Dynamics Committee, responsible for disseminating the results of the research and Advisory Group discussions to political leaders in all parties, international funding agencies, teachers and students, and MINED personnel, among others. The Advisory Group, and subsequently the Dynamics Committee, served as forums for dialogue that involved all the relevant actors in the education reform process, making possible the formulation of an appropriate action plan.

El Salvador's 1995 national education reform effort was initiated to target problems of limited access, systemic inefficiencies, and low quality. Three factors contribute significantly to the country's ongoing success in addressing those problems:

- Socioeconomic stability and steadfast government commitment to educational reform
- Increased local participation in education administration and management, and
- Active cultivation of a partnership between the government and the population that has supported and sustained the reform.

The 1995 Educational Reform and its principle strategic component, EDUCO, demonstrate the value of incorporating participation of all relevant organizations and actors in the reform of national education systems, a lesson applicable to all countries in the region seeking to reinvent educational services.

Sources: Bejar (1997) and Meza (1997).

Prospects for Reform

There is an increasing awareness on the part of society that a highly skilled labor force and its capacity to use knowledge flexibly will be key to a country's ability to compete in the global marketplace of the next century. This awareness has given education political visibility and has increased the political payoffs to leaders who undertake reforms. However, this payoff probably is considerably higher for initiating and legislating a reform than it is for implementing a reform already in place. And it remains true that reform incurs high political costs up front with the expectation that the educational benefits of the reform will take many years to surface. Still, the prospects for initiating the second phase of reforms are encouraging.

The focus on education is, also, not likely to recede in the near future. Several countries in the region have elected to participate in international testing of educational achievement and in the development of internationally comparable indicators of educational inputs, processes, and outcomes. These international comparisons have the potential to stimulate political debates on education and to increase the political payoffs to reform. One result may be an increase in the political prestige of the education minister, with increased likelihood that presidents will appoint politically skilled individuals and give them the tenure required to carry out reform.

The increased political visibility of education addresses, in part, the fact that the immediate beneficiaries of education reform—students, parents, school directors—are diffuse and not well organized, and the real educational benefits are long-term in nature. Meanwhile, teachers and their associations often view themselves as incurring the costs of the reform, and, as shown earlier, teachers are well-organized, vocal, and often represented by their own politically skilled leaders. A major challenge for governments wishing to introduce—and more importantly to implement—education reform is simultaneously to help the diffuse beneficiaries organize themselves for a more effective political voice and to win over the teachers to the cause of the reform.

Various actions are possible to help implement this strategy. The first phase of reforms created parent and school councils in many countries. Governments (or others, such as private business groups) could help these local councils create effective national councils who elevate the views and concerns of parents, drawing national attention. The first generation of reforms increased marginally the role and powers of the school director. Education ministries could, also, help these actors to organize themselves into more effective voices for further reform. Countries where education has been decentralized could help organize local authorities to lobby constituents more effectively for change.[3]

Another potentially effective action is the creation of effective systems of communication with parents and, especially, teachers to raise awareness about the benefits of reform. As noted earlier, education ministries have traditionally been ineffective in communicating the intentions and expected results of reform, especially relative to teacher associations. One example of how to do this comes from Victoria, Australia, where an education minister who wanted to aid reform efforts created a television studio in the basement of the ministry and began broadcasting programming of interest to teachers directly to schools at the end of every school day.

The dialogue between government and the teacher associations is, of course, a critical one, which is made more difficult by the fact that the associations may be aligned with political parties that oppose fundamental reform efforts and, hence, see little benefit in the government's succeeding in its reform efforts. Despite this political opposition, it is critically important for governments to have continual and open dialogue with teacher associations and to listen and be receptive to their views. Strong opposition by teacher associations to proposed education reforms at the very least means increased difficulty in implementation. To avoid resistance and conflict over reforms in El Salvador, the education minister created an advisory group comprising diverse actors in civil society to advise on the reform effort. The result was the development of a national consensus on reform.

Most reform efforts provide ways to compensate teachers for what they consider the costs of reform. In particular, the emphasis on upgrading the skills of teachers provides the opportunity to increase teacher compensation, linked to demonstrated improvement in teaching skills. Other reforms—for example, in Chile and Uruguay—entail the creation of single-shift schools, with increased hours of teaching and class preparation. These reforms can offer teachers both increased pay and improved professional status.

The educational institutions that exist now are the result of an evolution in which social learning has played a decisive role. The "rules of the game" and the standards and expected patterns of behavior cannot be changed except by a broad social and political learning process rather than by a mechanistic, often top-down, intervention. For any learning to occur, there will be a need for motivation and incentives as well as continuous reassessment and creativity. This represents the challenge of the educational reforms in LAC at the turn of the century.

Notes

1. While there are multiple associations, we assume, for purposes of exposition, there is only one.

2. There are many examples in Latin America of this power—and its consequences for education ministers. Recently, one minister was forced to resign because he planned to transfer teachers across schools to ensure a minimum class size.

3. The Brazilian Council of State Education Secretariats is a good example. The state education secretaries meet periodically, on their own, to exchange experience and to develop common positions on national educational issues. The Brazilian model contrasts with councils organized by and managed by education ministries.

CHAPTER 6

The Challenge of Judicial Reform

A S THE NATIONS OF THE LATIN AMERICAN AND CARIBBEAN REGION HAVE BEGUN TO modernize the machinery of government, reform of the courts, the public prosecutor, and the other organizations that together constitute the judicial system has emerged as a priority. This has been as true for those countries in the region whose legal systems are based on English common law as it has been for those whose systems are rooted in European civil law. Whatever a nation's legal tradition, its judiciary performs a set of functions essential to the governmental process: the enforcement of the criminal law, the resolution of conflicts between private citizens and those between the citizen and the state, and the determination of the law itself (Shapiro 1981). No political system can work well without a judicial system that preserves social order, fosters voluntary exchange, redresses complaints against the government, and contributes to the lawmaking process.[1]

The very nature of the judicial system makes reform difficult to realize. Judiciaries are deliberately insulated from short-term fluctuations in social preferences and the relative power of social groups. The aim is to ensure that judicial decisions are based on neutral legal principles, not the identity of the parties or the facts of the particular dispute. While the mechanisms that provide for judicial independence, and their effectiveness, vary greatly from nation to nation, in every instance they complicate the reform effort. Walling

off the judiciary from political pressure means that popular demands for reforms will not by themselves guarantee that reform is initiated.

Another obstacle to reform is the specialized nature of law and the judicial process. In every system, law is the domain of the professional expert: the jurist, the academic, the lawyer. It is this community that controls society's discourse about law and that enjoys a monopoly, or near monopoly, on the knowledge required to design and implement a reform project. Therefore, at least some members of this community must be enlisted in the reform project for it to succeed.

Professional roles and self-image also affect the judiciary's willingness to undertake reforms and the pace at which they are implemented. Unlike common-law judges, who typically are appointed to the bench after long careers

as practitioners, civil-law judges typically are career bureaucrats. But they share with their common-law counterparts an independent, craftsman's approach to their work, which conflicts with such basic management techniques as standardization of procedures, organizational guidelines for prioritizing attention to tasks, or quantified output targets. Furthermore, judges traditionally are kings (or queens) in their courtrooms and frequently reject the notion of officially delegating even logistical decisions to professional managers or of sharing support staff.[2] Professional norms and judicial independence (however much violated in fact) also conflict with measures to monitor performance, to increase accountability, or to deal openly with disciplinary and ethical issues. No profession likes to air its dirty laundry in public, but judges, to their collective detriment, seem particularly reluctant to do so.

This resistance to change manifests itself in many ways. Judiciaries have never been the leaders in adopting modern management techniques or new technologies, and it is not uncommon for them to be decades behind the rest of the public sector in this regard. Arcane personnel practices and procedural requirements are the norm, not the exception. So is antiquated equipment; the computer, the fax, or more efficient methods for recording data are usually adopted late and only after considerable hand-wringing over their "legality."

Finally, many systemic vices or distortions are commonly encountered across legal traditions. Judicial corruption, a retreat to legal formalism (deciding to the letter but not the spirit of the law) in the face of external threats, and decisions skewed by partisan or other biases are frequent complaints, especially in societies undergoing rapid and fundamental change. While often initiated by those outside the judiciary to cut individual transaction costs, they can become part of the informal organizational culture and thus embedded in a network of vested interests that will oppose their elimination. The opportunities for, forms of, and incidence of corruption vary widely, but there is no judicial system where corruption is unknown.

Not surprisingly, then, whether the legal system is based on common law or civil law, similar measures will improve the operation of the judicial system and the performance of the judges, clerks, and others who work within it. Common prescriptions include higher budgets and salaries; more staff, equipment, and infrastructure; training for judicial and administrative personnel; the adoption of modern administrative practices for individual courtrooms and entire judiciaries; the introduction of new categories of judicial and administrative staff; revised judicial appointment systems and qualifications for candidates; and the introduction of performance and ethical standards and monitoring as well as disciplinary systems. The rewriting of substantive and procedural laws is also a frequent element of a reform package.

Despite the commonalities of the issues, differences between civil- and common-law countries do produce a different mix of elements and a different emphasis. Reform in civil-law countries, for example, has often laid greater stress on procedural reforms. Civil-law systems traditionally rely on written rather than oral proceedings, but as caseloads have grown, the time and expense required to reduce everything to writing has exceeded system capacity.

Thus, there has been a move throughout the civil-law world to substitute oral for written procedures.

Judicial training is another example where the content, form, and integration into the judicial career differs depending on whether judges are politically appointed or whether they are career bureaucrats. Most reforms attempt to increase the merit element in appointments, but developing the criteria for assessing merit is still debated, even within individual systems. How countries define problems and what they deem acceptable remedies also affect reforms. American advisers working in Latin America in the early 1990s found that their local counterparts were often less concerned with reducing delays than with measures to combat corruption and increase judicial independence. While Latin Americans were interested in adopting more adversarial criminal proceedings (which they perceived as more effective and less susceptible to abuse), they were less receptive to the idea of plea bargaining, a procedure many U.S. jurists regard as critical to making Latin justice systems work better. While mediation, arbitration, and other forms of alternative dispute-resolution mechanisms have now achieved regionwide acceptance, even five years ago many judges and lawyers in the region saw them as abominations, arguing that they threatened judicial integrity and basic due-process rights.

It is the means for introducing change, however, that seem to vary most consistently between civil- and common-law traditions. In those countries where the legal system is based on common law, the judiciary is typically more independent of the political branches of government, and the judiciary itself more often takes the lead in introducing and implementing reform. In the United States, the legislature will often mandate reform but leave it up to the courts to design and apply the measures required to implement it. In civil-law systems, particularly those influenced by French law, the judiciary is much less independent (Merryman 1996). In these systems matters are more often left to the executive branch. This tends to be true whether the judiciary is managed by the executive branch or is responsible for its own governance. This has frequently produced conflicts in Latin American reforms because of their judiciaries' historical aspiration for more autonomy in the U.S. style and a long tradition of extensive if usually illegal executive intervention in court affairs.

These conflicts raise a final dilemma, which in one form or another confronts all judicial-reform efforts. Even reforms managed by a non-judicial agency, and certainly those headed by the judiciary, usually combine two goals—greater efficiency and greater independence. Both internally (at the level of individual judges) and externally (in relation to other political and economic forces), the judiciary is usually not conceived as a command system. Individual judges and judiciaries are expected to carry out their functions in compliance with the law, rather than because of the instructions of a superior or extra-judicial actor. As the Latin American case suggests, the two goals are related in that the judiciary's lesser efficiency is commonly blamed on external intervention. Nonetheless, whatever the difficulties of making an organization and its members either more efficient or more independent, accomplishing both at once is extraordinarily challenging.

Recent Changes in Latin American Judiciaries

Most judicial systems in Latin America and the Caribbean have suffered from a common set of failings. Resources to support courts and judges have been few. Procedures for resolving disputes have been slow and cumbersome. Appointment and promotion systems have been skewed by political interventions. And a variety of external pressures have often made it difficult for judges to produce neutral, unbiased decisions. One consequence of these flaws has been that citizens either have had to wait years for their cases to be heard or have been denied access to justice altogether. These problems have also fostered such public disdain for the system that many qualified individuals have been unwilling to become judges, while many private actors have preferred to use alternative, and often extralegal, mechanisms to resolve their conflicts. Worst of all, long delays in processing cases, biased decisions, and low public esteem have created a culture of corruption that has infested many Latin American and Caribbean justice systems.

Thanks to the spread of market forces and democratic political systems, judicial reform has become a priority in the region. Markets require a judiciary that can quickly and inexpensively resolve contract and property-rights disputes. The expansion of political participation has created a demand for greater access to justice. Rising rates of conventional and unconventional crime, with negative implications for both political and economic development, have also brought concerns about the systems' ineffectual response. These forces have spurred nations throughout the hemisphere to embark on long-term, systematic efforts to

modernize their justice systems and have encouraged external development agencies to provide funds and technical assistance to support them.

Whether because of the reform efforts themselves or the combined weight of societal pressures, the region's judicial systems have undergone a substantial transformation in recent years. In the past decade alone almost a dozen countries in the region have created judicial councils (*Consejos de la Magistratura*) to oversee judicial appointments and manage their judicial systems, and several more are considering them. Six nations have either amended their constitutions or adopted legislation requiring that a fixed percentage of the national budget, ranging from 6 percent in El Salvador to 2 percent in Panama, be earmarked for the judicial branch. More than a dozen have established judicial-training programs or separate schools to train judges, and over the past decade virtually every nation in the hemisphere has raised judicial salaries, added more courts, and introduced computers and other modern technologies (Correa Sutil 1998). Finally, almost all countries in the region have undertaken legal reform programs, rewriting the codes governing judicial procedures and the substance of the law.

It will be some time before the full impact of these changes can be assessed, but there are at least some preliminary signs that they are having an effect. Judiciaries have become more effective in curbing human rights abuses, including those once perpetrated by some of their members. Individual countries have reduced case backlogs and times for resolving at least some types of cases; more clients are being attended; judges appear more knowledgeable of the law, less arbitrary in their decisions, or at least less flagrant in their abuses; some courts have begun to remove corrupt and incompetent judges and administrators; countries where elites broke the law with impunity have begun to try prominent citizens and officials; and judicial governing bodies (supreme courts or judicial councils) appear to be taking their jobs more seriously.

Still, the amount of improvement has lagged behind the growing demand, and many of the traditional complaints persist, fed in part by heightened public expectations that reform efforts have encouraged. Despite the progress in accelerating the handling of some types of cases, most litigants continue to wait years for their cases to be heard, and the majority are frequently without any access to courts at all. Reports of systemic corruption persist, as do complaints that the augmented budgets are not being used efficiently, that at most production, but not productivity, has increased, and that access to donor funding has encouraged a proliferation of new offices and services that the recipient countries will be hard-pressed to sustain.

This poor performance is also reflected in public evaluations of the system. A World Bank survey of more than 3,600 entrepreneurs in 69 countries found that more than 70 percent of those in the Latin American and Caribbean region identified the judiciary as an impediment to doing business (World Bank 1997a). In Peru more than 90 percent of the respondents in a recent survey reported they had little confidence in the nation's judges, and in Argentina the figure was 87 percent (Dakolias 1996). A recent compilation of public opinion polls from 12 Latin American nations shows that only in Uruguay does a majority trust the courts (Martínez 1996).

There are several explanations for these disappointing results. First, reform takes time, and there is a still greater lag between its impact on judicial operations and on public perceptions. Where judiciaries are doing better, the public may be the last to recognize it. Second, the very societal forces encouraging reform have also complicated the task. Demand is not a fixed target but continues to increase, and meeting last year's goals may not satisfy this year's objectives. Promises of better, often subsidized services have exacerbated this problem, as have factors like the growing crime rate and economic privatization.

Third, reform has itself been a learning process, and it is only in the last few years that participants seem to have come close to assembling all the pieces. The initial tendency to rely on a few isolated interventions (computers, a new code, training programs, or a higher budget) has been replaced by a systemic strategy that acknowledges that multidimensional problems require multidimensional solutions, and that these in turn require the appropriate mix and sequencing. Just what that mix and sequencing are is still a matter for debate, but at least no one is any longer relying on magic bullets.

Fourth, reform has also had to confront some of these magic bullets or traditional solutions, which have hung on despite their having been discredited in practice. Most of them (earmarked percentages of national budgets, external judicial councils, new mechanisms for the selection and tenure of judges) offer partial remedies for real problems, but have been oversimplified or reduced to mere formulas. Many have already been set in national constitutions, mak-ing it still more difficult to modify them as their negative as well as positive consequences become evident.

Finally, it is likely that too much has been asked of reform. The best-performing judiciaries or entire justice sectors will not eliminate crime or gross social inequalities; nor will they compensate for inadequate physical infrastructure or resources in attracting external investment. In short, the task was far more difficult, lengthy, and uncertain than initially envisioned, and it thus is not surprising that the results are less than what was originally hoped.

Improving the Current Approach

There is surely room for improvement. One way is to facilitate greater exchange of information among reformers working in different countries. Few cross-national studies of reform have been published (for a notable exception see Correa Sutil 1994). As a result, too many national programs continue to repeat the same mistakes or reinvent the same procedures. Donors are critical here, since they have the best access to comparative experience, an advantage they unfortunately don't always use even in their own projects.

While the recent emphasis on a systematic approach to reform has increased the scope of recent reform projects, there is still considerable debate over the relative importance and timing of the different elements. Until this debate is resolved, or at least some progress made in that direction, doing what comes naturally or logically will lead to early paralysis (when the easy part is done, the reform ends), counterproductive or redundant results (a computer system is installed before procedures are changed), or a loss of the benefit of complementarities or synergies (while logic dictates that training programs should come later, there are additional benefits to doing some training early, to overcome resistance to change and to develop more information on the state of the system).

Another area for improvement is better and more realistic definition of objectives, both the problems to be resolved and what can be achieved. Judicial reform by itself will not resolve fundamental societal ills. Furthermore, many reform programs contain internal inconsistencies—goals which at least over the short run cannot be achieved simultaneously. For example, as a study of the Spanish judicial system demonstrates (Pastor Prieto 1993), providing subsidized services for all citizens may increase the level of demand so much that it will increase rather than reduce delays. It may also drive out the search for more effective alternatives that could reduce the pressure on courts by filtering or diverting some kinds of complaints or encouraging other means for reducing transaction costs.

The setting of realistic objectives must also address costs and the sustainability of new or higher levels of services. The apparent inattention to this issue has been exacerbated by the easy availability of donor funding. Once these funds begin to disappear, national systems may find they cannot sustain the special services, ambitious training programs, and equipment financed by external resources. In an era of cutbacks in public-sector budgets and staffing, justice institutions have enjoyed a special exemption, but it is one that is already being questioned.

A related consideration is the definition of judicial roles and powers. As programs produce more independent and often more activist judiciaries, some negative reactions have already been registered. These are especially evident where activism and independence have run ahead of more basic reforms, but they are also encountered where more professionalized judicial systems have come into conflict with executive and legislative bodies (e.g., Costa Rica). It was perhaps obvious that a more independent judiciary would affect the powers of other branches of government, and that this would lead to some unaccustomed clashes. However, a balance-of-power equation that is still evolving in the United States and Europe is having to be worked out much more rapidly in Latin America and the Caribbean and may be facilitated by a little more forethought as to where the respective societies wish it to go.

A Different Paradigm

All of the above suggestions for improvement work within the dominant systemic model, which even as regards its political choices still takes a fairly mechanistic, technocratic approach to introducing change. Once the basic choices are made, it places enormous faith in the powers of formal rules, organizational structures, and technological innovations to reorient behavior. The current reform agenda could be enriched by the addition of another perspective, one that draws on the insights of institutional economics in its depiction of institutions, "the rules of the game," as "the humanly devised constraints that shape human interaction" (North 1990, p. 3). This would allow a focus on some of the more perplexing issues of reform: how an organization comes to transform itself, and what that means for its leadership, its members, and those who benefit from the existing pattern of activities.

Whatever their wider social costs, the persistence of dysfunctional organizations rests on vested interests, incentive structures, and ingrained patterns of behavior and expectations, none of which will be reversed automatically and many of which can be easily transferred to "reformed" organizational settings. Sometimes this is because reformers have placed too much faith in the power of technology (as in the frequent observation that computers are simply used to automate inefficient systems, leading to automated inefficiency) or legal norms. More often it is because social engineers have not looked deeply enough into the factors reinforcing undesirable behaviors; they change the form or titles of organizations without altering the pressures and incentives shaping the actions of their members. An external judicial council composed of judge-like members is no more likely to oversee administrative matters any differently or any better than the internal governing body (court or council) it replaced. More highly paid judges may have one less reason to succumb to bribes; the other reasons, unfortunately, are still in place.

Some of the resistance to change is self-interest, always difficult to overcome but especially challenging where the likely losers are also the organizational and political leaders charged with directing reform. When leaders commit to a reform, they frequently do not realize the full implications of that commitment. Once they do, their enthusiasm may decrease sharply, either because of what they will lose directly (privileges, power, rent-seeking opportunities) or because of the costs they incur in fighting the resistance of others. Not all resistance is calculated self-interest. In the design and implementation of reform programs, the very institutional constraints targeted for elimination are likely to impede progress.[3] Aside from the obvious problem of endemic corruption and thus the threat that reforms will be misused or directed to private gain, these include factors like weak planning and management skills, a lack of understanding or appreciation of non-traditional disciplines and technologies, excessive reliance on relational networks as opposed to merit or expertise in selecting staff, and an approach to setting goals that is formalistic or principle-driven rather than instrumentalist or results-based.

Increasingly attention has thus focused on who should direct a judicial reform and how to ensure a continued "political will" to change. The obvious choices—the judiciary itself or the executive, or some kind of judicial council—all have drawbacks. Most likely, a better solution will have to draw in other stakeholders, including the general public and organized civil society, to create a sort of ad hoc principal. But including more interests does not resolve the problems of inadequate subjective models and other cultural constraints, inexperience, or more broadly inclusive but still self-serving agendas. This is an area where the participation of external donors may be useful in supporting the formation of these ad hoc principals, providing them with technical input, and helping to set and enforce the procedural rules shaping their operation. Still, if reform is to succeed, in addition to a good strategy, an agency or principal who can oversee its enactment is obviously essential, and this is equally true whether the reform enjoys external assistance or is entirely domestically supported.

A second set of questions, deriving in part from the first, has to do with the nature and internal governance of the new judiciary itself and its relationship to its broader institutional environment. Whatever its prior level of dependence or independence and whatever the external participation in its reform program, the judiciary has its own formal and informal rules of operation, institutionalized roles, and culture. These internal characteristics are shaped by the larger institutional setting, but they also distinguish members' understandings, motivations, and behavior from those of any other social actor. Although the ultimate goal of reform is to transform the organization's impact on its environment—its output—this obviously requires changing internal relationships and understandings and the environment's impact on them.

It may be true that "organizations will be designed to further the objectives of their creators" (North 1990, p. 73), but in the case of the judiciary the situation is far more complicated—first, because the creator (reform principal) is at best a proxy for (or agent of) the public or society, but also because this organization and its members are intended to have some degree of external and internal autonomy. A simple hierarchical chain of command between the agent (judiciary or individual judge) and principal (the "public" or a court or council) will not work, and thus a more complex internal structure and set of external relations are required. The goal at all levels is enhanced independence and accountability in pursuit of a common set of objectives. To date the objectives remain as unclear as the means for setting them and the identity of those who will do it; the mechanisms for internal and external accountability are just beginning to be debated, and the

question of greater independence is still caught up in a series of traditional and seemingly oversimplified formulas. However, before much progress is made in addressing the third, more technically based set of questions—on how to reorient judicial actions—considerably more attention should be directed to the issues of what the reformed judiciary will look like as an organization, how its objectives and values will be defined, and how it will reconcile the goals of increased independence and accountability, both internally and externally. Unless these issues can be answered more creatively, the most likely alternative developments are either total bureaucratization or independent irrelevance.

The third area, and one where institutional analysis supplies some answers as well as questions, is that of shaping the actions of individual judges. One reason why so many of the region's judicial reforms are failing to meet expectations is that they have largely ignored a central insight of the new learning on public-sector reform: that an organization is ultimately a collection of individuals with their own goals, and that unless these goals are aligned with those of the organization itself, performance will lag. The assumption implicit in most reform initiatives has been that judges, lawyers, and others within the judicial system are motivated solely by an interest in satisfying the public demand for a reliable, reasonably priced justice system. From this it has followed that if the system is not fulfilling this demand, it is for want of adequate resources, lack of properly trained personnel, or because of problems with the way the judiciary is organized. The continuing problems many systems are experiencing in spite of almost a decade of reforms argue for reconsidering this assumption. Successful reforms of other parts of the public sector show that reform is far more likely to succeed if it begins with a realistic assessment of the incentives faced by the people who make up the system, and if it is followed by measures that bring these incentives into line with the public's goals (Boston et al. 1996; T. Moe 1984).

An Incentive-Based Approach to Redirecting Judicial Behavior

This section suggests how this approach can be applied to a central problem in judicial reform: increasing judicial productivity. It bears repeating, however, that applying the techniques without resolving some of the foregoing questions—as to overall goals and internal organizational dynamics—may well produce more obedience in the pursuit of the wrong objectives. Unfortunately, their resolution is far more difficult, and far more political, than what follows.

Attracting the Right Candidates

Judges are the heart of the judicial system. Unless they apply themselves diligently and honestly to the resolution of the cases brought before them, procedural reforms, computerization, and other changes to the system will have little impact. But while many reform measures try to boost judicial output by providing judges with better tools and more training, comparatively little attention has been given to the reasons why people become judges, what motivates them to work hard once they are a judge, and how this hard work translates into better performance of the judicial system as a whole.

Job security, pay, prestige, ego, and a sense of public service are among the reasons why law school graduates might choose a judicial career. Whether these are in fact what attracts individuals to seek a judgeship, whether there are other reasons, and what the relative importance of the different reasons are, has yet to be explored in any systematic fashion. Doing so is critical, because the rewards a job offers determine the kind of individual who will apply for a position. If the current set of rewards are attracting the wrong kinds of candidates for the judiciary, they need to be altered.

Brennan (1996) uses the example of tenure for university professors to illustrate how this can be accomplished. Universities wish to grant tenure only to those interested in genuine scholarship, but some portion of those applying want tenure solely because it offers them the quiet life. One way universities can change the distribution of true scholars and shirkers in the applicant pool is to offer a lower wage but supplement it with graduate student assistants, better research facilities, and other non-cash perquisites appealing to the true scholar. Shirkers would presumably be interested only in the cash wage, and thus such a compensation package should change the distribution of scholars and shirkers in the applicant pool.

Just as universities could vary the package of financial and non-financial rewards offered to those seeking tenure to screen for desirable applicants, the region's judicial systems could likewise vary the compensation package offered prospective judges to attract candidates with the desired characteristics. The first step is to identify what those characteristics are. Judicial systems vary in the demands they put on judges and therefore on the kind of individual best-suited for a judicial career. At one extreme is the American-style judiciary, where politically appointed judges wield significant power over the other branches of government. At the other lies some civil-law systems, where career judges typically defer to legislative or executive action. The profile of a person who will perform well under the one system is unlikely to resemble the profile of one who would perform well in the other.

One trait that would seem to be desirable regardless of the system is a willingness to expend a significant amount of time and effort early in one's career mastering a large body of learning. Judges in any system need to know a great deal about the law to do their job well. Those willing to put in long hours early in their professional life studying the law are the kinds of individuals whom judicial systems should try to attract. A second trait would be a willingness to forgo short-term gain in favor of longer-term rewards. Like many professions, the rewards from being a good judge—peer respect, a sense of craftsmanship, and professional accomplishment—accumulate over time. Those looking for a quick payoff are unlikely to perform well. They are also more likely to succumb to the temptation to accept a bribe than those with a longer time horizon.

Arruñada (1996) argues that a profession that requires applicants to pass a stiff entrance exam for admission, that gives them an opportunity to advance during their career by scoring well on additional exams, and that pays less than what they could earn elsewhere early in their career but more than what they could earn later, will attract individuals with these traits. The exam requirement will screen out those unwilling to master a significant body of professional learning. Offering those already in the profession a chance for more rapid promotion if they do well on subsequent tests serves as a further screen. Deferring compensation until later in life will tend to select out those interested in short-term gains.

Incentives for the Best Judges

Just as more research is required to determine what kinds of incentives now make judging attractive and whether these need to be altered to affect the kind of individual seeking to become a judge, so too is research required to ascertain what incentives to work hard those who are already judges have, and whether and how they might be altered to encourage better performance. In Latin America, FIEL (1996) has identified the factors that create *disincentives* for Argentine judges to perform well, but research on an appropriate *incentive* structure remains to be done. Work conducted in the United States shows that trial-court judges are motivated by the chance of promotion to a higher court, the desire to exercise discretion in their rulings, and a wish to avoid heavy workloads. To these, an American appellate judge, Richard Posner (1995), adds considerations of prestige and reputation, the ability to exercise power, the deference accorded judges, and the intellectual and emotional pleasures associated with resolving conflicts. Given the differences between the U.S. judicial system and those in the LAC region, without empirical research it is impossible to say whether these same factors are important determinants of judicial behavior in LAC.

Once these factors are identified, a second priority is to find ways to capitalize on them when crafting reform measures. Some steps in this direction are already being taken. Whereas in the past promotion to a higher court was frequently based on personal or political ties, El Salvador, Honduras, Colombia, and Chile are among those countries that have recently introduced merit-based promotion systems. Establishing the appropriate criteria is proving to be a challenge, but if it turns out that the chance for promotion is as powerful an incentive for first-instance judges in LAC to work hard as it is for American trial-court judges, the effort will be well worth it.

Besides the possibility of promotion, Posner suggests that greater transparency in the conduct of judicial business is a way a judge's interest in a good reputation and desire for prestige can be harnessed to improve judicial productivity. When judges must conduct trials and other proceedings in the open, their conduct is exposed to scrutiny by lawyers, litigants, the press, and the public, and to the extent they value reputation and prestige, they have an incentive to acquit themselves well in public proceedings. Evidence to support this link between public scrutiny and better performance comes from a recent report of a committee weighing the merits of allowing trials in New York state to be televised. It found that when cameras were present in the courtroom, judges did a better job of conducting trials and other proceedings, and were also likely to behave in ways that fostered respect for the judicial system (New York State Committee 1997).

Disclosing how individual judges voted when decisions are made by a panel of judges could have a similar effect. Secret balloting can foster irresponsible voting, whereas disclosure, by facilitating public scrutiny and criticism, may again supply a motive for a judge concerned with reputation and prestige to decide cases carefully. In some countries in the region decisions are issued in the name of the full court and dissenting votes suppressed. If further research confirms the link between transparency and better performance, this practice should be reconsidered.

Traditionally, the chief means for holding a judge's work up to public examination has been the written opinion. It discloses why the judge ruled for one party and not the other and the reasons for the ruling. But in many countries in the region little attention is given to judicial opinions, particularly those of the lower courts. They usually are not published, and it can often be difficult to obtain a copy of an opinion even from the judge who wrote it. Again, if public scrutiny creates an incentive for judges to work harder, reform measures ought to lay greater stress on the publication, dissemination, and public evaluation of the judicial opinions of lower-court judges.

The Remuneration Issue

Ironically, although it is commonly thought that financial incentives play a secondary role in motivating judges, most of the attention that has been paid to how the existing reward system affects judicial behavior has focused almost exclusively on the financial side of the equation, and in particular on the relationship between salary and corrupt behavior. The theory has been that if judges are paid better, they will be less likely to take a bribe. Yet even on the narrow issue of salary level and corruption, reform measures have failed to apply what is known about the impact pay has on employee loyalty to maximize the deterrent effect higher pay can have on an individual's willingness to accept a bribe.

A judge offered a bribe must decide on economic grounds whether the amount offered is worth the risk. The gain is the size of the proffered payment. Assuming that a judge discovered taking a bribe would be immediately discharged, his or her loss equals the amount of income that would be forgone if fired. A judge who would earn $100,000 for the rest of his or her judicial career, but only $50,000 for the same period if forced off the bench, thus risks losing $50,000 by accepting a bribe. But while this

BOX 6.1

Measuring the Performance of a Judicial System

One way to measure the performance of a judicial system is through *opinion surveys*. Litigants or others who have had direct contact with the system can be asked about their experiences. In evaluating its judiciary last year, the government of New South Wales asked 255 individuals who had brought lawsuits in the civil courts how fair they thought the proceedings had been and whether they were satisfied with the resolution of their cases. Alternatively, the public at large can be surveyed about its perception of the courts and the other components of their country's justice system, a technique the World Bank sometimes uses when assessing a nation's judiciary.

A second way to measure performance is through *quantitative indicators of output*. Data on caseloads and court expenses can be used to develop measures of the speed with which courts resolve cases and the costs involved. Particularly in Latin America, one of the most important indicators of judicial performance is the average delay litigants encounter before their case is resolved. A simple measure is the ratio of the number of cases pending to the number adjudicated or withdrawn in a given period. A more precise measure, as Buscaglia and Dakolias (1996) note, can be calculated using time standards for different types of cases and then calculating the percentage of cases that fall outside a band around the average time.

Other quantitative measures include the percentage of cases reversed on appeal and the number of judges subject to disciplinary action in a given period. The former is a rough measure of the error rate of the lower courts while the latter is an indicator of the integrity of judicial personnel. In its recent study of the Argentine judiciary (1996), Fundacion de Investigaciones Economicas Latinoamericanas (FIEL) argued that both were important measures of the performance of a judicial system.

Efforts to evaluate judicial systems are very recent. The World Bank has a project underway to develop uniform, cross-national measures of judicial performance. Probably the most ambitious attempt so far to measure judicial performance is the annual review of the Australian federal, state, and territorial courts conducted by the Steering Committee for the Review of Commonwealth/State Provision. In its most recent performance review (1988), data on court filings, time to disposition, and cost for Australia's different court systems was combined with available survey data. Two measures of access to justice were also included, one based on court costs and a second on how accessible the courts were to those living in remote areas.

would suggest that a judge would have to be offered at least a $50,000 bribe before it would be even worth his or her while to consider it, a second factor enters into the calculation as well: the probability of detection. If the chances of detection are 50–50, then the amount of the bribe would only have to exceed $25,000 (½($100,000 − $50,000)) for it to be in the judge's economic interest to take it. Likewise, if the chances of detection were very small, say 1 in 20, it would be worth accepting any bribe over $2,500.

Although this example might seem to be merely a way of illustrating numerically the common intuition about corruption and wage levels, putting it this way brings out certain dimensions that might not be so obvious. One is that pay raises aimed at dampening the incentive to take bribes will have little impact so long as the risk of detec-

tion and censure remains very low. Pay increases must be complemented by measures that beef up enforcement efforts, and where pay levels are already reasonable, additional increases might be put off in favor of greater spending on policing corruption.

A second implication is that the economic incentive to take a bribe can be dampened just as much by measures that reduce what those removed for corruption can earn after leaving the bench as it can by a pay raise. In the example above, cutting the amount a judge forced off the bench can earn from $50,000 to $40,000 has the same effect as raising pay $10,000. The surest way of reducing post-judicial income is by incarcerating those discovered taking bribes, yet judges suspected of corrupt behavior are frequently permitted to resign quietly. The stigma of resignation may be sufficient by itself to keep post-judicial income low, but where it is not, incarceration is essential to maintain the deterrent effect the threat of lost income provides.

What this analysis also shows is that a judge's economic incentive to decline a bribe depends on tenure, age, and pension income as well. Those appointed to the bench for a fixed term have far less to lose in terms of future judicial income than those with lifetime tenure. Among those with tenure, older judges, because they are closer to retirement age, would forgo less in future income if forced from the bench than younger judges. Similarly, the size of the pension affects the calculation. When the pension is generous, even older judges may be deterred on economic grounds from considering a bribe.

Where judicial corruption continues to be a problem, reformers should incorporate these factors into their program. There may be advantages to appointing judges for a fixed term, or replacing some or all of the bench periodically, but these advantages must be weighed against the impact such policies have on the economic incentive to accept bribes. Salary differentials between younger and older judges should be also reviewed. If the wage scale has been compressed, consideration should be given to raising the pay of older judges. Where a general pay increase is contemplated, some or all of it might better be deferred until retirement.

Boosting Productivity

While level of pay and the way total compensation is distributed over time can help deter corrupt behavior, experience from the private and the public sectors shows that pay levels can also be manipulated to boost productivity. A common way of motivating workers in the private sector is to make their compensation depend on how hard they work. Rather than paying a fixed wage, the employer rewards them on the basis of output. Public-sector reforms have adapted this technique to government bureaucracies. In England, for example, teacher pay is linked to test scores. The better the students do, the more the teacher earns.

Judicial pay could also be tied to output. Those judges who produced more than their colleagues would be paid more, or be given bonuses, while those producing less would be penalized. Linking judicial pay to judicial performance requires measuring judicial output, however, and this exercise is not nearly as straightforward as tying pay to factory output. First of all, what is it that judges produce?

Although the primary function of a judge is to decide cases, judges may have other responsibilities as well. In some countries in the region they not only resolve disputes but confirm name changes, issue land titles, and administer estates as well.

As a first approximation when designing a pay-for-performance scheme for judges, judicial output might be defined solely in terms of the core judicial function of dispute resolution. This output can be measured in a couple of ways. There are several methods, for example, by which the speed with which a judge resolves disputes can be measured. How many cases a judge decides in a given period is one. The number awaiting decision, the judge's case backlog, is a second. A third is the number of cases that have been pending for more than a given period, say one year or more.

If judges were paid solely by the number of cases decided or the size of their backlog, this would create an incentive to resolve cases without sufficient deliberation just to meet numerical targets. Clearly some measure of the quality of the judge's decisions is required as well. For lower courts, the traditional measure of the quality of a judicial decision is whether it is reversed on appeal. The more time and effort the judge puts into determining the facts and the applicable law, the less the chance a higher court will find reversible error. Thus, to offset the bias that would be introduced if only speed were considered, the percentage of cases reversed on appeal could be made a part of an index of performance measurement, too.

Good judging, however, consists of more than the speedy and accurate disposition of cases. The way a judge treats lawyers, litigants, and witnesses can either promote respect for law or foster cynicism and disdain. Such intangible factors as temperament and demeanor are thus important, too. Although these can't be measured directly, surveys of the lawyers, litigants, and witnesses that have appeared in the judge's court is one way to take them into account.

Drawbacks

All these measures have their drawbacks. Collecting and maintaining the information needed to measure the speed with which judges dispose of cases is costly, and until the recent wave of reforms few judicial systems in the region took the time and trouble to gather it. Also, no matter how hard and how efficiently a judge works, his or her caseload may grow because the legislature failed to add new courts, because of a rise in the number of cases filed, and so on. Isolating those variables that are under a judge's control from those that are not may not be possible.

The rate of reversal on appeal can be misleading as well. A judge may do a poor job of deciding a case but reach a result the appeals court agrees with by chance. The cases appealed may not be a representative sample of the judge's work. And even when the judge is reversed, it may be for reasons outside his or her control: changes in the law, mistakes by the appellate court, and so forth.

There are problems with user surveys, too. It may be difficult to get a representative sample of litigants or witnesses to participate in the survey. If lawyers were to rate judges, judges might begin handling cases in ways that pleased the attorneys, say by drawing out the proceedings to increase fees.

Combining these different measures into a single index of judicial performance also raises questions of weighting. Is it more important that judges process cases quickly, or that their rate of reversal on appeal is low? What is the tradeoff between the two? How should low scores on both be balanced against high ratings on user surveys?

Despite all these difficulties, a performance measure that combined survey responses with rates of reversal on appeal and one or more measures of speed could well provide important information about judicial productivity. If nothing else, the scores of judges sitting on the same court could be compared. Those with high rates of reversal, large backlogs, and poor scores on user surveys are almost certainly putting in less effort than those who do well on three indicators.

Only very recently have policy-makers in the region considered making judges' pay depend upon their performance. FIEL's 1996 study suggested using a combination of performance measures to rate Argentine judges. A recent Chilean statute provides that a portion of judicial pay is to be based upon performance, although how the law is to be implemented is still under consideration. The approach is new and the hazards outlined above suggest that performance-pay schemes must be approached with caution, but no serious reform program concerned with judicial productivity should overlook the possibilities they offer.

Conclusions

The new learning on public-sector reform is still in its infancy, and many of the techniques it has borrowed from the private sector are still being adapted to the unique circumstances found in the public sector. This is even truer when it comes to applying them to the judiciary. But this chapter has suggested that the task is not impossible. There are surely risks—including the danger that a judiciary will come to resemble a tax-collection agency rather than an independent branch of government. However, assuming those shaping the reform have nobler objectives in mind, a little demystification of the judicial role might be just what is needed. It may also help address some of the more transcendent questions as to the direction of reform, who will oversee it, and what the reformed judicial organization will look like. The job will not be easy, but if the result is a better functioning judicial system, then surely the effort will be worthwhile.

Notes

1. Even in France, whose legal tradition formally denies judges any role in the lawmaking process, it is now widely acknowledged that the judicial function inevitably entails lawmaking (Salas 1998).

2. Of course, unofficial and even illegal delegation is a common problem, but aside from denying its existence, judges usually prefer to retain formal control.

3. North (1990, p. 111) observes that "ideas and ideologies" shape the way individuals "interpret the world around them and make choices." A more concrete application became the official justification for Peru's current reform program, much criticized for its erosion of judicial independence. As President Fujimori noted in confronting his critics, "When we begin a reform, we don't consult with its targets."

CHAPTER 7

Public Administration in Latin America and the Caribbean: In Search of a Reform Paradigm

THERE IS NOW A GROWING CONSENSUS, AS WAS REFLECTED IN *THE LONG MARCH*, THAT public administrations urgently need to change if the process of economic and social reform in the LAC region is to succeed. The public administrations of many countries of the region are typically inefficient, unable to deliver services to the most needy, and bastions of opportunistic behavior. Without effective public administration, how can services be delivered more efficiently? How can governments regulate effectively? How can they reach the poor? And how can they function in a way that does not threaten fiscal discipline?

The need for reform may be indisputable, but the way to do it is not. Governments and donors (particularly since the 1980s) have put a good deal of effort into reform, in LAC as in other areas of the developing world. But no clear reform paradigm has emerged, certainly not to the extent it has in such areas as macroeconomic policy, market regulation, and privatization. The success stories are limited, and the jury is still out on how effective the current variety of reform efforts in LAC will prove. The *World Development Report 1997* provides a good tour of the state of the art of reform. Its perspective is institutional, and it takes a realistic view of the problems. Box 7.1 provides a précis of the report's main messages about reforming the state and its administrative apparatus.

This chapter uses an institutional approach (see Chapter 1) to examine the performance of public administrations in LAC. Public administrations are those permanent bodies within government that execute policies made by a political executive or by a legislature. The chapter's main concern is how public administrations do their work, rather than what tasks governments should perform (and how they should devolve tasks). Its concern is primarily the national public administration, although most of the issues are also relevant for subnational administrations.

The problem of public administration: an institutional perspective, the first section of the chapter, outlines a framework for diagnosis of the problems of effectiveness, efficiency, and responsiveness that face public administrations. This framework relies largely on an institutional perspective in which politics play a central role. *"Models" of public*

administration characterizes the "models" of public administration that have emerged in the more advanced countries to tackle these problems, contrasting a classical, "hierarchical" model with an emerging set of ideas and practices coming under the umbrella of the "New Public Management." The new ideas are the fruit of a lively debate that has been cross-fertilized by ideas from other fields, especially theories from the new institutional economics. *Public administration in Latin America and the Caribbean* and *the regional reform experience* examine the LAC region's experience of public administration and its reform, and how it is difficult to fit into any of these models. In fact, in many LAC countries the rules are not what they seem. The underlying informal rules that guide the public administration are the product of institutional conditions that typically differ from those of the more advanced countries.

BOX 7.1
Public-Sector Reform: A World Bank View

The 1997 *World Development Report* was the first wholly devoted to the role of the state. It makes a number of recommendations for reform that provide some guidelines for countries of the LAC region:

- Rethink the role of the state, what it "produces" and how it "produces." The state should, where possible, be a market facilitator.
- Match the role of the state to its capability—and use the resources of the market and of civil society. Weak states should concentrate on the fundamentals—property rights, macroeconomic stability, control of diseases, safe water, roads, and protection of the destitute.
- Build a better public sector by:
  - Promoting a central capacity for formulating and coordinating policy
  - Promoting efficient and effective service-delivery systems through a variety of means (performance-oriented measures, better meritocracies, better information, strengthening "voice") tailored to the circumstances of the activity and the country
  - Fighting corruption through a multipronged approach, including reduced regulation, greater transparency and use of markets, and better enforcement
  - Promoting motivated and capable staff, by using appropriate compensation policies and building esprit de corps.
- Think how to sequence reforms:
  - Make sure that the announced rules, especially for macroeconomic control, are the real ones.
  - Be cautious in introducing the new techniques of public management. For instance, full-blown contracting within the public sector might be preceded by performance measurement. Greater flexibility will be possible only when effective input controls are in place.
  - While an effective, professionalized civil service is being put in place, improve policy-making and coordination; where possible use market mechanisms, such as contracting out and "voice" mechanisms.

The reform models of the more advanced countries thus provide an uncertain guide, and as shown in *reform: constraints and possibilities*, there is still much to learn about effective methods of reform of LAC's public administrations. What is clear is that politics are central.

The Problem of Public Administration: An Institutional Perspective

Good democratic government provides the products the electorate wants effectively, efficiently, and honestly.[1] The problems in doing this can be grouped under two headings, monopoly and the "principal-agent" problem.

The monopoly problem is straightforward and well known. The government mostly provides services for which it is a monopoly supplier. This is by definition the case with public goods: The government's monopoly of legitimate force makes it the dominant purveyor of defense, internal security, judicial services, and so on. Governments also have dominated the production of many other services, such as health, education, and communications. Monopoly provides an incentive to produce inefficiently.

The principal-agent problem, which occurs in market contracts as well as in contracts within hierarchies (see Chapter 1),[2] is more complex. It arises when the agent (who is being compensated to provide goods or services to the principal) has information about product quality (or changing states of nature) that the principal does not. Because the agents wish to extract from the principals as much net value as they can (in the form of rent, ability to shirk, political power, and so on), the asymmetric information problem enables the agents not to act in the principals' interest.

In the public sector, the principal-agent relationship is encompassed by the long chain of accountability that runs from voters, through political representatives and public bodies, down to public bureaucrats. There are thus at least two stages to the principal-agent relationship in democratic government.[3] In a first stage, voters are principals, and political actors (individuals, parties, and elected officials) are their agents. In a second stage, elected politicians (and parties) or government actors (such as presidents and ministers, legislatures, or judiciaries) are principals, and the public bureaucrats or their agencies (such as ministries, statutory boards, or state-owned enterprises) are their agents. At this level of generalization, the two-stage principal-agent problem is the same as the well-known problem of the shareholder-owned firm in which the shareholders exercise their ownership rights, through a representative board, over the firm's managers who in turn have to manage their employees.

In Stage 1, voters' control over politicians is usually imperfect for several reasons. First, there is a problem of collective action (see Chapter 1): It is difficult for individual agents to cooperate to further their common interests. Second, the political institutions purporting to represent voters—the political parties—also face problems of collective action. Third, voters' information on the appropriateness, quantity, and quality of public goods (and technological options for producing them) is imperfect.

In Stage 2 it is similarly difficult for politicians to control public employees. The particular difficulty lies in the problem of defining and measuring with any precision many of the outputs of public administration (a problem greater than in the private firm)—hence the difficulty of monitoring the performance of employees. It is not easy to submit typical government goods and services to the test of the market.[4]

Constraints on Collective Action of Voters

Collective action by voters seeking to have politicians represent their interests (Stage 1) is difficult for several reasons. First, voting rules that encourage fragmentation and multiplication of parties serve particular interests (provision of private goods), rather than the general interest (provision of public goods). The more the fragmentation, the more parties will represent particular rather than general interests, while in order to create governing coalitions, parties will trade particular interests (Cox and McCubbins 1996; Geddes 1994).

Second, information asymmetry may harm the "true" interests of voters and lead to a clientelist system of trading personal favors for votes. Low voter education and poor communications and information, including deficient media, will enable politicians and parties to win votes by providing private goods, such as access to state benefits, at the partial (though not complete) expense of public goods. Politicians and political parties need an army of people to provide these favors, and they need to reward this army in return, typically with government jobs (Geddes 1994; see also Box 6.2 of World Bank 1997a, which describes the "political machine" that characterized many U.S. cities in the nineteenth century).

Third—and related to the information asymmetry— rules and practices of political parties affect their responsiveness to voters. Candidates selected by "closed" parties dominated by oligopolies have greater latitude to act in their own particular interest, or those of the interest groups that provide financial backing, rather than in the interests of voters. Candidates chosen by the broader membership of "mass" parties will be able to change party leadership, and thereby influence the party's policies, presumably in the direction of the general interest.

Finally, successful collective action is "path-dependent" (North 1990): Different countries start from different historical situations; informal norms change more slowly than formal rules; and success is achieved after repeated attempts at collective action. So, even if formal political rules can be easily written, the practice that ensures compliance with the spirit of these rules takes time. Thus, democratic practice will take time to mature.

Special Interests and Other Problems

To the extent that voters lack control, special interests— economic, political, or civil—become important. They can, typically through campaign financing, influence politicians (Stage 1) and they can, by "colonizing" government agencies (through money or influence) limit politicians' control of the public administration (Stage 2). Where democratic practice is weak (i.e., where voters have a collective-action problem) and where societies are fragmented—notably by economic, social, ideological, or ethnic differences—public goods, including good public administration, are under-produced. This is akin to Olson's (1993) argument about the conditions giving rise to "roving bandits," rulers whose hold on power is sufficiently weak that they consume public revenues rather than invest them in producing public goods. ("Stationary bandits," rulers with a better hold on power, have an interest in providing some growth-inducing public goods so that they can continue to tax in the future.) This underproduction of public goods occurs for two reasons: First, fragmentation of power, as we already argued in the case of party fragmentation, leads to the trading of particular interests in political decision-making. Second, when fragmentation expresses itself in terms of political instability and discontinuity over time, politicians, mindful of their low probability of staying in power for long, will look to providing private goods that create a short-term advantage for them, rather than to public goods that would be more likely to assure their longer-term support by the citizenry. Constitutional arrangements often have "veto points" in the name of checks and balances (Cox and McCubbins 1996), such as presidential-congressional checks, judicial review, and term limits on presidents. These checks and balances exist in the name of prudent governance, but they also often reflect competing interests that do not trust each other.

In addition to the problems posed by interest groups, Stage 2 problems are exactly the same as those faced in any organization. And the larger the organization and the more difficult its outputs and behaviors are to monitor, the deeper will be the problem. Organizations seek to overcome the problem through arrangements that determine how authority is exercised (the nature of the implicit contract with employees); offer rewards; promote loyalty to the organization; and promote standards of behavior (Simon 1991).[5] The difficulties of imposing these kinds of arrangements are no doubt affected by different "cultural" traits. Notably, in societies where social capital—"norms of reciprocity and networks of civic engagement" (Putnam 1993, p. 169)—is greater, it is likely that the management of organizations will be easier.

"Models" of Public Administration

The Hierarchical Model

The first modern model of public administration came into being among the modernizing countries of the North Atlantic area in the nineteenth century. It developed as a response to prevalent political interference, corruption, and lack of professionalism—honesty, discipline, and competence—in the then-public service. This now-classical model, which we will call the hierarchical model, is still broadly intact in its essentials. It uses two principal-agent "techniques" to foster more efficient and honest government in the public interest—political checks and balances, and a hierarchical form of organization with centralized control.

Checks and balances are usually embedded in a constitutional separation of powers, which provides for specialization of functions, "second opinions" in decision-making, and oversight of behavior. Elected politicians in the executive and the legislature have a dominant role in making policies.[6] The politicians oversee the execution of policies, but they are bound by rules that limit their interference in

the professional public administration. Other institutions, notably the judiciary and a public comptroller, provide independent, external oversight.

Hierarchical and centralized forms of organization of the public administration ("command-and-control") are meant to provide a means of creating professionalized public servants who are responsive to a broad political mandate, but who are insulated from individualized political influence. In its idealized form, more or less as Weber (1968) defined it, the hierarchical model is characterized as follows:

- Functions are organized into specialized units where accurate financial and technical information flows up, down, and across. Commands are obeyed, agencies cooperate, and decision-making is delegated to the appropriate level (including decentralization to politically independent units of government).

- Qualified personnel are employed on a strict merit basis and under rules that relate pay scales to defined jobs and provide open and fair procedures for hiring, firing, and promotion. Typically, they offer a system of lifetime tenure and other non-pay incentives.

- Budgets (planned income and expenditure) are accurately forecast, and financial systems check that expenditures are made honestly and in accordance with these budgets.

- Records are accurate and procedures are codified.

In general, the hierarchical model has worked well in the more advanced countries to circumscribe the freedom of politicians and public servants to act outside the public interest and to create a professionalized public service. Although political interference, corruption, incompetence, and so on, do exist in the public administrations of these countries, generally they have honest and competent public administrations delivering a wide range of public services.

The hierarchical model is nonetheless under extreme pressure. It was born when government was small. In 1890, less than 10 percent of expenditures in today's OECD countries came from the public sector. But the role of the state expanded enormously—until the 1980s, at least—and by 1995 this share had grown to almost 50 percent (Figure 1 of World Bank 1997a). This growth has led to large public organizations difficult to control and easier for special interests to "capture." It has led to inefficiency and inflexibility. And citizens, more distrustful of government than in bygone times, have expressed increasing dissatisfaction.

The New Public Management

For these reasons all the advanced countries have experimented to modify the hierarchical model. The same checks and balances remain, and the experiments have been on the hierarchy itself. But it is difficult to identify any unique pattern (see Laking 1996). Governments have constantly experimented in new budget techniques, but not always successfully—indeed, new techniques have often led to a loss of budgetary control. They have exploited new information and communications technology. And more recently, they have exercised greater control over the growth of public employment.

Now, however, two particular reform themes—one concerning what governments do, the other how they do it—herald the emergence of radical new ideas that move in the direction of a new model.

- Virtually all advanced-country governments have experimented with increasing "contestability"—i.e., by putting activities back into markets or simulating market conditions. "Contestability" includes privatization and corporatization, voucher schemes (where the state finances a service, typically education, but the market provides it), contracting out, having government departments charge for their services (even to other departments), transferring funds to users, and devolution of activities to lower levels of government.

- A smaller number of governments is pursuing a range of options and experiments to change the way they do business (see Reid and Scott 1994; Holmes and Shand 1995; Nunberg 1995; Laking 1996). A ferment of new ideas focuses on improving performance—by switching the emphasis from controlling inputs to controlling outputs, thereby allowing greater managerial discretion—and on promoting greater transparency and accountability. The new ideas have been serviced by a lively academic debate reflecting competing approaches. A public choice approach emphasizes the need to constrain bureaucrats' freedom through top-down controls. A principal-agent approach concentrates, somewhat to the contrary, on the use of incentives and information to allow bureaucrats more freedom (see Aucoin 1990 on the tensions between these approaches). Some authors have examined the limitations of the new ideas in addressing the problems of advanced countries' public administrations (see, for instance, R. Moe 1994 and Savoie 1995).

It is premature to talk of any consensus, but there is a coalescence of ideas around a promising new model emerging from the debate. We shall refer to the new approach as the New Public Management.[7] It has evoked widespread interest in LAC, as well as other developing and transitional economies. The emerging model, as it applies to public administration, can be characterized along four lines, whose common theme is to borrow from the managerial methods of the private sector:[8]

- *Devolution of decision-making.* Reducing the burden of hierarchical rules and fostering greater discretion at lower points in the hierarchy—operating agencies, regional agencies, subnational governments—allows decisions to be made effectively because decision-makers are closer to the problem and have clearer objectives.

- *Performance orientation.* Changing the accountability relationship from an emphasis on inputs and legal compliance to one on outputs provides incentives that lead to greater effectiveness.

- *Client focus.* Reporting to and "listening" to the clients of the public sector allows governments to understand more systematically what citizens want and to respond with more appropriate outputs.

- *Market orientation.* Making greater use of markets or quasi-markets—typically through management and personnel contracts, competition between public agencies, inter-agency fee-charging, and outsourcing—improves the incentives for performance orientation.

As these kinds of reforms are progressively applied, they are typically intended to change the organizational characteristics of public administrations in the direction of:

- A more strategic orientation to policy-making

- A change in the way agencies are arranged, for instance splitting policy-making from implementation and financing from service delivery

- A financial-management system that emphasizes outputs, provides a full costing of inputs and outputs, and decentralizes ex ante expenditure controls; typically, controls become less specific (broader budget categories, for instance) and external controls are not eliminated, but shift from ex ante to ex post, and

- A decentralized personnel system placing larger emphasis on rewarding performance.

Since the 1980s, most industrialized countries have advanced on various fronts related to the new model. A small number of them, most prominently Australia, New Zealand, and the United Kingdom, have carried out large, integrated reforms in the spirit of the new model. Iceland, Sweden, Chile, and Singapore have also undertaken reform in a similar vein. Australia, for instance, has redefined cabinet, ministerial, and departmental management responsibilities to create stronger central control (through strategic decision-making, budgets, and evaluation) and to give greater managerial discretion to departments. The United Kingdom has so far devolved two-thirds of public employment to executive agencies in order to separate policy-making and implementation and to provide those agencies with greater managerial discretion related to performance. The New Zealand case is of special interest. It is the country that has applied the model in the most complete, conceptually rigorous, and integrated way (Box 7.2).[9]

Reforms in New Zealand, Australia, and the United Kingdom are reaping many benefits of greater efficiency and better services, though not always without controversy. New Zealand and the United Kingdom are the only OECD countries that have been able to cut core public-sector employment in the 1980s and early 1990s. Surveys in New Zealand and Australia generally support the view that the benefits of improved efficiency outweigh the costs. But it is too early for a comprehensive verdict on the desirability or feasibility of the new approach.

Some advanced countries remain wary of the New Public Management (see Nunberg 1995 and Laking 1996). Japan, Germany, and France have been careful to maintain basic bureaucratic traditions, though with some piecemeal reforms in the direction of performance orientation (such as more intensive use of formal evaluation of existing policies, greater use of performance measures, at least in reporting, decentralization, more extensive contracting out of contestable services, and more attention to quality of service). They have maintained a hierarchical tradition on the grounds that it is necessary to maintain an ethic of public service, equitable administration of public law and policy, efficient management of the public service, and control of the size of the public sector and of public finances.

Voice

The New Public Management emphasizes a client focus. One way it does this is through what we call a "voice" model, which emphasizes improved public-sector performance through "listening" or "participatory" techniques

rather than public-sector reform per se.[10] Paul (1998) describes the successful use of a "report card" to provide feedback on public services in Bangalore, India, and thereby to apply pressure to get services improved. Using "voice" shares some common ground with the customer-orientation shown in many New Public Management initiatives, such as the Citizen's Charter in the United Kingdom. But its proponents tend to emphasize its use where populations are politically marginalized—in our terminology, where the principal-voter cannot control the agent-government.

Public Administration in Latin America and the Caribbean

The Performance of Public Administrations

The countries of LAC have more or less copied the hierarchical model in creating their own public administrations. But the hierarchical model has not worked well. In fact, the dominant diagnosis is that the region's public administrations are overcontrolled, and most of them remain poor in the delivery of public services. It is thus not surprising that the techniques of the New Public Management have attracted attention.

A starting point is to ask how well the governments and public administrations of the LAC region have responded to the crises that have beset them since the 1980s. The answer, which has to be impressionistic, is mixed. Many governments of the region have a reputation for the poor quality of their services and excessive regulation. But there is another side: The region has made substantial achievements in economic stabilization. It has also done much to change the role of the state through structural reforms that emphasize privatization and deregulation. Many countries have developed effective regulatory institutions, including autonomous central banks, supervisory agencies in financial markets, and agencies to safeguard competitive markets and regulate natural monopolies. And these countries have considerably decentralized their governments. The region is the only one in the world to have reversed the growth of government in recent years: Public expenditure in the countries of the LAC region averaged 14 percent of GDP in the early 1960s; it rose to 26 percent in the early 1980s, but fell to 22 percent in the first half of the 1990s (World Bank 1997a, Figure 1.2). But this may be as much a sign of fiscal crisis as it is of fiscal responsibility. The over-

BOX 7.2

New Zealand: A Leading Example of New Public Management

The government that came to power in New Zealand in 1984, facing a deep economic crisis, undertook a program of fundamental macroeconomic and structural reforms, but it still found itself saddled with a large, inefficient, and unresponsive public sector. The first step was to institute a widespread program to corporatize, then privatize a large part of the public sector (utilities, manufacturing, services). Next, with the aid of new theories of public management, the government embarked from 1988 on a process of core public-sector reform more radical than has been seen in any other country during this century. The reforms were inspired by the idea that the incentives in the public sector were wrong and that they could be improved by replicating what was found in the private sector. The reform has been dominated by the idea of establishing contract-like relations between the government as purchasers and government agencies as suppliers (i.e., the Stage 2 principal-agent relationship described in this chapter).

The New Zealand public-sector reforms are characterized by the following main elements.

- *Accountability and employee relations.* Department (i.e., ministry) heads lose their lifetime tenure and now work as chief executives with specific performance contracts negotiated with the relevant minister. The department heads are free to run their departments

as they wish. Employees in the public sector now work under private labor law (and under the same conditions as any private firm).

- *Defining performance and delegating authority.* Chief executives are responsible to ministers, under annual purchase contracts, for outputs (actual goods and services); ministers are responsible for outcomes (the effect of these on the community). Ministers are free to buy services from other public or private sources. Chief executives make all current and capital expenditure decisions. To avoid conflicts of interest, policy advice and service delivery have mostly been separated into different agencies.
- *Reporting, monitoring, and coordination.* Monitoring performance requires—as the quid pro quo of enhanced autonomy for chief executives—financial budgeting and regular financial reporting on an accrual basis, exactly as in the private sector (including the treatment of assets and depreciation). Ministers coordinate strategic policy by specifying and publishing the targeted outcomes, through specialized inter-ministerial committees, and by splitting the provision of policy advice and services.

Sources: Bale and Dale (1998) and Schick (1998)

all impression is of a set of countries that, with some exceptions, has had the capacity to dismantle much of the old state, but has not had the resources or capacity to reconstruct a public administration appropriate to the new state.

The problems of government are reflected in the measurement of investors' perceptions of the quality of governance in the region. In terms of three indicators of foreign investors' perceptions reported in Chapter 1—the level of corruption (Figure 1.5), law and order (Figure 1.6), and the quality of the bureaucracy (Figure 1.7)—the average score for the countries of the LAC region in 1998 is low. Even though the indicators have seen notable improvement since 1984, they still show levels of governance comparable to those of Africa and the Middle East, and well below those of East Asia and the industrial countries.[11]

What lies behind this poor performance? Again, a familiar, anecdotal picture is painted in different studies of an overcentralized, overregulated, overrigid, under-motivated public administration:

Many studies of bureaucracy and public administration in Latin America conclude that certain characteristics appear to be persistent despite constant reform efforts. Among the frequently cited characteristics are excessive centralization of authority, supervisory instability, legalism, inadequate communication, and incomplete staff management (Hopkins 1991, p. 701).

Most Latin American public sectors are bedeviled with counterproductive civil service policies and practices that impede their efforts to recruit and retain highly qualified employees and motivate them to perform to the best of their abilities. ... Excessively rigid procedures and practices impede the ability of public managers in LAC to significantly affect the performance of their employees. ... Finally, the institutional structure within which the public sector managers must operate in LAC is often so full of red tape and overlapping responsibilities that it is extraordinarily difficult to take any significant actions, let alone effectively manage complex programs and large numbers of employees (Reid and Scott 1994, p. 39).

It is not surprising, in light of such views, that the dominant diagnosis of many LAC governments is that their public administrations suffer from overcontrol—a diagnosis shared, to an extent, by the international financial institutions. This diagnosis says, at least implicitly, that the traditional approach to public administration has failed. This is why the new market-based approaches to managerial flexibility are attractive, and, thus, there is a close parallel with the diagnosis that has been made for the public administrations of more advanced countries.

Informality in the Public Administration

For the LAC region, however, this diagnosis appears premature. In particular, it does not take account of the institutions in the region that drive performance. The administrations of LAC possess formal rules and structures very much consistent with the hierarchical (and centralized) model prevalent in more advanced countries. But actual bureaucratic behavior is different. As Evans (1992, pp. 176-177) remarks:

Bureaucracy is in *under*-, not over-, supply. This is not only a problem in the post-colonial societies of the sub-Sahara. Even in countries like Brazil that enjoy relatively abundant supplies of trained manpower and a long tradition of state involvement in the economy, predictable, coherent, Weberian bureaucracies are hard to find. The standard perception to the contrary flows from the common tendency for patrimonial organizations to masquerade as Weberian bureaucracies. There is an abundance of rule-making or administrative organizations, but most have neither the capability of pursuing collective goals in a predictable, coherent way nor an interest in doing so.

We shall characterize this difference between the apparent rules of Weberian hierarchy and the real rules as "informality." Informality occurs when actual informal bureaucratic behavior does not correspond with the formal rules. Bureaucracies often may appear to comply with rules, while in reality they are broken or bent. In effect, the rule of law is undermined.[12]

Informality can be characterized in terms of the main functions of government—decision-making, procedural rules, and personnel and financial-management systems (Box 7.3 provides the example of informality in Peruvian government):

- *Decision-making* processes are concentrated among a small number of people and agencies, and the benefits of delegation (and of contact with end users) are forgone. This reflects an absence of cooperation and trust. And yet decision-making is also fragmented; technicians at lower levels often hoard technical information.

- The formal *rules of procedure* are excessive, because managers do not trust public employees. Yet the rules have limited effect, either because an excess of rules means they are contradictory (sometimes reflecting a legal framework that has been designed in pieces that do not fit together; very often, when one law is seen to be ineffective, another is enacted, typically with insufficient effort to annul the first), or because there is no effective mechanism of enforcement, and written rules can simply be ignored. One effect is to minimize the number of administrative interactions (i.e., transactions). Another effect is to encourage informal solutions. If line-ministries do not work, new agencies outside the formal administrative structure are created. If career public servants are ineffective, ad hoc appointments are made to do the job. Another effect, of course, is to encourage opportunistic behavior—corruption and shirking.

- Merit-based *personnel rules* are circumvented in favor of procedures that allow employment for reasons of patronage or personal trust. Typically, the merit system is used as a cover to practice patronage or to choose employees who will be personally loyal. Or else the system is circumvented through ad hoc appointments.

BOX 7.3

Informality in the Peruvian Government

Two or three years after it took office in 1990, a new government in Peru implemented a sweeping program of economic, social, and political change. The government achieved some major steps in re-establishing credible and effective government. The size and scope of the public sector have been reduced to far more manageable proportions, and the nature of government has shifted substantially from ownership and intervention to market regulation and provision of services targeted to the poor. But most public services are still of poor quality. Reforms of the public sector have been highly selective, bypassing existing ineffective agencies to concentrate on a few privileged agencies (some ministries and some autonomous agencies) that have spearheaded the reforms of the government.

The most evident feature of Peru's system of public administration—and one that has not changed with the new government—is that the de jure system is in reality mostly overtaken by a very different de facto, or informal, system. A first level of law (the constitution and leading laws) prescribes an "ideal form" of public administration in the image of the advanced industrial countries, characterized by checks and balances, public accountability, hierarchical forms of organization, and a professionalized public service. But the first level of law is systematically circumvented by second-level law; sometimes these are actual laws, but usually they are lower-level implementing rules. This second level produces, in effect, elements of parallel government with several main attributes:

- First, a parallel organizational structure (especially key autonomous agencies) substantially by-passes the cabinet and ministerial structure.

- Second, temporary appointments are important, particularly in the key posts, in the absence of effective staffing from the permanent public service. There is weak compliance with merit-promoting rules in the civil service, and the salary structure has lost any semblance of unity.

- Third, the budget and financial-management system is the counterpart of the parallel organizational structure: A highly centralized system weakens the role of cabinet and congress in the process; there is little effective oversight; and a cash-management system allows the government to concentrate on its chosen targets.

In an effort to resolve the tensions between written law and informal practice, Peruvian governments have had the habit of seeking to correct manifest defects by writing more laws, very often without properly eliminating old laws. This has led to legal confusion—an "excess" of laws, which undermines the rule of law. One manifestation of this is the redundancy and overlap within government. For instance, different ministries, autonomous agencies, and municipalities have conflicting, uncoordinated jurisdictions in the same business (especially in the area of social services and infrastructure investment). There is a vicious circle of rule-making as new controls are added to existing legislation, such as personnel or budgetary legislation, in an effort to make it work as it ought. But the outcome is, instead, a regulatory jungle. In addition, laws are often poorly enforced. Poor enforcement and legal confusion feed off each other, and their combination powerfully undermines the rule of law—known, clear, and universally applied rules—within the public administration.

- The *management* rules for setting and executing budgets often have little meaning. Many public initiatives, such as tax breaks, escape the budget.[13] Budgets are unrealistic; unexpected increases in spending and sudden decreases in revenues are the norm. Information from agencies on expenditures is inaccurate, often deliberately so. Thus the budget as executed does not resemble what was originally planned. Box 7.4 provides Caiden and Wildavsky's (1974) synthetic description of the vicious circle of fiscal uncertainty and informality characterizing budget systems in developing countries.

Informality is an institutional arrangement with national costs and benefits. Opportunism (corruption, fraud, patronage, and rent-seeking) and inefficiency flourish and are "institutionalized," while the costs of bureaucratic transactions are raised. On the other hand, informality allows some essential transactions to be completed, in

BOX 7.4
Budgeting and Informality in Developing Countries

"Governments that are too strong for the liberties of their subjects may nevertheless be too weak to budget effectively. The weakness of government in poor countries lies at the heart of their budgetary troubles. Unable to collect taxes in sufficient amounts, and lacking control over a significant portion of the resources they do collect, governments work in a perpetual aura of financial crisis. When the moment comes to separate rhetoric from reality, the finance ministry usually buries the burden of decision. Fearful of being blamed when the money runs out and anxious to respond to what it sees as real priorities for existing governments, the finance ministry desperately seeks protection against the unexpected. Maintaining liquidity becomes the main motive of its activities. Under normal conditions of extreme uncertainty (if not plain ignorance), this understandable desire leads to the sequence of the conservative estimating devices, the repetitive budgeting, the delays in releasing funds, and the inordinate amounts of paper work that we have already described. These procedures accomplish their purposes at first; a surplus is protected for the time being, the finance ministry is able to adapt to changing circumstances by delaying decision, and the causes of uncertainty are pushed onto the operating departments. They respond, in turn, by trying to stabilize their own environment. Departments withhold information on unexpended balances, thus increasing underspending, in order to retain some flexibility. They become more political because they must engage in ceaseless efforts to hold on to the money ostensibly allocated to them, lest the finance ministry claw it back. Ultimately, they seek their own form of financing through earmarked taxes, or they break off to form autonomous organizations—a sequence of events encouraged by foreign donors seeking stability through creating recipient organizations with whom they can have more predictable relations. Because the official budget is not a reliable guide as to what they actually can spend, departments are not motivated to take it seriously. Padding takes on huge dimensions, and it reinforces the tendencies of the finance ministry to mistrust departments and to put them in a variety of straitjackets."

—Caiden and Wildavsky (1974), p. 302

spite of burdensome rules. There is often a vicious circle whereby the failure of the state breeds more corrective rules, which both reformer and opportunist applaud, the reformer under mistaken formalistic notions about how to reform and the opportunist in the knowledge that reform will be frustrated and his opportunism can continue. Indeed, the existence of many laws—"legal pollution"—can be the antithesis of the rule of law. Informality seems to reflect the gap between expectations of what the state should be doing and the reality of what it can do.

To characterize informality is not, of course, a complete diagnosis of problems of public administration in LAC. There are other important elements, such as low wages and skills and a corrupted wage structure, that, though no doubt linked with informality, have not been mentioned above. Moreover, our characterization of a dominant mode of informal behavior has been stylized and generalized. In reality, informality is a worldwide phenomenon of public administration in developing countries. It is not absent in the advanced countries, and some Latin American and Caribbean countries are doing better than others.

Chile, for instance, has reduced informality through a long process of construction and reform, and today it is close to the practice of the more advanced countries (see Box 7.5). Costa Rica, Colombia, and to an extent Brazil and Venezuela are also countries that have benefited from a history of relative stability that has allowed a better public service to emerge (though political crisis in Colombia has recently meant some deterioration). Some of the small English-speaking countries of the Caribbean also provide an interesting foil. These countries tend to have clearer legal frameworks (with less overlap between agencies), a more professionalized public service, more centralized and better enforced personnel and financial controls, and less opportunistic behavior than in other LAC countries. Indeed, the control system works to the point that effective centralization and the inflexibility associated with this is—somewhat as in the more advanced countries—one of the principal problems that reformers have to tackle in the English-speaking Caribbean and in Chile.

The Origins of Informality

Informality, in this sense of a weak rule of law, is a fundamental characteristic of many countries of the region, pervading the public and private sectors. It is not simply a technical problem that can be corrected by better rules. Some point to its origins in colonial history (see de Soto 1989 and Hopkins 1991), although this may apply more to the Spanish-speaking countries than to Brazil or the English-speaking countries. Others point to the low level of generalized trust, or social capital, that sometimes characterizes these societies and, correspondingly, the importance of private networks in transacting in the modern sector. But when governments do not want to, or cannot, obey the rules they themselves have set, surely informality must also be seen as political. A recent study by ECLAC (United Nations Economic Commission for Latin America and the Caribbean 1998) argues that non-transparent—in our language, informal—fiscal arrangements typify many countries of the region. These arrangements, the study argues, are ways of getting around the lack of political consensus in society on the role of the state, including its size and how it is financed.

The political problem can be addressed in institutional terms. Earlier, in *the problem of public administration: an institutional perspective*, we suggested that the voter-principal would have difficulty controlling the politician-agent *if* voting rules led to fragmentation within or between political parties; *if* information asymmetry helped preserve clientelist patterns of political activity; *if* party rules created closed, oligopolistically controlled parties (rather than open, mass-based parties); and *to the extent that* democracies were "young." While it is difficult to collect conclusive evidence on the matter, it must be a strong hypothesis that many countries of the LAC region meet these criteria.

Comparing six countries under democratic rule in postwar Latin America, Geddes (1994, Chapter 5) shows that civil service reform was more likely to be legislated and extended when power was more evenly and stably divided among a small number of parties.

Typically lower educational levels, poorer communications, and less developed media in the LAC region than in more advanced countries may lead to the kind of information asymmetry that allows clientelist—or machine—politics to flourish. Geddes (1994, pp. 86-89) describes how the political machine works in Brazil: Politicians win votes, in part, by using *cabos eleitorais* ("electoral corporals") as intermediaries who provide private favors, such as access to state benefits, from public resources. This system requires extensive patronage, in the form of public jobs, to work.

Democracy in the LAC region is typically younger, and has been more punctuated by non-democratic interludes, than in the OECD countries. For instance, universal male suffrage was achieved by 1921 in most of Western Europe and North America but not until the 1970s in a sample of Latin American countries (Engerman, Haber, and Sokoloff 1998).

As is expected under these conditions of a weak voter-principal, interest groups dominate the political scene. To the extent that interests were fragmented and none of these had the expectation of commanding power over a longer period of time, it might furthermore be expected that public goods would be underproduced (and public administration weakened), because these interests would have the incentives to act as "roving bandits" rather than "stationary bandits."

Despite the indications that this is the case in LAC, there is a strong tide of democratization in the region, and as voters are becoming more effective, the pressures to formalize the public sector are growing (see below).

The Regional Reform Experience

There have been various approaches to public-sector reform in the region. Although we still need to learn far more about how successful these initiatives have been, we nevertheless can make a few generalizations, or at least put forward some hypotheses. Reforms affecting the public sector can be classified in two dimensions. First, these reforms are either discrete (or "one-off")—a downsizing, for instance— or they represent permanent changes in process—for instance, the rules and procedures that control the size of the civil-service establishment. Second, reforms have been implemented either through "enclaves"—typically, special-purpose bodies insulated from the rest of the public administration—or across the board, i.e., in the public administration as a whole.

The Successes: "One-Off" and Enclave Reforms

Many countries of the region have, since the 1980s, succeeded in many of the areas of "first-generation" reforms,

BOX 7.5

Chile's Long March to Sustain an Effective Public Administration

Chile's public administration is one of the best in Latin America. It is effective in delivering public services, its public servants are professionalized—competent and honest—and its operations are predictable. Chile's case shows that "effective public institutions are not created out of a pure act of political good will, but by the accumulation of experience and capabilities over long periods" (Marcel 1997) and it shows a long sequential development—albeit punctuated by cyclical factors—culminating in the introduction of important reforms in the style of the New Public Management. A professionalized public service began to develop early on in Chile's post-independence history. As the size of government has increased and its role has changed, this professionalism has been vital in maintaining good government. But there has been a political cycle of deterioration and remediation. On two occasions—in the 1930s and the 1970s—following some decades of rapid expansion of the bureaucracy and an accompanying loss of discipline and control, strong, sometimes authoritarian, governments have had to discipline the public administration. And for the last few years, the public administration has been progressively exposed—more than any other country in the region—to performance-oriented reforms. These reforms represent a response to the rigidities that can result from effective controls, and they have been fueled by strong democratic pressures for better government.

Chile's public administration was born in the context of the liberal, minimalist state that evolved soon after independence. Under an authoritarian form of civilian government, the administration was hierarchically organized, a financial-management system was introduced, and rules were established to professionalize the civil ser-

vice. These modernizing measures came earlier and proved more effective and durable than in most other Latin American countries.

The operating environment for the public administration deteriorated from the end of the nineteenth century. As congress came to play a larger role, an increasing use of patronage began to undermine the public administration. At the same time, a newly emerging middle class and a growing urban working class were demanding larger government. The increase in public services led to an uncontrolled expansion of government agencies, employment, and spending. The government took a number of centralizing measures in the 1930s to regain control of the public administration: Strict civil service rules were introduced to limit patronage, strong hierarchical financial controls (such as centralization of tax collection and accounting in a Treasury) were established, and a strong Comptroller General with extensive ex ante control powers was introduced.

From the late 1930s, the Chilean state took on a socially and economically more developmentalist role. Much of this was done by creating a number of autonomous agencies (for planning, service delivery, infrastructure development, and so on) as legal "exceptions" made by the executive in order to avoid the interference of the legislature. These new agencies became the dominant form of public agency in Chile. But their proliferation also contributed to growing problems in the public administration. Indeed, successive governments after the 1930s lacked the power to check the progressive loss of financial control, the proliferation of agencies, the loss of coherence and discipline in the public service, and the growth in patronage practices that accompanied the

(Box continues on following page)

including macroeconomic stabilization, downsizing the public administration, deregulation, privatization, and decentralization.[14] There have also been some successful reforms in specific areas of service delivery, notably Social Investment Funds.

Typically, first-generation reforms—"one-off" reforms often involved in dismantling public interventions rather

than constructing and implementing them—have been achieved by small groups of people, usually technocrats and usually not permanent civil servants. Service-delivery successes often have been achieved by creating enclaves that sit outside the ministerial structure and often answer directly to the president, so that they are protected from outside interests; moreover, they have protected funding

BOX 7.5
(Continued)

growth of the public sector. But governments were able to make some modest compensating gains through the improvement of the skills-base of public servants, rationalization of budget procedures, and improvement in the public administration's capacity for self-diagnosis. Moreover, by the 1960s policy-makers were seeing the autonomous agencies in a more favorable light.

The military government that seized power in 1973 sought to turn back the frontiers of the state, but as much as anything else it changed the way the state did business—from owner and service provider to regulator, and from centralized to decentralized service provider. To do this, it benefited from a professionalized civil service (which came under much pressure from the harsh fiscal adjustments of the mid-1970s and most of the 1980s). But to sustain the reforms, the government also had to deal with the severe problems it inherited of a deteriorated public administration. It carried out a number of reforms to centralize financial control within the executive and reduce the influence of interest groups; unify civil-servant pay scales and strengthen meritocratic rules; and simplify the organizational structure and decentralize activities or devolve them to the private sector. (In 1986 the government formalized into law the distinction between policy-making ministries and autonomous agencies providing services, thus creating a system akin to Sweden's and to some of the innovative elements of public administration introduced in the United Kingdom and New Zealand in the 1980s.) These reforms led to a system characterized by the combination of a centralized, rigid control of resources (i.e., inputs) with decentralized implementation—budget execution, personnel management, and procurement. (Chile's decentralized implementation, which is not char-

acteristic of many developing countries, makes the public administration more dependent on the honesty and dedication of its civil servants.) This reformed system was largely effective, but more in macroeconomic control than in allocation of resources or delivery of services, because of its reliance on input controls.

After the end of military government in 1990, the new democratic government sought to devolve further public services to the private sector, improve the performance of regulatory agencies, and resuscitate some social services. It also came to realize the need for a more performance-oriented style of public administration to address the rigidities arising from hierarchical decision-making, the emphasis on input controls, and the ambiguity in public-sector objectives. Characteristic of the analytical but pragmatic approach to reform typified by previous reform efforts, the government has gone about reform in a gradualist, stepwise manner. A participative form of strategic planning was introduced in 1993. In 1994, modernization agreements between the President and individual agencies were introduced; these were substantially fulfilled and are now being extended. In the same year, experiments in performance-based pay were introduced in some agencies and will cover all agencies by 1999. In 1995 budget-based performance indicators were introduced, covering 67 agencies and 291 indicators by 1996. At the end of 1996, agencies started producing annual performance reports and a system of evaluating public programs was introduced. These reforms have been accompanied by substantial increases in the resources applied to training.

Sources: Aylwin et al. (1990); Marcel (1997); Valencia (1996); Villalobos (1983).

and are subject to different control rules, which usually allow greater latitude in salary policies and greater management flexibility in using resources and rewarding performance.

Enclaves have played important developmental roles in a number of countries. Geddes (1994, Chapter 3) cites Brazil, and President Vargas's success in using such an

approach to promote administrative reform in the 1930s and President Kubitschek's success in using agencies to promote his industrial program in the 1950s.[15] Autonomous agencies also played an important role in Chile's development since the late 1930s (Marcel 1997). Peru has had substantial success in reforming its tax and customs administrations and in regulating competition, consumer protection, and utilities through autonomous agencies (Keefer 1995). But the enclave approach is problematic, for two main reasons (see Manning 1998).

First, enclaves undermine efforts to reform the core public administration because they undermine the rules of the core. This is to say that enclaves are a manifestation of informality. The donor community bears some of the responsibility; the project units promoted by foreign aid-donors and the habit of bringing in consultants paid by donors (as in Bolivia) to work alongside higher-level civil servants constitute an extreme version of this problem.

Second, enclaves do not provide a permanent solution. In general, they have proved difficult to sustain (or at least to sustain as productive agencies) once their champion—usually a president—has left office. Jamaica's autonomous agencies have in the past, for instance, created a substantial fiscal challenge (Manning 1998). The successful efforts of one mayor of the city of La Paz, Bolivia, to combat corruption in the early 1990s stalled after he left office (Klitgaard and Baser 1997).

Autonomous agencies are not bad per se. In fact, the autonomous agency and the executive-agency arrangements favored by proponents of the New Public Management have much in common. The problem arises when the autonomous agency operates under a different institutional umbrella. More than other countries of the LAC region, Chile has been able to bring its enclaves within the general structure of government.

Reforms of the Core Public Administration: A Mixed Picture

We do not know enough about more ambitious attempts to reform public administration across the board. There have been many of these in recent decades. Some have shown disappointing results, but the jury is still out on current efforts. Reform attempts have taken a variety of forms, including strategic planning, better civil service systems and training, better budget and financial management systems, performance-oriented management techniques, greater use of "voice," and so on. Large amounts of resources have been spent on designing and installing integrated financial-management systems in most of the larger countries of the region. But with a few exceptions, such as Brazil, these systems have not yet shown that they can be effective in rationalizing public financial management (see Reid 1998 on overambitious efforts in Bolivia and

Venezuela). Chile provides the region's best example of a country that has successfully reformed its core public administration across the board (see Box 7.5).

There have also been some attempts to apply newer models. These, too, have had a mixed success, or else the outcome is not yet clear (see Chapter X of United Nations Economic Commission for Latin America and the Caribbean 1998). On the plus side, since the early 1990s, Chile's public administration has adopted a progressively broader array of New Public Management instruments, including strategic planning, modernization agreements with individual agencies, performance pay, performance indicators, and evaluation of public programs. And the Brazilian State of Ceará, over the period of a few years after 1987, achieved dramatic improvements in the quality and coverage of its services, much of this through a transformation of its civil service (Tendler 1997 and World Bank 1997a, Box 5.7). Through civil-service rewards and careful recruitment, flexible organization, and community monitoring—a mixture of the New Public Management and "voice" reforms—the Ceará government created a sense of mission and participation among its workers. But there was a failure in Ecuador, where an attempt to introduce, sequentially, a contractual approach to administrative reform in all the ministries quickly foundered. Two months after finalizing the rules, the government declared all central administration entities "restructured," in order to grant a salary increase, although none had met the eligibility conditions (Reid 1998).

A World Bank project is helping Jamaica transform 11 existing entities into executive agencies on the U.K. model, but it is too early to gauge the results of this experiment. Brazil also has a system of performance contracts between the central government and agencies. In addition, Colombia is building a National Evaluation System for Public Sector Performance (see World Bank 1997b), and Costa Rica has also introduced a system of performance measurement and related incentives.

There also have been a number of successes in applying newer methods to the reform of individual agencies. The Brazilian Treasury has introduced a system of salary rewards based partly on team performance. Results-oriented budgeting has been introduced with some success in the province of Mendoza, Argentina. Several autonomous agencies have benefited from increased managerial discretion and contract-like arrangements (see Keefer 1995 for Peru).

In a nutshell, many LAC countries have done well in "one-off" and enclave-based reforms and less well on process reforms and across-the-board reforms. The successes, achieved by circumventing the public administration, have come about because they changed the principal-agent problem. Typically, the president puts the operation in his direct backyard, bypassing the cabinet and the ministries—or at most only using a few trusted people in the ministries. But enclaves are a problematic instrument and typically lose their effectiveness, or die, when political regimes change. By contrast, many across-the-board reforms have not been good at addressing the principal-agent problem. Chile's careful (though not always linear) advance—its effectiveness in achieving core public-administration reforms, its ability to sustain autonomous agencies, and its current experiments in mitigating the rigidities of hierarchy—probably comes nearest to a model of reform for the region.

Reform: Constraints and Possibilities

Informality and Reform

The core difficulty in getting good public administration in democratic countries can be usefully expressed in principal-agent terms: how to make the chain of accountability work—from voters, through their political representatives, down to public bureaucrats. To simplify, we could say that the advanced countries have answered this with two models: the older hierarchical model, which combines checks and balances (deriving from the separation of powers) and command-and-control structures, and the recent New Public Management model which combines checks and balances and market-friendly performance-oriented arrangements. The second is an offshoot of the first (and by no means eschews hierarchy). Both are based on the application of universal rules, including the same checks-and-balances arrangements. And there might be more convergence, in modern practice, than the champions of either school care to admit.

Informality lies deep within the fabric of society, pervading both the public and private sectors, and reflects political structures. It follows that reforming public administration in the countries of LAC is not merely, not even principally, a technical issue. Changing the formal rules will not help if incentives do not change. Providing hardware or systems to improve information or trans-parency will also have only a marginal contribution under these circumstances. Fred Riggs made this point more than 30 years ago with the hypothetical example of a would-be reformer "called upon to correct the evils of a chaotic filing system in a formalistic bureau. His technology takes for granted the existence of an effective demand for good written communications. The most modern and scientific procedures and equipment will not remedy the situation if such a demand does not exist" (Riggs 1964, pp. 17–18).

Reforms that Address Informality

A precondition to any modern system of public administration based on rules and checks and balances is a change in the political conditions that encourage informality. The LAC region is clearly moving in the direction of change, as a result of two powerful pressures—democratization and globalization (see Chapter 2).

The democratization of the LAC region since the late 1970s—the replacement of authoritarian governments, constitutional change, democratization of subnational government—has been remarkable and consistent. The changes have been as deep as in any other region of the world (see Figure 7.1 of World Bank 1997a) and paralleled only by the more abrupt democratization of Eastern Europe and Central Asia. Globalization, meanwhile, has helped bring about the opening of the LAC region's economies to the forces of international competition. These forces are putting pressure on the very interests that have benefited from informality in the past to improve public services—education, communications, dispute resolution, market regulation and so on—so that their economies can compete. Thus, we can expect that the space for public administration reform will continue to grow.

The political demand for formalization can be supplemented by public actions such as these:

- Electoral reforms might help improve the chain of accountability: Some political-science research suggests that reforms which lead to fewer, stronger parties could strengthen the constituency for reform of the public administration.
- "Voice" mechanisms—client surveys and scorecards, participatory practices—circumvent the poorly functioning chain of accountability. Reforms that increase the information available to the public, provide public undertakings on service standards, create mechanisms for the government to "listen" to clients, or

technically strengthen other branches of government, such as the legislature or the office of the auditor general, can all contribute.

- Policies that move the "informal sector" nearer to the modern sector—formalization of property rights, deregulation of business practices, tax reforms—may also have the result of better incorporating the "excluded" into the political system.
- Economic reforms that "level the playing field," open up modern-sector activities to new entrants, and weaken oligopolies, may create a demand from the private sector for better services from the public sector. Schick (1998, p. 127) argues that "[n]orms, practices, and ideas migrate from one sector to the other," and that "[t]he emergence of open, robust markets is as much a precondition for modernizing the public sector as it is for developing the private economy."

If this is an eclectic list of reform possibilities, it points to the need for continuing to improve our understanding of the interaction of political arrangements (who holds the power in countries and under what conditions), economic arrangements (the economic rules and their impact on who the economic players are), and bureaucratic arrangements (principal-agent relationships in the governance process).

Reform Options

The New Public Management provides a powerful set of ideas about the uses of hierarchies, markets, and voice that have reset the agenda for public sector reform. Many OECD countries, and a number of developing countries, have begun to move in the new direction. Devolution of activities—to the private sector, to corporatized bodies, or to lower levels of government—is an important common element. But as for the reform of the core of the public administration, there is as yet no consensus on the new model—in particular how far to go in the direction of "marketizing" functions and systems. Nonetheless, there are some key ideas that provide something of an idealized menu for reform in the countries of the LAC region. The ideas relate to the setting of strategic priorities; reorganizing the way that public services are delivered; moving to a performance-based (or results-based) system of accountability; and backing up this system through financial-management and personnel reforms. These ideas are set out in more detail in Box 7.6.

How should the countries of the region move in this direction? How comprehensive should the reforms be? What is the best order of reform? The answers depend, of course, on specific conditions in each country—on politics, leadership, windows of opportunity, and the current state of the public administration. But there is also a lively generic debate on how far and how fast the reform process should go in developing countries. Caution is a common theme. The *World Development Report 1997* (World Bank 1997a and Box 7.1) advocates many aspects of the new thinking, but advises caution in some areas. Reid (1998) discusses the steps necessary to make New Public Management reforms work in Latin America, and also advises caution. Schick's (1998) advice is that "most developing countries should not try New Zealand's reforms." Bale and Dale (1998), on the other hand, maintain that developing countries can, if careful, learn from New Zealand's success.[16]

For countries where informality still rules in the public sector, the issue of sequencing is difficult to avoid. Formal rules must prevail before the system can be improved. Several sequencing variants have been suggested. Schick (1998, pp. 129–131) sketches out a possible sequential path. He sees private-sector economic reform as a necessary initial condition. This should be followed by the establishment of reliable external control (centralized, top-down financial controls), realistic budgeting, and some investment in a professional civil service. These basics will allow politicians to take control of public management on the basis of effective control of inputs: "They must be able to control inputs before they are called upon to control outputs." Once this stage has been mastered, the system could move to internal controls, where agencies police themselves and are subject to ex post audit from the center. This would give the agencies substantial managerial flexibility. After independence in 1963, Singapore rapidly followed this route from internal to external controls, and it was then able, by the mid-1990s, to adopt a "budgeting-for-results" system that implements several elements of the New Zealand model.

Some have criticized sequentialism as a recipe for inaction. A variant is to propose that different agencies "graduate" at different times to a more performance-oriented set of rules, and that the timing depend on the ability of these agencies to shift from external to internal control. Reid (1998) describes such an approach and how it has been used in the LAC region. It is being applied in Brazil, Ecuador, and Jamaica.

BOX 7.6

A Set of Reform Issues Emerging from New Public Management

A recent World Bank report on results-oriented public-sector reform in Colombia considered some issues in reforming public management systems, structures, and incentives. From this emerges a set of issues that are relevant to the reform of public administrations of the LAC region (Annex 3 of World Bank 1997b).

- *Clear strategic priorities.* Governments must decide on strategic priorities and use budget allocations, incentives, and monitoring to achieve these.
- *Optimal ways of delivering public services.* Governments must decide whether public goods and services are best delivered through regulation, regulated private production, or public production.
- *Optimal ways of organizing public agencies.* Incentives may be clarified and information may flow better by "rearranging the boxes." (For instance, an agency that both implements and provides policy advice may provide biased advice.) Performance may be enhanced by creating competition within the government.
- *Specification of relevant objectives.* Performance can be enhanced if objectives are set and there are incentives to achieve them.

- *Modern management systems.* Effective management requires a package of elements, including leadership, resources, incentives, freedom to manage, and congruent values.
- *Effective financial management.* Financial-management systems should integrate planning, budgeting, execution, and audit functions. A performance orientation also requires that these systems allocate resources on an output basis, fully account for all resources used (including capital), and provide for decentralized execution that balances managerial freedom and accountability for resource use.
- *Performance-information systems.* Performance-based systems require information that is integrated with the financial management system.
- *Institutional capacity.* Performance-based systems require a change in mindset from a compliance culture to a performance culture.
- *Effective personnel systems.* Decentralization of personnel functions is necessary if managers are to be held accountable for results.

Those countries in the region where some success, however limited, has come from the creation of autonomous agencies may face an additional option—to improve the sustainability of autonomous agencies by incorporating them more effectively within the rules of the state, i.e., by "formalizing" them. This might be achieved, for example, by transforming autonomous agencies into executive agencies by creating a uniform set of accountability rules and establishing client-service standards. Part of Chile's successful public-administration reforms has been through incorporating its autonomous agencies.

The new reform ideas provide a challenge to many countries of the LAC region because of the informality of their current systems of public administration. But under the thrust of democratizing and globalizing forces, these ideas also provide many opportunities for the region to move forward.

Notes

1. This characterization is meant to encompass what a political scientist might expect from good government in terms of decisiveness, capability, and responsiveness (see Cox and McCubbins 1996) and what an economist might expect in terms of macroeconomic stability, strategic prioritization, and efficient and responsive service delivery (see Campos and Pradhan 1996).

2. The principal-agent literature addresses how a principal designs a contract that will provide the best incentives for (i.e. best likelihood of) an agent's carrying out the principal's wishes. For applications of principal-agent literature to the functioning of the public sector, see Blau (1974); Morgan (1986); Scott and Gorringe (1989); and Lane and Nyen (1995).

3. See also Annex 3 of World Bank (1997b) for a similar presentation.

4. To present only two stages is, of course, to simplify. Not only are there many stages (voter, politician, party, executive/president, minister, agency head, civil servant...), but the process is not linear, nor is it unidirectional: Executives, legislatures, and judiciaries all have degrees of control over each other and can have competing control over agencies.

5. Wade (1997) seeks to explain the superior performance in the management of Korean irrigation systems compared with Indian systems by showing how the organizations in each country used differing arrangements to tackle the principal-agent problem.

6. Sometimes the executive is subordinate to the legislature; at other times, notably in the United States, it is independent.

7. Others call it "the new managerialism" or "performance-based management."

8. The four topics follow a schema suggested by David Shand.

9. For a treatment of these reforms, see Scott and Gorringe (1989), McCulloch and Ball (1992), Schick (1996 and 1998), and Bale and Dale (1998).

10. Paul (1991), Salmen (1992), and World Bank (1992) have adapted the concepts of "exit" and "voice" from Hirschman (1970). In broad terms, they use "exit" as the ability of the customer/citizen to choose alternatives (i.e., within a market) and "voice" as the ability of the customer/citizen (through the government's "listening") to exercise influence over the type and quality of service.

11. These averages, of course, mask a substantial variation among the countries of the region.

12. De Soto (1989) played a leading role in characterizing informality as it affected the private sector and the populace. Informality in the public sector has not been newly discovered, though the specific terminology may not have been used much. Riggs (1964) expounds a concept of "formalism," a term frequently used to characterize Latin America's legal systems, more or less the same as informality: laws that are not put into practice. Following de Soto, Schick (1998) applies the idea of informality to the public sectors of developing countries, arguing that there is a parallel incidence of informality in the public and private sectors. Klitgaard (1998, p. 336) characterizes "sick institutions" by "weak information, ineffective incentives, and chronic shirking and malfeasance."

13. The United Nations Economic Commission for Latin America and the Caribbean (1998) characterizes these kinds of budget problems as indicating the weakness of the "fiscal covenant" between government and citizens.

14. However, decentralization, which has been especially strong in health and education services, has a mixed record in terms of its efficiency effects and has often created fiscal disequilibria.

15. See also Evans (1992) on other "pockets of efficiency" in Brazil.

16. There are several reasons for particular caution about applying a New-Zealand-style model emphasizing contracting. Contracting is technically demanding and risky: Public-sector outputs are typically difficult to measure, as is the performance of individuals; and since intra-government contracts are not at arm's length, they could be difficult to enforce. For these reasons, some fear that greater managerial discretion could open the door to greater opportunism. A study of state-owned enterprises in developing countries (World Bank 1995b) showed that the use of performance contracts did not do much to improve enterprise performance because they did not reduce managers' information advantage, they rarely included effective rewards or penalties, and governments showed little commitment to contract terms.

TECHNICAL APPENDIX:

Concepts for Analyzing and Designing Institutions

Economists have developed some useful concepts and insights to help analyze and design appropriate institutions. In this appendix we review concepts associated with six sets of issues: First, we cover issues related to asymmetric information and resulting principal-agent problems. Second, we describe exit and voice strategies as feedback devices. Third, we discuss the relationship between transactions, property rights, contracts, and enforcement mechanisms. Fourth, we evaluate the implications of the existence of transaction costs for the design of institutions for markets and hierarchies. Fifth, we highlight the importance of institutions for the provision of public or collective goods. Sixth, we briefly discuss the importance of the predictability and credibility of institutions for economic and social development.

Asymmetric Information and Principal-Agent Problems

Two closely related concepts are those of asymmetric or imperfect information and principal-agent problems. The basic information problem described the financial and education sectors is that agents (school teachers or directors and firm managers) possess much more information about what they do (teach or use other people's money) than those who take their children to school or own shares from a firm, lend to it or deposit money in a bank.

Asymmetric and imperfect information are facts of life. Asymmetric information exists whenever one or more parties in a transaction have information about the quality of their inputs, outputs, or other aspects of the economic undertaking that is not readily available to the others (or that is too costly for the others to assess). Likewise, imperfect information afflicts all economic or business transac-

tions whenever relevant information about a particular transaction is not fixed. If the relevant information tends to change over time as conditions change, then there will tend to be imperfect information.

Principal-agent problems arise whenever an interested party (the principal) delegates the responsibility to act on his or her behalf to an agent, but, due to information asymmetries, the agent can relinquish such responsibility without the agent's knowledge. This type of problem affects numerous relationships: Politicians sometimes do not adequately represent the interests of voters; bureaucrats or regulators do not always act in accordance with the mandates of politicians or voters; teachers may not act in the interest of students and parents; and judges may not always defend the interests of parties engaged in a legal dispute or the "public interest" (T. Moe 1984, Pratt and Zeckhauser 1985). The negative welfare consequences of principal-agent problems can be prevented or reduced through institutions that establish effective monitoring or feedback mechanisms and that make performance and outcomes more transparent and measurable. Ideally, monitoring mechanisms should also be accompanied by enforcement mechanisms that effectively punish opportunistic behavior and reward good performance.

These problems can lead to **adverse selection, moral hazards**, and **incomplete markets**. These economic phenomena were described informally in the previous section. In our example of the problems faced by bankers and borrowers when they do not have sufficient information regarding the borrowers' creditworthiness, we emphasized that in the context of imperfect information only risky borrowers may be willing to take on loans at the high rates of interest charged by the banks. Hence this type of situation has been called **adverse selection**, reflecting the tendency for the market to be dominated by exactly the riskiest customers. This type of problem has been extensively analyzed in the case of insurance markets, where only the worst risks tend to purchase private insurance (Rothschild and Stiglitz 1976).

Likewise, due to asymmetric information, firms may tend to undertake too risky operations, expecting to benefit fully from good results while shifting, at least partially, potential losses to their lenders. Banks can engage in the same behavior, expecting to shift eventual losses, at least partially, to depositors. These are the so-called **moral hazards**. In the context of insufficient information about the health of banks, governments often provide deposit insurance to protect the banking system from potential panics by depositors who may rush to withdraw their deposits in response to events that may or may not have affected a specific bank. However, the government-provided insurance may reduce the depositor's incentive to avoid risky banks or to monitor the entity's financial health, increasing the moral hazard problem. Thus, disclosure requirements, prudential regulation, and supervision are essential institutions to cope with such problems. (These issues are discussed in detail in Chapter 3.) Moral hazards can also emerge in the context of hierarchies. For example, tenured employment contracts within organizations (including public bureaucracies) tend to create an incentive to work less since employment is guaranteed.[1]

Also, as illustrated earlier, some markets in the context of information asymmetries may never develop. In general terms, whenever private markets fail to provide goods or services at costs below the price that individuals are willing to pay, economists refer to this phenomenon as **incomplete markets** (Stiglitz 1986).

One of the critical roles of institutions, then, is to reduce the information asymmetry and overcome principal-agent problems. For example, teachers can be made more responsive to the concerns and interests of parents by establishing performance contracts that pay teachers according to their performance (and even attendance) in the classroom; the government may conduct standardized academic tests across public and private schools in order to provide parents with information regarding the academic progress of the children in each school relative to others, etc. In the case of capital markets, providing minority shareholders rights, establishing disclosure rules, and promoting the use of rating agencies enable shareholders to effectively "voice" their informed opinions about management decisions, or "exit" the firm, which in turn can provide incentives for managers to behave in a way that promotes minority shareholders interests and to provide them with better and fuller information. Organizations like securities exchange commissions are part of the institutional set to regulate and supervise the implementation of such requirements.

Exit and Voice as Feedback Devices

In general terms, shareholders or households can provide incentives for improving the management of firms and schools respectively by either *exit* or *voice* strategies.[2] In the former, shareholders or households use the market to defend their interests if they are dissatisfied with their agents' decisions; they simply divest from the firm in question, take their deposits to a different bank, or, theoretically, withdraw their children from the school. In contrast, the voice strategy implies the use of control devices, whereby the shareholders or parents in our examples can induce changes in management of the firm or school.

With this distinction in mind, it is worthwhile to explore some of the challenges associated with education, where exit is often not an available strategy. For example, in rural areas of developed and developing countries, it is difficult to find more than one school within a reasonable distance from household clusters. In addition, due to familial and cultural ties to certain regions, households often are tied to their "roots," which again limits the exit strategy. Thus, in addition to the aforementioned problems of insufficient information available for parents to make decisions about where to send their children to school, these considerations about the lack of household mobility seem to limit the scope for a market-driven education system, such as public education vouchers.[3] In such situations, "voice" mechanisms, through parent or community involvement in the decision-making in schools—as in the EDUCO program in El Salvador—are useful complements to "exit" mechanisms.

Transactions, Property Rights, Contracts, and Enforcement

Transactions in an economy (through markets or hierarchies) consist of transfers of *property rights* on assets, goods, or services. Such transactions permit the exploitation of the potential gains from trade (internal and external) and specialization (both within markets and hierarchies), which are essential to economic development. It is precisely one of the basic roles of institutions to specify who owns what (property rights) and how property can be combined or exchanged through transactions.

Transactions are regulated by formal or informal **contracts** that determine the conditions under which property rights are transferred, including prices, conditions for payment, the venue for finalizing the transaction, and so on. Contracts are institutions—that is, *rules* that establish the conditions that the parties must satisfy to reap the benefits of the exchange in question. Contracts, in turn, are regulated by higher institutions—both formal rules (the legal system, regulations, bureaucratic procedures) and informal rules (trust and acceptable business practices)—and are enforceable through courts or other arbitration mechanisms.

Although informal rules for resolving property and contract disputes are used throughout the world, especially in developing countries with unreliable enforcement of formal rules, it can be argued that in today's world of impersonal transactions and non-barter economies, it is increasingly important to develop the formal rules establishing property rights and contractual obligations. Some analysts have argued that developing countries should focus on the development of substantive and procedural rules of property and contract as much as on creating a first-class judiciary (Posner 1998).

Transaction Costs

It must be clear by now that transactions involve significant costs. *Transaction costs* include *costs of obtaining and verifying information* about the quantity and quality of goods and services, the partners in a transaction (and verifying their reputation, records, etc.), and the quality of their property rights to be transferred, including the legal and contractual framework; as well as *costs of designing, monitoring, and enforcing the contract* of transfer, including any costs incurred in litigation and dispute resolution. Some of the risks involved in a transaction are insurable; that is, *insurance costs* are also part of transaction costs.[4]

For some transactions these costs may be small, as reflected in our previous discussion of shopping for groceries in supermarkets or spot-market transactions. In others, transaction costs can be huge for all parties involved. Consider, for example, the bidding or negotiations of a pri-

vatization, a mining concession, or an acquisition or a merger among private firms. In these cases, the information and enforcement requirements can be enormous.

In general, the magnitude of transaction costs depends partially on technology. For instance, the information revolution has reduced the costs of transferring and evaluating information. However, while the information superhighway makes it easier to access information, it has not necessarily provided incentives for entities to provide information. Thus, the magnitude of transaction costs also critically depends on the quality of institutions.

Indeed, their magnitude depends on the transparency and efficacy of the rules that establish and protect property rights and the characteristics of contracts, including the efficiency and reliability of the judiciary and alternative dispute-resolution systems, and on the extent to which they reduce the costs of information gathering, by establishing clear incentives for actors to provide and seek information relevant to their particular undertakings—or to those of others, in the case of credit bureaus, rating agencies, entities that rank the quality of universities, or any organization or individual that makes a living out of providing information. In addition, the rules that establish markets and hierarchies affect the incentives to participate in market activities (including risk-taking) and for members of an organization (both private and public) to act collectively in pursuit of common objectives.

In the case of financial and capital markets, the adoption of sound internationally accepted accounting standards, external audit requirements, disclosure rules for banks and corporations, and consolidated balance sheets for financial groups can reduce the scope of asymmetric information that afflicts these markets. Also, promoting the operation of credit bureaus and rating agencies for the same markets can help to improve the availability of relevant information that can then be used by depositors or shareholders to make informed decisions about where to put their money. In the commercial area, there are also important quality standards for trade, especially concerning international trade, which ensure that traders are getting what they paid for. In the field of education, we have already mentioned the potentially constructive role of standardized exams for teachers and students, and the relevance of certification requirements to ensure a minimum level of quality for schools and universities.

Unfortunately, there are also numerous examples of "excessive" regulations and information pollution that increase transaction costs. For instance, licensing requirements for establishing businesses, with heavy and costly information requirements, are often imposed as revenue-raising or protectionist measures (they can unduly increase entry costs) rather than for solving real information or enforcement problems. Also, very often reporting requirements within the public sector take enormous efforts to produce massive ill-designed data that nobody can use or cares to use in an efficient way. In addition, there are institutions that induce excessive "risk-taking" by the private sector, such as the case of blanket universal deposit insurance schemes in the banking sector.

A useful way to assess the quantitative importance of an economy's transaction costs (and thus institutions) is by disaggregating total costs of production into *transformation costs* (determined by technology, factor, and input prices) and *transaction costs* (determined by institutions and technology). Wallis and North (1986), for example, estimated that transaction costs exceeded 40 percent of total production costs (GNP) in the United States in 1970. Although it should be acknowledged that in practice there are difficulties in making the distinction between transformation and transaction costs, such an estimate underscores the critical importance of institutions for efficiency in an economy.[5]

According to the transaction-cost literature, hierarchies are instituted to reduce the transaction costs that would be involved if the relevant transactions had been conducted through the market (O. Williamson 1989). Nonetheless, transaction costs within hierarchies can still be significant, especially in large organizations. For example, many governments spend a significant amount of resources auditing and controlling the expenditures of public agencies. As mentioned, public organizations are often used as political instruments, which may lead to opportunistic behavior by politicians. Of course, this type of opportunistic behavior can also be ameliorated by designing institutions that effectively monitor performance, and perhaps that link remuneration or the length of employment to such performance. Indeed, as already mentioned, many countries around the globe are currently experimenting with various forms of performance contracts.

Collective Action and Public Goods

A key role of institutions relates to incentives for people to shirk on their contractual or collective-action commitments. In other words, institutions may reduce transaction costs by eliminating the capacity of organizations and individuals to act in an opportunistic fashion. This role is particularly important for the production of *public goods*.

Broadly defined, public goods have two important characteristics. First, they are **non-excludable**: Once they are provided to one member of a group, they cannot be denied to the others. Second, public goods are characterized by a **non-rival consumption** feature; that is, the consumption of a public good or service by one individual or organization does not reduce the supply of such good or service for other potential beneficiaries.[6] For example, the benefits of police—greater personal security—cannot be denied to any member of the community once it is provided to others. Similarly, economic and institutional reforms can be analyzed as public goods, because the benefits from reforms will be absorbed by society as a whole.

A problem arises in ensuring that all beneficiaries of a public good will pay for its production. Since consumers cannot be excluded from its benefits, they have an incentive not to pay for providing it. This is the so-called **free-rider** problem, where beneficiaries have an incentive not to pay because benefits are not linked to contributions. Olson (1965, p. 14) equates public goods with **collective goods**, implying that organizations or groups of individuals with common interests may face free-rider problems. Often organizations impose membership requirements in the form of mandatory contributions, such as dues imposed by labor unions around the world (frequently supported in law; i.e. coerced by the state). Another potential solution for free riders is to establish monitoring mechanisms to ensure that members are not shirking on their collective commitments.

Institutions, Predictability, and Credibility

In previous sections we argued that institutions matter for long-term economic development because they establish the incentive structure (constraints) for economic and political actors. Consequently they determine the incentives that actors face to undertake business transactions, to invest in productive activities and human development, to innovate, and to take economic/financial risks. Institutions determine the perceived profitability of undertaking economic and political activities by affecting the risks, costs, and benefits of economic transactions, by defining who owns what (i.e., property rights) and by establishing the conditions for undertaking the transactions (i.e., contracts). In addition, institutions also determine the penalties and other consequences for parties that do not satisfy the terms of an agreed transaction (i.e., enforcement mechanisms). The main role of institutions (or institutional reforms), therefore, is to minimize transaction costs, thus facilitating exchange and promoting investment in the production of private as well as public goods. *In summary, well-designed institutions reduce transaction costs by ameliorating information and enforcement problems. Thus, they make possible the existence, efficiency, and depth of markets and organizations.*

In addition, the quality (and stability) of institutions may be important for maintaining stable, predictable, and credible "rules of the game" in economic and political life, which may affect the overall performance of an economy, both in the long run and in the short run. Surveys of investors and recent studies (see Chapter 1) have proved that investment decisions and growth are affected by the predictability and credibility of governmental policies.[7] Thus, institutions that improve the predictability and credibility of policies are essential to reap the benefits of "sound" policies.

The efforts by governments of developing countries to "lock in" their structural reforms and market access through external commitments that increase exit costs—such as membership in the World Trade Organization (WTO), Regional Trade Agreements (RTAs), and the like—is partially explained by the desire to convince investors that the current authorities or future governments will not display opportunistic behavior and roll back the reforms. Without such credibility, investors may not take the decisions that permit reaping the fruits of freer trade and investment environments.[8]

A similar problem arises in private participation in infrastructure and utilities. Privatization must be accompanied by substantial institutional reforms (regulatory laws and by-laws, autonomous regulatory agencies) that set adequate incentives and give predictability and credibility to the new policies. Without them, private investment would not be forthcoming in the desired amounts or it will require excessive governmental guarantees that may impair the very objectives of private participation in infrastructure (shifting risks to the private sector to encourage efficiency and allow the state to concentrate scarce public funds in the provision of basic social services and public goods) and create huge fiscal contingencies.[9]

Credibility has also proved to be critical for the success of stabilization policies.[10] One important institutional development that has arisen from this fact is a drive toward central bank autonomy in constitutional and legal reforms in LAC and around the world. The drive toward improved budgetary institutions is also influenced by such considerations.

In turn, recent analyses of the East Asian crisis of 1997 have highlighted the role that inadequate institutions had in inducing banks and corporations to undertake excessive risks.[11] The existence of "perverse" incentives, that induced excessive risk-taking, resulted in catastrophic consequences when their effects were magnified by recent exposure to huge short-term capital inflows through capital account liberalization. It is clear by now that reforming and strengthening of financial-sector and corporate-governance institutions is absolutely critical for developing countries if they wish to reduce the risks of costly financial and currency crisis associated with financial integration. Countries that have not liberalized their capital account should do it in a gradual and careful way, while keeping pace with such institutional reforms.

Notes

1. Pearce (1992) defines "moral hazard" as "the effect of certain types of insurance systems in causing a divergence between the private marginal cost of some action and the marginal social cost of that action…"

2. See Hirschman (1970) for an insightful analysis of these strategies in a variety of economic and political scenarios.

3. Education voucher schemes had been proposed a long time ago by Friedman (1955), and have been tried across the United States and in several developing countries. On the controversies associated with these experiments, see Carnoy (1997) and West (1997).

4. O. Williamson (1989, p. 142) defines transaction costs as "the comparative costs of planning, adapting, and monitoring completion under alternative governance structures." North (1990, p. 27) defines them as "the costs of measuring the valuable attributes of what is being exchanged and the costs of protecting rights and policing and enforcing agreements."

5. It should be noted, for example, that total transaction costs in an economy can be readily confused with the legal, accounting, and management services that are part of the services sector of the economy.

6. A succinct definition along these lines can be found in Pearce (1992).

7. World Bank (1997a) presents evidence on the relationship between credibility and predictability of policies and laws, based on Brunetti et al. (1997a and 1997b).

8. See Burki and Perry (1998) and Fernández (1997).

9. See Irwin et al. (1997).

10. Kydland and Prescott (1977), Calvo (1989), and Rodrik (1989)

11. See, for example, Krugman (1998); Corsetti, Pesenti, and Roubini (1998); IMF (1998); World Bank (1998a); and Perry and Lederman (1998).

DATA APPENDIX:

Institutional Indicators Used in Figures 1–17

The data used were obtained from the monthly publication *International Country Risk Guide* (ICRG), published by Political Risk Services (PRS), a private international investment risk service company that employs analysts to provide political, financial, and economic risk ratings of countries.

The "composite institutional index" used in Chapter 1 is made up of five components given in the ICRG: (1) repudiation of contracts by government, (2) expropriation risk, (3) bureaucracy quality, (4) corruption, and (5) law-and-order tradition. PRS defines the five components as follows:

Repudiation of contracts by government: The minimum and maximum amount of points given to this component are zero and 10 respectively. A low score in this component means that the commitment by a country's government to fulfill previous or present contracts is low.

Expropriation risk: It measures the risk of "forced nationalization." As in the case of repudiation of contracts, a minimum of zero points and a maximum of 10 points are given. A high score in this component indicates a low risk of expropriation or confiscation of enterprise equity by government.

Bureaucracy quality: This component measures the expertise and autonomy of the bureaucracy. A country with a competent bureaucracy that is independent of "political pressure" receives a high score in the ICRG. The minimum and maximum points assigned to this component were zero and six from 1984 to 1997. Starting in 1998, they are zero and four respectively.

Corruption: This measures the extent to which bribery is present "within the political system." The higher the corruption level in a country the less the efficiency of governments and the lower the score. Forms of corruption given in the ICRG are related to bribes in areas of exchange controls, tax assessments, police protection, loans, and licensing of exports and imports. The points of this component range between zero and six, where low scores indicate high levels of corruption.

Law-and-order tradition: This component is a measure of a country's legal system and rule of law. The range of points given to this component is between zero and six. A high score indicates the existence of a highly strong and impartial legal system and the citizens' acceptance of legal mechanisms to settle disputes.

The above components measure the quality of public institutions and the quality of public services. The "composite institutional index" was created with them for each country where there was data available from 1984 to 1998. The index is the sum of the five components in each year. In order to be able to add up the five components, the last three components were transformed to 10-point scales; therefore, the total number of points possible for a country is 50, where a country with a perfect quality of public institutions and quality of public services would have a score of 50. Annual averages of the five components were available for the countries in the sample from 1984 to 1996, 1997 data are from the January 1997 issue of the ICRG, and 1998 data are from the February 1998 issue. Table A1 has the list of the countries by regions and table A2 has the list of countries in the sub-regions of LAC.

TABLE A1

Countries Included in the Sample

ASIA	EUROPE AND CENTRAL ASIA	LATIN AMERICA AND THE CARIBBEAN	MIDDLE EAST AND NORTH AFRICA	OECD	SUB-SAHARAN AFRICA
Bangladesh	Albania	Argentina	Algeria	Australia	Angola
Brunei	Bulgaria	Bolivia	Bahrain	Austria	Botswana
China	Czech Republic	Brazil	Egypt, Arab Rep. of	Belgium	Cameroon
Hong Kong, China	Greece	Chile	Iran, Islamic Rep. of	Canada	Côte d'Ivoire
India	Hungary	Colombia	Iraq	Denmark	Gabon
Indonesia	Poland	Costa Rica	Israel	Finland	Ghana
Malaysia	Romania	Dominican Republic	Jordan	France	Guinea
Pakistan	Russian Fed.	Ecuador	Kuwait	Germany	Kenya
Papua New Guinea	Turkey	El Salvador	Lebanon	Iceland	Liberia
Philippines	Yugoslavia	Guatemala	Libya	Ireland	Malawi
Singapore		Guyana	Morocco	Italy	Mali
Korea, Rep. of		Haiti	Oman	Japan	Mozambique
Sri Lanka		Honduras	Qatar	Netherlands	Nigeria
Taiwan, China		Jamaica	Saudi Arabia	New Zealand	Senegal
Thailand		Mexico	Syrian Arab Rep.	Norway	South Africa
Vietnam		Nicaragua	Tunisia	Portugal	Sudan
		Panama	United Arab Emirates	Spain	Tanzania
		Paraguay	Yemen, Rep. of	Sweden	Togo
		Peru		Switzerland	Uganda
		Trinidad and Tobago		United Kingdom	Zambia
		Uruguay		United States	Zimbabwe
		Venezuela			

TABLE A2

LAC Sub-regions

SOUTHERN CONE	NORTHERN CONE	CENTRAL AMERICA AND PANAMA	MEXICO AND THE CARIBBEAN
Argentina	Bolivia	Costa Rica	Dominican Republic
Brazil	Colombia	El Salvador	Guyana
Chile	Ecuador	Guatemala	Haiti
Paraguay	Peru	Honduras	Jamaica
Uruguay	Venezuela	Nicaragua	Mexico
		Panama	Trinidad and Tobago

TABLE A3

Description and Sources of Variables Used in Regression for Figure 1.1b

VARIABLE	DESCRIPTION	PERIOD	SOURCE
1. GDP growth	Average annual growth of GDP per capita in constant local prices. This was measured as the log difference of the per capita GDP in 1984 and 1995 divided by the elapsed time period	1984–95	WDI, World Bank
2. Initial per capita GDP	Log of initial per capita GDP in constant 1987 US$	1984	WDI, World Bank
3. Education	Average schooling years in the total population of ages 15 years and over	1985	Barro and Lee (1996)
4. (Export + Import) / GDP	Ratio of the sum of exports and imports of goods and services to GDP	1984	WDI, World Bank and International Financial Statistics, IMF
5. M2/GDP	Ratio of money and quasi money to GDP	1984	WDI, World Bank and International Financial Statistics, IMF
6. Gross investment	Gross domestic investment as a percentage of GDP	1984	WDI, World Bank and International Financial Statistics, IMF
7. Inflation	The annual percentage inflation measured in consumer prices averaged over 1984 to 1995. A Laspeyres index formula is used	1984–95	WDI, World Bank and International Financial Statistics, IMF
8. Terms of trade – average	The annual percentage change in the net barter terms of trade averaged over the entire period – 1984–95. Net barter terms of trade are the ratio of the export price index to the corresponding import price index (1987 = 100)	1984–95	WDI, World Bank
9. Terms of trade – standard deviation	The standard deviation of the net barter terms of trade over the period 1984–95	1984–95	WDI, World Bank
10. ICRG 84	*Composite institutional index, as described above*	1984	*See above*

TABLE A4

Countries Included in the Sample of Figure 1.1b

ASIA	EUROPE AND CENTRAL ASIA	LATIN AMERICA AND CARIBBEAN	MIDDLE EAST AND NORTH AFRICA	OECD	SUB-SAHARAN AFRICA
Bangladesh	Greece	Argentina	Algeria	Australia	Cameroon
China	Hungary	Bolivia	Egypt, Arab Rep.	Austria	Gabon
India	Poland	Brazil	Iran, Islamic Rep. of	Canada	Ghana
Indonesia	Romania	Chile	Israel	Denmark	Kenya
Malaysia	Turkey	Colombia	Kuwait	Finland	Malawi
Pakistan		Costa Rica	Syrian Arab Rep.	France	Mali
Philippines		Dominican Republic	Tunisia	Iceland	Senegal
Singapore		Ecuador		Italy	South Africa
Korea, Rep. of		El Salvador		Japan	Togo
Sri Lanka		Guatemala		Netherlands	Zambia
Thailand		Guyana		New Zealand	
		Honduras		Norway	
		Jamaica		Spain	
		Mexico		Sweden	
		Nicaragua		Switzerland	
		Paraguay		United States	
		Peru			
		Trinidad and Tobago			
		Uruguay			

References

Academy for Educational Development (AED) (1996). *Educational Reform Projects Supported by the World Bank, the Inter-American Development Bank, and USAID in Latin America and the Caribbean*. Washington, D.C.: Academy for Educational Development.

Akerlof, George (1970). "The Market for Lemons, Qualitative Uncertainty and the Market Mechanism." *Quarterly Journal of Economics*, 59:473–494.

Akerlof, G., and P. Romer (1993). "Looting: The Economic Underworld of Bankruptcy for Profit." *Brookings Papers on Economic Activity*, 2:1–73.

Alesina, Alberto, and Allan Drazen (1991). "Why Are Stabilizations Delayed?" *The American Economic Review*, 81(5):1170–1188.

Alexander, William E.; Jeffrey M. Davis; Liam P. Ebrill; and Carl-Johan Lindgren (1997). *Systemic Bank Restructuring and Macroeconomic Policy*. Washington, D.C.: International Monetary Fund.

Alvarez, Benjamin (1998). "Life Cycle and Legacy of the Educational Reforms in Latin America and the Caribbean." *International Journal of Educational Reform*, 7(1):34–45 (January).

Alvarez, Benjamin, and Monica Ruiz-Casares (eds.) (1997). *Paths of Change: Education Reforms Under Way in Latin America and the Caribbean*. Washington, D.C.: U.S. Agency for International Development/Agency for Educational Development.

American Bar Association (1989 and 1993). *Multinational Commercial Insolvency*. Wisconsin: MG Publishing.

Ames, Barry (1998). "Institutions and Democracy in Brazil." Mimeograph. Pittsburgh, Penn.: Department of Political Science, University of Pittsburgh.

Angell, Alan (1996). "Improving the Quality and Equity of Education in Chile: The Program 900 Escuelas and the MECE-Básica." In *Implementing Policy Innovations in Latin America: Politics, Economics and Techniques*, edited by Antonia Silva. Washington, D.C.: Inter-American Development Bank Social Agenda Policy Group.

Arrow, Kenneth J. (1985). "The Economics of Agency." In J. Pratt and R. Zeckhauser, eds., *Principals and Agents: The Structure of Business*. Cambridge, Mass.: Harvard Business School Press.

Arruñada, Benito (1996). "The Economics of Notaries." *European Journal of Law and Economics*, 3(1):5–37.

Ascher, William (1984). *Scheming for the Poor: The Politics of Redistribution in Latin America*. Cambridge, Mass., and London: Harvard University Press.

Aucoin, Peter (1990). "Administrative Reform in Public Management: Paradigms, Principles, Paradoxes and Pendulums." *Governance: An International Journal of Policy and Administration*, 3(2):115–137.

Aylwin, Mariana; Carlos Bascuñan; Sofia Correa; Cristian Gazmuri; Sole Serrano; and Matias Tagle (1990). *Chile en el Siglo XX*. Santiago: Planeta.

Bale, Malcolm, and Tony Dale (1998). "Public Sector Reform in New Zealand and Its Relevance to Developing Countries." *The World Bank Research Observer*, 13(1):103–122.

Bardhan, Pranab (1997). "The Nature of Institutional Impediments to Economic Development." Mimeograph. Berkeley, Calif.: Department of Economics, University of California, Berkeley.

Barro, Robert, and Jong-Wha Lee (1996). "New Measures of Educational Attainment." Mimeograph. Cambridge, Mass.: Department of Economics, Harvard University.

Beaton, Albert E.; Ina V. S. Mullis; Michael O. Martin; Eugenio J. Gonzalez; Dana L. Kelly; and Teresa A. Smith (1996). *Mathematics Achievement in the Middle School Years: IEA's Third International Mathematics and Science Study (TIMSS)*. Chestnut Hill, Mass.: International Association for the Evaluation of Educational Achievement.

Becker, Gary (1983). "A Theory of Competition Among Pressure Groups for Political Influence." *Quarterly Journal of Economics*, 98(3):371–400.

Benston, George J.; Robert A. Eisenbeis; Paul M. Horvitz; Edward J. Kane; and George G. Kaufman (1986). *Perspectives on Safe and Sound Banking: Past, Present, and Future*. Cambridge, Mass.: MIT Press.

Blau, Peter M. (1974). *On the Nature of Organizations*. New York: Wiley.

Boston, Jonathan, et al. (1996). *Public Management: The New Zealand Model*. Auckland: Oxford University Press.

Brennan, Geoffrey (1996). "Selection and the Currency of Reward." Chapter 10 in Robert E. Goodin, ed., *The Theory of Institutional Design*. Cambridge: Cambridge University Press.

Brock, Philip L., ed. (1992a). *If Texas Were Chile: A Primer on Banking Reform*. San Francisco: ICS Press.

Brock, Philip L. (1992b). "The Government-Sponsored Securitization of Mortgages in Nineteenth Century Chile: The Macroeconomic Consequences of the Caja de Crédito Hipotecario, 1855–1880." Working paper.

Brock, Philip L. (1998). "Financial Safety Nets and Incentive Structures in Latin America." Paper commissioned for this chapter.

Brunetti, Aymo; Gregory Kisunko; and Beatrice Weder (1997a). "Credibility of Rules and Economic Growth." Policy Research Working Paper No. 1760. Washington, D.C.: World Bank.

Brunetti, Aymo; Gregory Kisunko; and Beatrice Weder (1997b). "Institutional Obstacles to Doing Business: Region-by-Region Results from a Worldwide Survey of the Private Sector." Policy Research Working Paper No. 1759. Washington, D.C.: World Bank.

Burki, Shahid Javed, and Guillermo Perry (1997). *The Long March: A Reform Agenda for Latin America and the Caribbean in the Next Decade*. Washington, D.C.: World Bank, Latin American and Caribbean Studies Viewpoints Series.

Burki, Shahid Javed, and Guillermo Perry (1998). "Towards Open Regionalism in Latin America and the Caribbean." In Shahid Javed Burki, Guillermo Perry, and Sara Calvo (eds.), *Proceedings of the Annual Bank Conference on Development in Latin America, 1997*. Washington, D.C.: World Bank.

Buscaglia, Edgardo, and Maria Dakolias (1996). Judicial Reform in Latin American Courts: The Experience in Argentina and Ecuador. World Bank Technical Paper No. 350. Washington, D.C.: World Bank.

Caiden, Naomi, and Aaron Wildavsky (1974). *Planning and Budgeting in Poor Countries*. New York: Wiley.

Calomiris, Charles W. (1996). "Building an Incentive-Compatible Safety Net: Special Problems for Developing Countries." New York: Columbia University.

Calomiris, Charles W. (1997). *The Postmodern Bank Safety Net: Lessons from Developed and Developing Economies*. Washington, D.C.: The AEI Press.

Calomiris, Charles W., and Gary Gorton (1991). "The Origins of Banking Panics: Models, Facts, and Bank Regulation." In R. Glenn Hubbard, ed., *Financial Markets and Financial Crises*. Chicago: University of Chicago Press.

Calvo, Guillermo (1989). "Incredible Reforms." In *Debt, Stabilization, and Development: Essays in Memory of Carlos Diaz-Alejandro*, edited by G. Calvo, et al. Oxford, England, and Cambridge, Mass: Basil Blackwell.

Campos, Ed, and Sanjay Pradhan (1996). "Budgetary Institutions and Expenditure Outcomes: Binding Governments to Fiscal Performance," Policy Research Working Paper 1646. Washington, D.C.: World Bank, Policy Research Department, Public Economics Division, September.

Caprio, Gerard Jr., and Daniela Klingebiel (1996). "Bank Insolvency: Bad Luck, Bad Policy, or Bad Banking?" Washington, D.C.: Development Research Group, World Bank.

Caprio, Gerard Jr.; Michael Dooley; Danny Leipziger; and Carl Walsh (1996). "The Lender of Last Resort Function under a Currency Board: The Case of Argentina." Washington, D.C.: World Bank.

Caprio, Gerard Jr., and Philip Keefer (1998). "Regulations, Institutions and Country Responses to Bank Insolvency." Reserarch Proposal (work in progress). Washington, D.C.: Development Research Group, World Bank.

Cariola, Patricio, S.J. (1996). "New Criteria for Educational Policies in Chile." In *Conference Report on Revital-*

ization of Education in the Americas, December 4–6, 1995, edited by Benjamin Alvarez. U.S. Agency for International Development Education and Human Resources Technical Services Working Paper No. 11. Washington, D.C.: U.S. Agency for International Development.

Carlton, Dennis W., and Jeffrey M. Perloff (1990). *Modern Industrial Organization*. Harper Collins.

Carnoy, Martin (1997). "Is Privatization through Education Vouchers Really the Answer? A Comment on the West." *The World Bank Research Observer*, 12(1):105–116.

Carnoy, Martin, and Patrick McEwan (1997). *Public Investments or Private Schools? A Reconstruction of Educational Improvements in Chile*. (November 1997 draft): Stanford, Calif.: Stanford University.

Chandavarkar, Anand G. (1996). *Central Banking in Developing Countries*. Great Britain: Macmillan Press Ltd.

Chong, Alberto, and Cesar Calderón (1997a). "Empirical Tests on the Causality and Feedback Between Institutional Measures and Economic Growth." Mimeograph. Washington, D.C.: World Bank.

Chong, Alberto, and Cesar Calderón (1997b). "Institutional Change and Poverty, or Why is it Worth it to Reform the State?" Mimeograph. Washington, D.C.: World Bank.

Chong, Alberto, and Cesar Calderón (1998). "Institutional Efficiency and Income Inequality: Cross Country Empirical Evidence." Mimeograph. Washington, D.C.: World Bank.

Coase, Ronald (1937). "The Nature of the Firm." *Economica*, 4:386–405.

Correa Sutil, Jorge (ed.) (1994). *Situación y Políticas Judiciales en América Latina*. Santiago: Universidad Diego Portalis, Cuadernos de Análisis Jurídico.

Correa Sutil, Jorge (1998). "Judicial Reforms in Latin America: Good News for the Underprivileged?" In *The (Un)Rule of Law in Latin America*. Notre Dame: Notre Dame University Press.

Corsetti, Giancarlo; Paolo Pesenti; and Nouriel Roubini (1998). "What Caused the Asian Currency and Financial Crisis?" Mimeograph. Yale University, Princeton University, and New York University.

Cox, Cristian (1998). "Estrategias de Cambio y Factores de Éxito: Chile en la Década de 1990." In *Educación: La Agenda del Siglo XXI, Hacia un Desarrollo Humano*. Bogotá: Programa de Naciones Unidas para el Desarrollo/Tercer Mundo Editores.

Cox, Gary W., and Mathew D. McCubbins (1996). "Structure and Policy: The Institutional Determinants of Policy Outcomes." Mimeograph. San Diego, Calif.: Department of Political Science, University of California, San Diego.

Cull, Robert (1998). "How Deposit Insurance Affects Financial Depth." Policy Research Working Paper No. 1875. Washington, D.C.: World Bank.

Dakolias, Maria (1996). *The Judicial Sector in Latin America and the Caribbean: Elements of Reform*. Washington, D.C.: World Bank, World Bank Technical Paper No. 319.

de Juan, Aristóbulo (1987). "From Good Bankers to Bad Bankers." Washington D.C.: World Bank.

de Juan, Aristóbulo (1995). "A Sum Up of 'False Friends' in Banking Reform." Seminar on Building Sound Banking in Transition Economies. EDRD Annual Meeting.

de Soto, Hernando (1989). *The Other Path: The Invisible Revolution in the Third World*. New York: Harper & Row.

Demirgüç-Kunt, Asli, and Enrica Detragiache (1998). "Financial Liberalization and Financial Fragility." Washington, D.C.: Development Research Group, World Bank.

Dewatripont, Mathias, and Jean Tirole (1993). "Efficient Governance Structure: Implications for Banking Regulation." In *Capital Markets and Financial Intermediation*, C. Mayer and X. Vives, eds. Cambridge: Cambridge University Press, pp. 12–35.

Dewatripont, Mathias, and Jean Tirole (1994). *The Prudential Regulation of Banks*. Cambridge, Mass.: MIT Press.

Diamond, Douglas (1989). "Reputation Acquisition in Debt Markets." *Journal of Political Economy*, 97:828–862

Diamond, Douglas (1991). "Debt Maturity Structure and Liquidity Risk," *Quarterly Journal of Economics*, 106:1027–1054.

Dixit, Avinash K. (1996). *The Making of Economic Policy: A Transaction-Cost Politics Perspective*. Cambridge, Mass., and London: The MIT Press.

Domínguez, Jorge (1997). "Latin America's Crisis of Representation." *Foreign Affairs*, 76(1):100–113.

Drazen, Allan, and Vittorio Grilli (1993). "The Benefit of Crises for Economic Reforms." *The American Economic Review*, 83:598–607.

Easterbrook, Frank, and Daniel Fischel (1991). *The Economic Structure of Corporate Law*. Cambridge, Mass.: Harvard University Press.

Edwards, Sebastian (1984). "The Order of Liberalization of the External Sector in Developing Countries." *Princeton*

Essays in International Finance, 156. Princeton, N.J.: Princeton University.

Edwards, Sebastian, and Daniel Lederman (1998). "The Political Economy of Unilateral Trade Liberalization: The Case of Chile." In *Going Alone: The Case for Relaxed Reciprocity*, edited by J. Bhagwati. Forthcoming. Cambridge, Mass., and Washington, D.C.: MIT Press and American Enterprise Institute. Also published as National Bureau of Economic Research Working Paper Series No. 6510, Cambridge, Mass., April.

Edwards, Sebastian, and Moisés Naím, editors (1997). *Mexico 1994: Anatomy of an Emerging Market Crash*. Washington, D.C.: Carnegie Endowment for International Peace.

Engerman, Stanley L.; Stephen H. Haber; and Kenneth L. Sokoloff (1998). "Inequality, Institutions, and Differential Paths of Growth Among New World Economies." Working Paper. Los Angeles: University of California, Los Angeles.

Espinola, Viola (1997). *Descentralización del Sistema Educativo en Chile: Impacto en la Gestión de las Escuelas*. Human Capital Development Group for Latin America and the Caribbean, Informe No. 10. Washington, D.C.: World Bank.

Evans, Peter (1992). "The State as Problem and Solution: Predation, Embedded Autonomy and Structural Change." In Stephan Haggard and Robert R. Kaufman, eds., *The Politics of Economic Adjustment: International Constraints, Distributive Conflicts and the State*. Princeton, N.J.: Princeton University Press.

Federal Deposit Insurance Corporation (1997). "Resolutions Handbook: Methods for Resolving Troubled Financial Institutions in the United States."

Fernández, Raquel (1997). "Returns to Regionalism: An Evaluation of Non-Traditional Gains from RTAs." Mimeograph. Washington, D.C.: International Trade Division, World Bank, February.

Fernández, Raquel, and Dani Rodrik (1991). "Resistance to Reform: Status Quo Bias in the Presence of Individual-Specific Uncertainty." *American Economic Review*, 81(5):1146–1155.

Fetter, Frank W. (1931). *Monetary Inflation in Chile*. Princeton: Princeton University Press.

Filmer, D.; L. Pritchett; and Tan Jee-Peng (1998). *Educational Attainment Profiles of the Poor (and Rich): DHS Evidence from around the Globe*. Unpublished paper. Washington, D.C.: World Bank.

Foster, John; John Greer; and Erick Thorbecke (1984). "A Class of Decomposable Poverty Measures." *Econometrica*, 52(3):761–765.

Friedman, Milton (1955). "The Role of Government in Education." In *Economics and the Public Interest*, edited by R. Solow. New Jersey: Rutgers University Press.

Fundacion de Investigaciones Economicas Latinoamericanas [FIEL] (1996). *La Reforma del Poder Judicial en la Argentina*. Buenos Aires: FIEL.

Garber, Peter M. (1997). "The Transition to a Functional Financial Safety Net." In Liliana Rojas-Suárez, ed. *Safe and Sound Financial Systems: What Works for Latin America*. Washington, D.C.: Inter-American Development Bank.

Garber, Peter M., and Steven R. Weisbrod (1992). *The Economics of Banking, Liquidity, and Money*. Lexington, Mass.: D.C. Heath and Company.

Gavin, Michael, and Ricardo Hausmann (1997). "Make or Buy? Approaches to Financial Market Integration." In Liliana Rojas-Suárez, ed., *Safe and Sound Financial Systems: What Works for Latin America*. Washington D.C.: Inter-American Development Bank.

Geddes, Barbara (1994). *Politician's Dilemma: Building State Capacity in Latin America*. Berkeley, Los Angeles, and London: University of California Press.

Giammarino, Ronald M.; Tracy R. Lewis; and David E. M. Sappington (1993). "An Incentive Approach to Banking Regulation." *The Journal of Finance*, 48 (4): 1523–1539.

Gomes, Armando (1996). "The Dynamics of Stock Prices, Manager Ownership, and Private Benefits of Control." Manuscript. Cambridge, Mass.: Harvard University.

Graham, Carol, and Moises Naím (1998). "The Political Economy of Institutional Reforms in Latin America." In *Beyond Trade-Offs: Market Reforms and Equitable Growth in Latin America*, edited by N. Birdsall, C. Graham, and R. Sabot. Washington, D.C.: The Brookings Institution.

Greene, William H. (1993). *Econometric Analysis, Second Edition*. New Jersey: Prentice Hall.

Grossman, Sanford, and Oliver Hart (1986). "The Costs and Benefits of Ownership: A Theory of Vertical and Lateral Integration." *Journal of Political Economy*, 94:175–202.

Guido Bejar, Rafael (1997). "The Dynamics of Education Reform in El Salvador, 1989–1996." In *Paths of Change: Education Reforms Under Way in Latin America and the Caribbean*, edited by Benjamin Alvarez and Monica

Ruiz-Casares. Washington, D.C.: U.S. Agency for International Development/Agency for Educational Development.

Hanson, E. Mark (1995). "Best (and Worst) Practices in Education Decentralization." Washington, D.C.: World Bank.

Hart, Oliver; Rafael La Porta; Florencio López-de-Silanes; and John Moore (1997). "A New Bankruptcy Procedure that Uses Multiple Auctions." *European Economic Review*, 41:461–473.

Hausmann, Ricardo, and Liliana Rojas-Suárez (1996). *Banking Crises in Latin America*. Washington, D.C.: Inter-American Development Bank.

Hirschman, Albert O. (1970). *Exit, Voice, and Loyalty: Responses to Decline in Firms, Organizations, and States*. Cambridge, Mass., and London: Harvard University Press.

Hobbs, Cynthia, and Kathryn Rentel (1997). "The Paraguayan Education Reform: A Collective Effort," In *Paths of Change: Education Reforms Under Way in Latin America and the Caribbean*, edited by Benjamin Alvarez and Monica Ruiz-Casares. Washington, D.C.: U.S. Agency for International Development/Agency for Educational Development.

Holmes, Malcolm, and David Shand (1995). *Management Reform: Some Practitioner Perspectives on the Past Ten Years*. The SOG Ten-Year Reunion "Ten Years of Change," draft not for quotation, May 9.

Hopkins, Jack W. (1991). "Evolution and Revolution: Enduring Patterns and the Transformation of Latin American Bureaucracies." In Ali Farazmand, ed., *Handbook of Comparative and Development Public Administration*. New York: M. Dekker.

Inglehart, Ronald (1994). *Codebook for World Values Surveys*. Ann Arbor, Mich.: Institute for Social Research.

Institutional Shareholder Services, Inc. (1994). *Proxy Voting Guidelines*. Several countries, ISS Global Proxy Services.

Inter-American Development Bank (1996). *Economic and Social Progress in Latin America, 1996*. Washington, D.C.: Inter-American Development Bank.

International Monetary Fund (1998). "The Asian Crisis: Causes and Cures." *Finance and Development*, 35(1): 18–21.

Investor Responsibility Research Center (1994). Proxy Voting Guide. *Global Shareholder Service*, Washington, D.C.: I.R.R.C.

Irwin, Timothy; Michael Klein; Guillermo E. Perry; and Mateen Thobani, eds. (1997). *Dealing with Public Risk in Private Infrastructure*. Washington, D.C.: World Bank, Latin American and Caribbean Studies Viewpoints.

Jensen, Michael, and William Meckling (1976). "Theory of the Firm: Managerial Behavior, Agency Costs, and Ownership Structure." *Journal of Financial Economics*, 3:305–360 (October).

Kane, Edward J. (1977). "Good Intentions and Unintended Evil: The Case Against Selective Credit Allocation." Journal of Money, Credit, and Banking, 9: 55–69.

Kane, Edward J. (1989). "How Incentive-Incompatible Deposit Insurance Funds Fail." National Bureau of Economic Research Working Paper No. 2836. Cambridge, Mass., February.

Keefer, Philip (1995). "Reforming the State: The Sustainability and Replicability of Peruvian Reforms of its Public Administration." Paper presented at the Conference on the Reform of the State, El Pueblo Hotel, Peru, June; second draft, September.

Kellaghan, Thomas; Kathryn Sloane; Benjamin Alvarez; and Benjamin S. Bloom (eds.) (1993). *The Home Environment & School Learning: Promoting Parental Involvement in the Education of Children*. San Francisco: Jossey–Bass Publishers.

Klein, B., and K. Leffler (1981). "The Role of Market Forces in Assuring Contractual Performance." *Journal of Political Economy*, 81:815–841.

Klitgaard, Robert, and Heather Baser (1997). "Working Together to Fight Corruption: State, Society and the Private Sector in Partnership," in Suzanne Taschereau and José Edgardo L. Campos, eds., *Governance Innovations (Lessons from Experience: Building Government-Citizen-Business Partnerships)*. Ottawa: Institute of Governance.

Klitgaard, Robert (1998). "Healing Sick Institutions." In Silvio Borner and Martin Paldam, eds., *The Political Dimension of Economic Growth*. Basingstoke: Macmillan.

Knack, Stephen, and Philip Keefer (1995). "Institutions and Economic Performance: Cross-Country Tests Using Alternative Institutional Measures." *Economics and Politics*, 7(3):207–227.

Knack, Stephen, and Philip Keefer (1997a). "Why Don't Poor Countries Catch Up? A Cross-National Test of an Institutional Explanation." *Economic Inquiry*, 35:590–602 (July).

Knack, Stephen, and Philip Keefer (1997b). "Does Social Capital Have an Economic Payoff? A Cross-Country

Investigation." *Quarterly Journal of Economics*, 112:1251–1288 (November).

Koch, Timothy W. (1992). *Bank Management*. Second Edition. Florida: The Dydren Press.

Krugman, Paul (1998). "What Happened to Asia." Mimeograph. Cambridge, Mass.: Massachusetts Institute of Technology.

Kydland, Finn, and Edward Prescott (1977). "Rules Rather than Discretion: The Inconsistency of Optimal Plans." *Journal of Political Economy*, 85:473–491.

La Porta, Rafael; Florencio López-de-Silanes; Andrei Shleifer; and Robert W. Vishny (1997a). "Legal Determinants of External Finance." *Journal of Finance*, 52(3):1131–1150.

La Porta, Rafael; Florencio López-de-Silanes; Andrei Shleifer; and Robert W. Vishny (1997b). "Trust in Large Organizations." *AEA Papers and Proceedings*, 87(2):333–338.

La Porta, Rafael; Florencio López-de-Silanes; Andrei Shleifer; and Robert W. Vishny (1998a). "Law and Finance." *Journal of Political Economy*, December. An earlier version was published as National Bureau of Economic Research Working Paper No. 5661. Cambridge, Mass., July 1996.

La Porta, Rafael; Florencio López-de-Silanes; Andrei Shleifer; and Robert W. Vishny (1998b). "Corporate Ownership Around the World." Mimeograph. Harvard University, March.

La Porta, Rafael; Florencio López-de-Silanes; Andrei Shleifer; and Robert W. Vishny (1998c). "Agency Problems and Dividend Policies Around the World." National Bureau of Economic Research Working Paper No. 6594. Cambridge, Mass., June.

Laking, Rob (1996). "Public Management Lessons for Developing Countries and the World Bank." Mimeograph.

Lane, Jan-Erik, and Torgeir Nyen (1995). "On the Relevance of Neo-Institutionalism to the Public Sector." In Pal Foss, ed., *Economic Approaches to Organizations and Institutions: An Introduction*. Vermont: Dartmouth Publishing Co.

Larrañaga, Oswaldo (1997). "Chile: A Hybrid Approach." In *The Public-Private Mix in Social Services*, edited by Elaine Zuckerman and Emanuel de Kadt. Washington, D.C.: Inter-American Development Bank.

Levine, Ross (1997a). "Financial Development and Economic Growth: Views and Agenda." *Journal of Economic Literature*, 35 (2):688–726 (June).

Levine, Ross (1997b). "Napoleon, Bourses, and Growth in Latin America." Conference on The Development of Securities Markets in Emerging Economies: Obstacles and Preconditions for Success. Washington: October 28–29.

Levine, Ross (1997c). "Law, Finance, and Economic Growth." Mimeograph. Washington, D.C.: World Bank.

Lindgren, Carl-Johan; Gillian García; and Matthew Saal (1996). *Bank Soundness and Macroeconomic Policy*. Washington, D.C.: International Monetary Fund.

Lowden, Pamela (1996). "The *Escuelas Integrales* Reform Program in Venezuela." In Implementing Policy Innovations in *Latin America: Politics, Economics and Techniques*, edited by Antonia Silva. Washington, D.C.: Inter–American Development Bank, Social Agenda Policy Group.

Machado, Ana Luiza (1998). "La Política Educacional de Minas Gerais, Brasil," *Educación: La Agenda del Siglo XXI, Hacia un Desarrollo Humano*. Bogotá: Program de Naciones Unidas para el Desarrollo/Tercer Mundo Editores.

Mainwaring, Scott, and Timothy R. Scully (1995). "Introduction: Party Systems in Latin America." In *Building Democratic Institutions: Party Systems in Latin America*, edited by S. Mainwaring and T. Scully. Stanford, Calif.: Stanford University Press.

Mainwaring, Scott, and Mathew S. Shugart, eds. (1997). *Presidentialism and Democracy in Latin America*. New York: Cambridge University Press.

Manning, Nick (1998). "Unbundling the State: Autonomous Agencies and Service Delivery." Draft. Washington, D.C.: Economic Development Institute, World Bank, April 29.

Marcel, Mario (1997). "Effectiveness of the State and Development Lessons from the Chilean Experience." Paper prepared for World Bank Seminar, "Chile Development Lessons and Challenges."

Martínez, Nestor Humberto (1996). "Judicial Councils in Latin America." Chapter 1 in *Lessons Learned*, Madeleine Crohn, and William E. Davis, eds. Williamsburg, Va.: National Center for State Courts.

Mauro, Paolo (1995). "Corruption and Growth." *Quarterly Journal of Economics*, 110:681–712.

McCulloch, Brian W., and Ian Ball (1992). "Accounting in the Context of Public Sector Management Reform." *Financial Accountability & Management*, 8(1):7–12 (Spring).

McKinnon, Ronald (1973). *Money and Capital in Economic Development*. Washington, D.C.: Brookings Institution.

McKinnon, Ronald (1991). *The Order of Economic Liberalization: Financial Control in the Transition to a Market Economy*. Baltimore, Md.: Johns Hopkins University Press.

Merryman, John H. (1996). "The French Deviation," *American Journal of Comparative Law*, 44(1):109–119.

Meza, Darlyn (1997). *Descentralización Educativa, Organización y Manejo de las Escuelas a Nivel Local—el Caso de El Salvador: EDUCO*. Human Development Group for Latin America and the Caribbean Informe No. 9 (May). Washington, D.C: World Bank.

Mishkin, Frederic S. (1991). "Asymmetric Information and Financial Crises: A Historical Perspective." In *Financial Markets and Financial Crises*, edited by R. H. Hubbard. Chicago: University of Chicago Press.

Mishkin, Frederic S. (1996). "Understanding Financial Crises: A Developing Country Perspective." National Bureau of Economic Research Working Paper No. 5600. Cambridge, Mass.

Mishkin, Frederic S. (1998). "Systemic Risk, Moral Hazard, and the International Lender of Last Resort." Prepared for the World Bank conference, Reinventing a Bretton Woods Committee Conference on the Aftermath of the Asian Financial Crisis, March 13–14, Washington, D.C.

Modigliani, Franco, and Merton Miller (1958). "The Cost of Capital, Corporation Finance, and the Theory of Investment." *American Economic Review*, 48:261–297 (June).

Moe, Ronald C. (1994). "The 'Reinventing Government' Exercise: Misinterpreting the Problem, Misjudging the Consequences." *Public Administration Review*, 54(2):111–122 (March/April).

Moe, Terry M. (1984). "The New Economics of Organization." *American Journal of Political Science*, 28:739–775.

Moe, Terry M. (1990). "Political Institutions: The Neglected Side of the Story." *Journal of Law, Economics, and Organization*, 6:213–253.

Montenegro, Armando (1995). *An Incomplete Educational Reform: The Case of Colombia*. Human Capital Development and Operations Policy Working Papers No. 60 (August). Washington, D.C.: World Bank.

Morgan, Gareth (1986). *Images of Organization*. Beverly Hills, Calif.: Sage.

New York State Committee to Review Audio-Visual Coverage of Court Proceedings (1997). *An Open Courtroom: Cameras in New York Courts*. New York: Fordham University Press.

North, Douglass (1990). *Institutions, Institutional Change and Economic Performance*. New York: Cambridge University Press.

North, Douglass C. (1994). "Economic Performance through Time." *The American Economic Review*, 84(3):359–368.

Nunberg, Barbara (1995). *Managing the Civil Service: Reform Lessons from Advanced Industrialized Countries*. World Bank Discussion Papers 161. Washington, D.C.: World Bank.

Olson, Mancur (1965). *The Logic of Collective Action: Public Goods and the Theory of Groups*. Cambridge, Mass., and London: Harvard University Press.

Olson, Mancur (1993). "Dictatorship, Democracy, and Development." *American Political Science Review*, 87(3):567–576 (September).

Organización de los Estados Americanos (1998). *Educación en las Américas: Calidad y Equidad en el Proceso de Globalización*. Washington, D.C.: Organización de los Estados Americanos Secretaría General.

Pastor Prieto, Santos (1993). *¡Ah de la Justicia! Politica Judicial y Economia*. Madrid: Editorial Civitas, S.A.

Paul, Samuel (1991). "Accountability in Public Services: Exit, Voice, and Capture." PRE Working Paper 614.

Paul, Samuel (1998). "Making Voice Work: What Happened to the Report Card on Bangalore?" PREM Seminar Series, March 4.

Pearce, David W., ed. (1992). *The MIT Dictionary of Modern Economics*. Cambridge, Mass.: The MIT Press.

Perris, Lyall (1998). *Implementing Education Reforms in New Zealand: 1987–1997*. Education Reform and Management Series 1(1). Washington, D.C.: World Bank.

Perry, Guillermo (1997). "The Political Economy of Financial Reforms." Paper presented at the Conference on Building Robust Banking Systems, World Bank Annual Meetings, Hong Kong, China.

Perry, Guillermo, and Daniel Lederman (1998). *Financial Vulnerability, Spillover Effects, and Contagion: Lessons from the Asian Crises for Latin America*. Washington, D.C.: World Bank, Latin American and Caribbean Studies Viewpoint Series.

Plank, David (1996). *The Means of Our Salvation: Public Education in Brazil*. Boulder, Colo.: Westview Press.

Posner, Richard (1995). "What Do Judges Maximize?" Chapter 3 in *Overcoming Law*. Cambridge, Mass.: Harvard University Press.

Posner, Richard A. (1998). "Creating a Legal Framework for Economic Development." *The World Bank Research Observer*, 13(1):1–12.

Pratt, John, and Richard Zeckhauser, eds. (1985). *Principals and Agents: The Structure of Business*. Boston: Harvard Business School Press.

Programa de Naciones Unidas para el Desarrollo [PNUD] (1998). *Educación: La Agenda del Siglo XXI, Hacia un Desarrollo Humano*. Bogotá: Programa de Naciones Unidas para el Desarrollo/Tercer Mundo Editores.

Putnam, Robert D. (1993). *Making Democracy Work: Civic Traditions in Modern Italy*. Princeton, N.J.: Princeton University Press.

Rajan, Raghuram, and Luigi Zingales (1995). "What Do We Know about Capital Structure: Some Evidence from International Data." *Journal of Finance*, 50:1421–1460 (December).

Rama, German (1992). *¿Aprenden los Estudiantes en el Ciclo Básico de Educación Media?* Montevideo, Uruguay: CEPAL.

Reid, Gary J., and Graham Scott (1994). Public Sector Human Resource Management: Experience in Latin America and the Caribbean and Strategies for Reform. Washington, D.C.: World Bank, Green Cover, Report No. 12839, March 14.

Reid, Gary J. (1998). "Performance-Oriented Public Sector Modernization in Developing Countries: Meeting the Implementation Challenge." Forthcoming in *Research in Public Administration*, edited by Joseph C. M. Raadschelders and James L. Perry. Greenwich, Conn.: JAI Press.

Reynolds, Thomas, and Arturo Flores (1989). *Foreign Law: Current Sources of Basic Legislation in Jurisdictions of the World*. Littleton, Colo.: Rothman and Co.

Riggs, Fred W. (1964). *Administration in Developing Countries: the Theory of Prismatic Society*. Boston: Houghton Mifflin.

Rodrik, Dani (1989). "Promises, Promises: Credible Policy Reform via Signaling." *The Economic Journal*, 99:756–772.

Rojas, Carlos (forthcoming). "Las Sistemas de Medición de la Calidad de la Educación Latínoamericana." Washington, D.C.: World Bank.

Rojas, Carlos, and Juan Esquivel (1998). "Las Sistemas de Medición de la Calidad de la Educación Latínoamericana." Washington, D.C.: World Bank.

Rojas-Suárez, Liliana (1997). *Safe and Sound Financial Systems: What Works for Latin America*. Washington, D.C.: Inter-American Development Bank.

Rojas-Suárez, Liliana (1998). "Early Warnings Indicators for Banking Problems: What Works for Emerging Markets?" Working Paper. Inter-American Development Bank.

Rothschild, M. and Joseph E. Stiglitz (1976). "Equilibrium in Competitive Insurance Markets." *Quarterly Journal of Economics*, 90:629–50.

Salas, Denis (1998). *Le Tiers Pouvoir: Vers une Autre Justice*. Paris: Hachette Littératures.

Salmen, Lawrence F. (1992). *Reducing Poverty: An Institutional Perspective*. Poverty and Social Policy Series, Paper No. 1. Washington, D.C.: World Bank.

Savoie, Donald J. (1995). "What Is Wrong with the New Public Management?" *Canadian Public Administration*, 38(1):112–121 (Spring).

Schick, Allen (1996). *The Spirit of Reform: Managaing the New Zealand State Sector in a Time of Change*. Report prepared for the State Services Commission and the Treasury, New Zealand, August.

Schick, Allen (1998). "Why Most Developing Countries Should Not Try New Zealand's Reforms." *The World Bank Research Observer*, 13(1):123–132.

Schiefelbein, Ernesto (1995). "La Reforma Educativa en América Latina y el Caribe: Un Programa de Acción." In *Proyecto Principal de Educación en América Latina y el Caribe*. Santiago, Chile: UNESCO/OREALC, Boletín 37 (August): 3-34.

Scobie, Tanya D. (1998). "Agenda del Sindicato de Maestros." *Educación: La Agenda del Siglo XXI, Hacia un Desarrollo Humano*. Bogotá: Programa de Naciones Unidas para el Desarrollo/Tercer Mundo Editores.

Scott, Graham, and Peter Gorringe (1989). "Reform of the Core Public Sector: The New Zealand Experience." *Australian Journal of Public Administration*, 48(1):81–92 (March).

Shapiro, Martin (1981). *Courts: A Comparative and Political Analysis*. Chicago: The University of Chicago Press.

Sheng, Andrew (1996). *Bank Restructuring*. Washington, D.C.: World Bank.

Shepherd, Geoffrey, and Sofia Valencia (1996). "Modernizing the Public Administration in Latin America: Common Problems, No Easy Solutions." Paper prepared for the conference, "Reforma del estado en America Latina y Caribe." Madrid, October 14–17, 1996.

Shleifer, Andrei, and Robert W. Vishny (1986). "Large Shareholders and Corporate Control." *Journal of Political Economy*, 94:461–488 (June).

Simon, Herbert A. (1991). "Organization and Markets." *Journal of Economic Perspectives*, 5(2):25–44 (Spring).

Steering Committee for the Review of Commonwealth/ State Service Provision (1998), *Report on Government Services: 1998*. Melbourne: Government of Australia, Industry Commission.

Stigler, George J. (1971). "The Theory of Economic Regulation." *Bell Journal of Economic and Management Science*, 2:3–21.

Stiglitz, Joseph E., and Andrew Weiss (1981). "Credit Rationing in Markets with Imperfect Information." *American Economic Review*, 71:393–410 (June).

Stiglitz, Joseph E. (1986). *Economics of the Public Sector*. New York and London: W. W. Norton & Company.

Stiglitz, Joseph E. (1993). "The Role of the State in Financial Markets." Washington D.C.: World Bank's Annual Conference on Development Economics.

Stiglitz, Joseph E. (1994). *Whither Socialism?* Cambridge, Mass., and London: The MIT Press.

Summit of the Americas (1998). *Action Plan*. Santiago, Chile: Organization of American States.

Swope, John, and Marcela Latorre (1998). *El aporte de Fe y Alegría a la educación primaria en América Latina: un estudio comparativo longitudinal de la educación primaria impartida por Fe y alegría y las escuelas públicas en nueve países en América Latina*. Santiago, Chile: Centro de Investigación y Desarrollo Educativo/Agency for Educational Development/Inter-American Development Bank.

Talley, Samuel, and Ignacio Mas (1992). "The Role of Deposit Insurance." In Dimitri Vittas, ed. *Financial Regulation: Changing the Rules of the Game*. Washington, D.C.: Economic Development Institute, World Bank.

Tendler, Judith (1997). *Good Government in the Tropics*. Baltimore, Md.: Johns Hopkins University Press.

Tommasi, Mariano, and Andrés Velasco (1996). "Where Are We in the Political Economy of Reform?" *Journal of Policy Reform*, 1:187–238.

Tornell, Aaron (1995). "Are Economic Crises Necessary for Trade Liberalization and Fiscal Reform? The Mexican Experience." In *Reform, Recovery, and Growth: Latin America and the Middle East*, edited by R. Dornbusch and S. Edwards. Chicago and London: The University of Chicago Press.

United Nations, Economic Commission for Latin America and the Caribbean (1998). *The Fiscal Covenant: Strengths, Weaknesses, Challenges*. April 23, Santiago, Chile.

United Nations Educational, Scientific and Cultural Organization (1994). *World Education Report 1994*. Paris: United Nations Educational, Scientific and Cultural Organization.

United Nations Educational, Scientific and Cultural Organization (1995). *Proyecto Principal de Educación en América Latina y el Caribe*. Boletín 37 (August). Santiago, Chile: United Nations Educational, Scientific and Cultural Organization.

Valencia, Sofia (1996). "Public Sector Reforms in a Developing Country: an Analysis of the Chilean Experience." Mimeograph.

Villalobos R., Sergio (1983). *Breve Historia de Chile*. Santiago: Editorial Universitaria, S.A.

Villegas-Reimers, Eleonora (1998). "The Preparation of Teachers in Latin America: Challenges and Trends." LCSHD Paper Series No. 15. Washington, D.C.: World Bank.

Vishny, Paul (1994). *Guide to International Commerce Law*. New York: McGraw-Hill.

Wade, Robert (1997). "How Infrastructure Agencies Motivate Staff: Canal Irrigation in India and the Republic of Korea." In Ashoka Mody, ed., *Infrastructure Strategies in East Asia: The Untold Story*. EDI Learning Resource Series, Washington, D.C.: World Bank.

Wallis, John J., and Douglass C. North (1986). "Measuring the Transaction Sector in the American Economy, 1870–1970." In *Long-Term Factors in American Economic Growth*, edited by S. L. Engerman and R. E. Gallman. Chicago: University of Chicago Press.

Weber, Max (1968). *Economy and Society: An Outline of Interpretive Sociology*. New York: Bedminster Press.

West, Edwin G. (1997). "Education Vouchers in Principle and Practice: A Survey." *The World Bank Research Observer*, 12(1):83–104.

White, Michelle (1993). "The Costs of Corporate Bankruptcy: the U.S.-European Comparison." Manuscript. Ann Arbor: University of Michigan, Department of Economics.

Williamson, John (1990). "What Washington Means by Policy Reform." In *Latin American Adjustment: How*

Much Has Happened, edited by J. Williamson. Washington, D.C.: The Institute for International Economics.

Williamson, Oliver (1981). "The Modern Corporation." *Journal of Economic Literature*, 19:1537–1568.

Williamson, Oliver (1985). *The Economic Institutions of Capitalism: Firms, Markets, Relational Contracting*. New York: Free Press.

Williamson, Oliver (1989). "Transaction Cost Economics." Chapter 3 in *Handbook of Industrial Organization, Volume I*, edited by R. Schmalensee and R. D. Willig. New York: Elsevier Science Publishers.

Williamson, Oliver (1994). "The Institutions and Governance of Economic Development and Reform." *Proceedings of the World Bank Annual Conference on Development Economics, 1994*. Washington, D.C.: World Bank.

Winkler, Donald (1997). *Descentralización de la Educación: Participación en el Manejo de las Escuelas al Nivel Local*. Human Capital Development Group for Latin America and the Caribbean, Informe No. 8 (May). Washington, D.C.: World Bank.

World Bank (1990). *World Development Report 1990*. Washington, D.C.: World Bank.

World Bank (1992). *Governance and Development*. Washington, D.C.: World Bank.

World Bank (1993). *Social Indicators of Development 1991–1992*. Baltimore: Johns Hopkins University Press.

World Bank (1995a). *World Development Report 1995*. Washington, D.C.: Oxford University Press.

World Bank (1995b). *Bureaucrats in Business: the Economics and Politics of Government Ownership*, published for the World Bank by Oxford University Press.

World Bank (1996). *World Development Report 1996*. Washington, D.C.: Oxford University Press.

World Bank (1997a). *World Development Report 1997: The State in a Changing World*. New York: Oxford University Press.

World Bank (1997b). *Colombia: Paving the Way for a Results-Oriented Public Sector*. A World Bank Country Study, Washington, D.C.: World Bank.

World Bank (1997c). *Global Economic Prospects and the Developing Countries*. Washington, D.C.: World Bank.

World Bank (1997d). *Private Capital Flows to Developing Countries: The Road to Financial Integration*. Washington, D.C.: World Bank.

World Bank (1998a). *Global Development Finance*. Washington, D.C.: World Bank.

World Bank (1998b). *World Development Report 1998*. "Information and the Financial Markets: The Need for Support and Restraint from Policy." Chapter 6 (work in progress). Washington, D.C.: World Bank.

Zaiter, Josefina (1997). "Civil Society and Educational Reform: The Dominican Experience." In *Paths of Change: Education Reforms Under Way in Latin America and the Caribbean*, edited by Benjamin Alvarez and Monica Ruiz-Casares. Washington, D.C.: U.S. Agency for International Development/Agency for Educational Development.

Zuckerman, Elaine and Emanuel de Kadt (editors) (1997). *The Public-Private Mix in Social Services*. Washington, D.C.: Inter-American Development Bank.

WORLD BANK LATIN AMERICAN AND CARIBBEAN STUDIES

VIEWPOINTS SERIES

Latin America after Mexico: Quickening the Pace
by Shahid Javed Burki and Sebastian Edwards

Poverty, Inequality, and Human Capital Development in Latin America, 1950–2025
by Juan Luis Londoño
available in English and Spanish

Dismantling the Populist State: the Unfinished Revolution in Latin America and the Caribbean
by Shahid Javed Burki and Sebastian Edwards

Decentralization in Latin America: Learning through Experience
by George E. Peterson

Urban Poverty and Violence in Jamaica
by Caroline Moser and Jeremy Holland
available in English and Spanish

Prospects and Challenges for the Caribbean
by Steven B. Webb

Black December: Banking Instability, the Mexican Crisis and Its Effect on Argentina
by Valeriano Garcia

The Long March: A Reform Agenda for Latin America and the Caribbean in the Next Decade
by Shahid Javed Burki and Guillermo E. Perry
forthcoming in Spanish

Dealing with Public Risk in Private Infrastructure
Edited by Timothy Irwin, Michael Klein, Guillermo E. Perry, and Mateen Thobani

Crime and Violence as Development Issues in Latin America and the Caribbean
by Robert L. Ayres

Financial Vulnerability: Spillover Effects, and Contagion: Lessons from the Asian Crises for Latin America
by Guillermo E. Perry and Daniel Lederman

Determinants of Crime Rates in Latin America and the World: An Empirical Assessment
by Pablo Fajnzylber, Daniel Lederman, and Norman Loayza
forthcoming

Beyond the Washington Consensus: Institutions Matter
by Shahid Javed Burki and Guillermo E. Perry
available in English and Spanish

PROCEEDINGS SERIES

Currency Boards and External Shocks: How Much Pain, How Much Gain?
Edited by Guillermo Perry

Annual World Bank Conference on Development in Latin America and the Caribbean 1995: The Challenges of Development
Edited by Shahid Javed Burki, Sebastian Edwards, and Sri-Ram Aiyer

Annual World Bank Conference on Development in Latin America and the Caribbean 1996: Poverty and Inequality
Edited by Shahid Javed Burki, Sri-Ram Aiyer, and Rudolf Hommes

Annual World Bank Conference on Development in Latin America and the Caribbean 1997: Trade: Towards Open Regionalism
Edited by Shahid Javed Burki, Guillermo E. Perry, and Sara Calvo
forthcoming